The value in *Beyond Clinical Dehumanisation* lies in its daring call to community mental health care providers and researchers to confront the dehumanisation of the "vulnerable help seeker" (the patient, the client), and their own moral injury. The book offers an interdisciplinary and fascinating analysis of the issues Catherine Racine raises through moving personal testimony about her work as a clinician, and through an examination of "wonder" informed by the philosophy of Emmanuel Levinas. Racine illuminates the de-moralising, de-humanising subtext of the institution and points to the ethical clinical relationship that "ought to be". This thoughtful, well-argued and compelling book offers no simple answers. It is an intervention, a call to action, and an example of how the work of change can be approached. This is a worthy ethical primer and an inspiration for anyone working for structural and cultural reform inside or outside the walls of community mental health care.

—**Harold G. Koenig, MD**, Professor of Psychiatry and Behavioral Sciences; Associate Professor of Medicine; Director, Center for Spirituality, Theology and Health, Duke University Medical Center, Durham, North Carolina

At a time when health care professionals are increasingly stressed and health care systems under-resourced, what might result if the clinical encounter were to become a moment of wonder? Catherine Racine's beautifully observed, searchingly honest examination of community mental health care explores the nature of wonder by means of Levinas's ethical vision. It is both elegant testimony to autoethnography's disruptive potential in unmasking institutional power, and eloquent advocacy for a reimagining of the relationship between the medical professional and vulnerable help seeker in ways that could be profoundly humanizing for each.

—**Robert Song**, Professor of Theological Ethics, Department of Theology and Religion, Durham University, United Kingdom

Catherine Racine's book is an important and timely literary contribution. Her engagement with wonder, autoethnography, and Emmanuel Levinas adds a unique voice to the philosophy and the theology of wonder and manifests as a rich resource for mental health professionals, researchers, activists, students and service users worldwide challenging the problem of clinical dehumanisation.

—**Jan B. W. Pedersen**, author of *Balanced Wonder: Experiential Sources of Imagination, Virtue and Human Flourishing*

Beyond Clinical Dehumanisation towards the Other in Community Mental Health Care

Beyond Clinical Dehumanisation towards the Other in Community Mental Health Care offers a rare and intimate portrayal of the moral process of a mental health clinician that interrogates the intractable problem of systemic dehumanisation in community mental health care and looks to the notion of "wonder" and the visionary relational ethics of Emmanuel Levinas for a possible cure.

An interdisciplinary study with transdisciplinary aspirations, this book contributes an original and compelling voice to the emerging therapeutic conversation attempting to re-imagine and transcend the objectifying constraints of the dominant discourse and the reductive worldview that drives it. Chapters bring into dialogue the fields of community mental health care, psychology, psychology and the Other, the philosophy of wonder, Levinasian ethics, clinical ethics, the moral research of autoethnography and the medical humanities, to consider the defilement of the vulnerable help seeker, the moral injury of the clinician and look for answers beyond.

This book is an ethical primer for mental health professionals, researchers, educators, advocates and service users working to re-imagine and heal a broken system by challenging the underpinnings of entrenched dehumanisation and standing with those they "serve".

Catherine A. Racine is an independent Canadian scholar, feminist, ethicist and writer. She completed her PhD at Durham University in England in 2017.

THE PSYCHOLOGY AND THE OTHER BOOK SERIES

The *Psychology and the Other* Book Series highlights creative work at the intersections between psychology and the vast array of disciplines relevant to the human psyche. The interdisciplinary focus of this series brings psychology into conversation with continental philosophy, psychoanalysis, religious studies, anthropology, sociology, and social/critical theory. The cross-fertilization of theory and practice, encompassing such a range of perspectives, encourages the exploration of alternative paradigms and newly articulated vocabularies that speak to human identity, freedom, and suffering. Thus, we are encouraged to reimagine our encounters with difference, our notions of the "other", and what constitutes therapeutic modalities.

The study and practices of mental health practitioners, psychoanalysts, and scholars in the humanities will be sharpened, enhanced, and illuminated by these vibrant conversations, representing pluralistic methods of inquiry, including those typically identified as psychoanalytic, humanistic, qualitative, phenomenological, or existential.

Series Titles:

Unconscious Incarnations
Psychoanalytic and Philosophical Perspectives on the Body, 1st Ed
Edited by Brian W. Becker, John Panteleimon Manoussakis, David M. Goodman

Schelling, Freud, and the Philosophical Foundations of Psychoanalysis
Uncanny Belonging, 1st Edition
By Teresa Fenichel

Race, Rage, and Resistance
Philosophy, Psychology, and the Perils of Individualism, 1st Edition
Edited by David M. Goodman, Eric R. Severson, Heather Macdonald

Eros Crucified
Death, Desire, and the Divine in Psychoanalysis and Philosophy of Religion, 1st Edition
By Matthew Clemente

Dante and the Other
A Phenomenology of Love
By Aaron B. Daniels

Beyond Clinical Dehumanisation towards the Other in Community Mental Health Care
Levinas, Wonder and Autoethnography
By Catherine A. Racine

For a full list of titles in the series, please visit the Routledge website at: www.routledge.com/Psychology-and-the-Other/book-series/PSYOTH

Beyond Clinical Dehumanisation towards the Other in Community Mental Health Care

Levinas, Wonder and Autoethnography

Catherine A. Racine

LONDON AND NEW YORK

First published 2021
by Routledge
2 Park Square, Milton Park, Abingdon, Oxon OX14 4RN

and by Routledge
52 Vanderbilt Avenue, New York, NY 10017

Routledge is an imprint of the Taylor & Francis Group, an informa business

© 2021 Catherine A. Racine

The right of Catherine A. Racine to be identified as author of this work has been asserted by her in accordance with sections 77 and 78 of the Copyright, Designs and Patents Act 1988.

All rights reserved. No part of this book may be reprinted or reproduced or utilised in any form or by any electronic, mechanical, or other means, now known or hereafter invented, including photocopying and recording, or in any information storage or retrieval system, without permission in writing from the publishers.

Trademark notice: Product or corporate names may be trademarks or registered trademarks, and are used only for identification and explanation without intent to infringe.

British Library Cataloguing-in-Publication Data
A catalogue record for this book is available from the British Library

Library of Congress Cataloging-in-Publication Data
Names: Racine, Catherine A., author.
Title: Beyond clinical dehumanisation toward the other in community mental health care : levinas, wonder and autoethnography / Catherine A. Racine.
Description: Milton Park, Abingdon, Oxon ; New York, NY : Routledge, 2021. | Series: Psychology and the other | Includes bibliographical references and index.
Identifiers: LCCN 2020045878 (print) | LCCN 2020045879 (ebook) | ISBN 9780367511944 (hardback) | ISBN 9780367511937 (paperback) | ISBN 9781003052760 (ebook)
Subjects: LCSH: Psychiatric ethics. | Community mental health services—Moral and ethical aspects.
Classification: LCC RC455.2.E8 R32 2021 (print) | LCC RC455.2.E8 (ebook) | DDC 174.2/9689—dc23
LC record available at https://lccn.loc.gov/2020045878
LC ebook record available at https://lccn.loc.gov/2020045879

ISBN: 978-0-367-51194-4 (hbk)
ISBN: 978-0-367-51193-7 (pbk)
ISBN: 978-1-003-05276-0 (ebk)

Typeset in Times New Roman
by Apex CoVantage, LLC

 Printed in the United Kingdom by Henry Ling Limited

In memory of the lovers, my parents,
Muriel I. Hatch and F. Bruno Racine

And, in gratitude for A.W.'s shining example

Contents

	Acknowledgements	xi
	Introduction	xiii
1	James' Story	1
2	Three opponents of wonder	21
3	From behind the mask: Writing autoethnography	53
4	Wonder: A turn towards the divine	76
5	Levinas and the wholly/holy other	103
6	Clinical application and beyond: The function of the holy	135
7	The politics of need and desire	170
	Index	194

Acknowledgements

This book would not have seen the light of day without the support, wise counsel, friendship and kindness of family, friends, colleagues and academic mentors on both sides of the world from Canada and the United States to the United Kingdom, Denmark, and Kuwait.

To my circle in Canada, I extend loving thanks to Paul Racine, Stephen Racine, Stephanie Dugdale, Mardi Skuce, Natalie Lipson, Eileen Hendry, Mary Ellen Clarke, Akram Noorbakhsh, Golya Mirderikvand, Sharon Darlington, Shirley Buchan, Elaine Richmond, Barbara Edwards. To Durham friends and academic colleagues, my enduring gratitude for your generous hospitality, for welcoming me into your homes and communities and introducing me to a remarkable part of the world in the north east of England that I dearly miss. The adventure would have been half as great without you. Special thanks to Jill and Eric Bowerbank, Janiece and Paul Spence, Gillian Allnutt and Tom Midgley, Theo Harman, Val Fanoni, Val Standen, Kathleen Wood, Catherine Beaumont, Sarah Hills, Jodi Nelson-Tabor, Jan Pedersen. Loving thanks to Dori Beeler—Super Woman, true-blue friend and colleague. Finally, my eternal thanks to Tahani Alterkate, cherished friend and ally during my time in Durham, for her unflagging constancy and for singing in my kitchen.

At Durham University, many thanks to Prof. Robert Song and especially Dr Eleanor Loughlin for their compassion and assistance during a very challenging time of transition. Warmest thanks also to Prof. Ann Loades, whose early encouragement was so helpful, and to Prof. Sonya Sharma, trusted friend and mentor. I am also indebted to Prof. Martyn Evans for his scholarship on wonder and for nudging me towards the work of Emmanuel Levinas, which greatly influenced my thinking and the final shape of this book. Much gratitude also to those generous souls who carefully read and commented on early drafts of this work, particularly Dr Dori Beeler, Jill Bowerbank and Dr Campbell Robinson.

Unreserved thanks are due to Prof. Harold Koenig, whose prolific work, wonder-full research course on religion, spirituality and health at Duke University and kind encouragement were the genesis of the whole adventure.

My humblest gratitude goes to Prof. Gerard Loughlin, who received me as the stranger at the door and took me in. Thank you for your light guiding touch, your faith in the work and a great deal more; there are hardly enough words of appreciation and esteem.

I must also extend deep respect and affection to the many gifted and compassionate professional comrades with whom I toiled in the trenches as a frontline worker in community mental health care. Your friendship, support and patience never failed me. Among the most cherished are Sukhdev Sandhu, Debbie Suian, Sharmaine Van Staalduinen, Gunnel Tesfa, Robin Hutton, Richa Sharan, Cobus McCallaghan.

To David Goodman, my wonder-full editor for the Routledge Series on Psychology and the Other, and the brilliant editorial team, thank you so much for making it possible for this work to be published and bringing it into the world.

Finally, I give thanks to those individuals who should come first at every moment in the course of a mental health clinician's work—the vulnerable help seeker, the embodiment of the Other, to whom so much is owed. You are the ones whose lives and stories affected me and whose suffering, resilience and trust changed my life, inspired me and often broke my heart. Whatever imperfect offering I might have made in the context of my "clinical" role, I always received more than I gave. For this unmerited gift, I express my profound regret and gratitude.

Introduction

The urgency for community mental health care professionals, researchers, activists, students and service users to challenge the problem of clinical dehumanisation and to work for—and imagine—structural and philosophical reform has never been more significant nor the issues more contentious or complex. This book contributes a moral argument that is both salient and timely, given the ever-increasing call for better and more accessible mental health services in Canada, the United States and worldwide.

We do not need another critical commentary on the status quo to know that transformation is required. But the call for radical revision bears repeating in insistent, ethical and creative ways to infiltrate cultural consciousness further, deepen critical analysis and fuel political passions and imaginations so that, like water on stone, the seemingly implacable institution may give way to radically new possibilities, configurations and ethical imaginings *beyond*.

It is also true that if the system of community mental health care is flawed and broken, there is no indication it will be replaced soon by something significantly better. The growing call for more and improved mental health services will not likely abate in a world where a global pandemic of COVID-19 is still unfolding, along with a rise in right-leaning politics, the erosion of democracy, the increasing impact of climate change and the threat of economic collapse. As I add the final touches to this manuscript, the world has taken to the streets in protest against racism and police violence. There is ample reason for the distress, trauma and anguish we rush to pathologise as "mental illness". Nor may we anticipate community mental health care being quickly salvaged even by Emmanuel Levinas' astounding ethical vision. Levinas himself acknowledged his inability to see how it might be applied—in any context. Yet exciting possibilities are emerging given the ongoing labours of Levinasian scholars who, together with clinicians and researchers, continue the work of excavating his work and broadening the discourse.

Lest any part of this work be perceived as falling into a simple binary of "evil institution and doomed victim", there can be no doubt that community mental health care *should* be recognised for what it does offer—imperfect and dehumanising though it can be. Community mental health care *should* be acknowledged, especially for the army of skilled, caring, *loving*, frequently demoralised and weary clinicians and support staff who make it work. These are members of multidisciplinary teams who suffer with their patients, rejoice in their successes and, not infrequently, fight on their behalf for a better share of the dwindling resources and enough time to help. They do this while often struggling with a sense of urgency, guilt, inadequacy and resignation for what they are simply unable to accomplish or change within the "system".

There are increasing efforts to challenge and shift the paradigm and our construal of "mental illness" and its "treatment" found in such projects as *Mad in America: Science, Psychiatry and Social Justice* (www.madinamerica.com/) and the Hearing Voices Network (www.hearing-voices.org/) and in the work of psychiatrists like Joanna Moncrieff, founder of the Critical Psychiatry Network (https://joannamoncrieff.com/critical-psychiatry-network/). Moncrieff educates worldwide on the dangers and limitations of psychiatric medication in attempting to raise the bar of practice. Others, like Paul Farmer's organisation, Partners in Health, whose tagline is "Injustice has a cure", study the provision of health care worldwide, including mental health care. The focus is on health equity, the problem of structural violence and the social determinants of health (www.pih.org/pages/our-founders). Such efforts, together with the scholarship emerging from *Psychology and the Other* (www.psychologyandtheother.com/),[1] are informing new apprehensions of the vulnerable help seeker and an-*Other* way of seeing and addressing the dis-ease of systemic violence.

Author's note

In introducing "transcendent" and "wonder-full" terms of reference to an analysis and critique of institutional mental health care, I have tried to ensure a considered level of restraint and inclusivity. Regardless of the reader's professional or spiritual orientation, allusions to God and the Holy can make those working within the medical-scientific paradigm of mental health care instinctively wary. Consequently, some author transparency and a footnote on my own religious/spiritual biases are in order.

I now split modest spiritual loyalties between the Anglican Church and Buddhist practice from the Theravadan tradition. Like Richard Kearney, "I. . . call myself religious in the sense of seeking God in a way that neither excludes other religions nor purports to possess the final truth. . . . I would call myself a seeker of love and justice tout court".[2]

I have confronted lifelong ambivalence about the Church and the notion of "God" throughout this work. Yet I have discovered in Levinas' relational vision a rational ethical possibility that opens a promising space for the transcendent in community mental health care. The relationship he evokes constitutes a phenomenal "event" that has erupted through my own lived experience as a clinician and captures its essence both accurately and profoundly. Such a relationship also reveals the disturbing inadequacy of the institution of community mental health care while confirming the ultimacy of the most vulnerable person involved.

My ambivalence in closely identifying with any spiritual practice or religion reflects a feminist outlook and wariness of institutional authority and violence. In Canada alone, within the Christian tradition, we have two spectacular examples of such violence. These are found in the desecration of Canada's First Nations People by the former residential school system and in the historical problem of systemic sexual abuse and its egregious cover-up by the Church. There is no end in sight, given the recent revelations of the deceased and venerated Canadian humanitarian, Jean Vanier, which has left his name in disgrace and L'Arche, his lifelong project, in some question. The first half of Chapter 6 was to have been devoted to Vanier's work as one heartening example of Levinasian ethics in practice.

It is apparently part of our human nature to maintain the illusion about the "good ones", those "precious few" who—because we want them to—confirm our deepest longing for the goodness, solace and inspiration we seek and yearn to emulate and touch. Yet there can be no enduring place for cynicism or contempt in the labour of moving from de-moralisation to re-moralisation. Stating my biases may not preclude any risk of violence or unwarranted and unfair judgement of the community mental health system. But it hopefully communicates genuine hospitality for the secular and spiritual interests and concerns of the reader. Our shared task calls for porosity between borders, both academic and professional, and an openness to the deepening discourse about the possible role of wonder and the holy in the clinical relationship.

Above all, this study focuses on the *ethical* implications of the "therapeutic" relationship within the dehumanising institution of community mental health care. Its objective is realised through the moral, performative research of evocative autoethnography and an exploration of "wonder" based on Levinasian ethics. Its aim—allied with the project of *Psychology and the Other*—is towards re-humanisation of the vulnerable help seeker and the re-visioning of community mental health care, which looks steadfastly to the Face of the Other for direction.

The origins of this book

The origins of this book emerged in the Nitobe Japanese Garden at the University of British Columbia where I sat many years ago, one drizzly summer's afternoon, practising "empathy skills" in a rustic wooden rain shelter with a colleague from a counselling class. While listening to his story, I became increasingly enthralled with the deepening beauty suffusing my colleague's face that left me spellbound and shattered by a sense of presence.

I began looking for a language to help name and understand this marvellous encounter and to explore its implications for counselling practice and subsequently wrote my master's thesis on "The Mystical Experience of a Counsellor".[3] The intersection of mysticism with the emerging field of spirituality, theology and mental health confirmed my passion for this research. But it was Levinas' vision that invited me to go further and concluded my quest two decades later. Here, at last, was the key to the door through which the wonderfull Other had been calling all along, inviting me to the place beyond yearning and holding me responsible for everything.

The central claim of this interdisciplinary exploration is that wonder can interrupt the institutional entrancement of the clinician to exert a gravitational pull on her awareness that can "awaken" the clinician from the normalising perspective of clinical praxis. Such interruptions are vital within a clinical environment that can defile the vulnerable help seeker and contribute to the clinician's moral disengagement or paralysis. Through our discussion, we revisit many well-rehearsed ethical questions about the therapeutic relationship, the construct of mental illness and its care, the politics of power within the institution of community mental health care and the supposed and real dangers of emotional intimacy in the clinical relationship. Such questions can point uncomfortably—sometimes devastatingly—back to why and how the ethics of educated, dedicated, *caring* clinicians are diluted, for which we are examining the possible "cure" of wonder.

The book employs three intersecting approaches to unearth and illuminate the problem of systemic clinical dehumanisation. These are the notion of wonder, Emmanuel Levinas' ethical vision—which informs our final understanding of wonder, and evocative autoethnography. Autoethnography sparks the imperative of our ethical quest for radical institutional change, albeit enigmatically. But Levinas' ethical vision evokes and grounds the revelatory relationship for which the clinician also *yearns*. This relationship is discovered in the approach of the vulnerable help seeker, whose ethical invitation to the beleaguered clinician, while nearly irresistible, is predictably left unanswered or misconstrued.

Conceived and written as an ethical intervention and invitation, this study inclines towards what we have yet to imagine without offering any simple solutions. It speaks directly and urgently to clinical educators, researchers, students who intend to work in the field of mental health care, and to all clinical professionals working on multidisciplinary mental health teams—and in private practice. It also speaks to the threatened interests of those who seek or have sought community mental health care—and their advocates—and is accessible for a general readership. While scholarly, the book is also a cautionary tale, a call for reform, an intervention, an ethical plea, a memoir, a confession, a political analysis and a primer for those working for change. Equally, it is an indictment of a mental health system that can too easily exploit the largely disenfranchised cohort it purports to "serve".

Our study brings into conjunction the fields of community mental health care, psychology, theology, philosophy, autoethnography, medical ethics and the medical humanities to problematise clinical dehumanisation and consider a solution *beyond*. But as Grace Jantzen reminds us, this is not a simple matter of calling imagination into play "just to invent a new theory. . . in confrontation with the old one". It is a matter of bringing to consciousness what has been repressed—"the threat of desire and the imagination"—and *then*

Introduction xvii

to invoking imagination for new symbols and ways forward.[4] It is arguably within clinicians' reach to exponentially increase the hospitality and humanity of community mental health care by labouring—willingly and intentionally—to *see* the divinity of the disenfranchised vulnerable help seeker and, finally, to serve Her.

The chapters

In Chapter 1, "James' Story", the reader is immediately oriented to the narrative voice and the inner moral landscape of the author as a clinician/therapist working in a community mental health centre in British Columbia, Canada. This transformation narrative takes up the entire chapter to introduce the book's central themes and reflect on the moral implications that emerge between the helper and help seeker. The therapeutic bond, so fundamental to the process and outcome of clinical work, is focused almost exclusively on its benefits to the help seeker within clinical research. "James' Story" reveals the profound benefit of this bond to the *clinician* and unearths a complex of imperatives and dilemmas arising from this bounteous relationship that *transcends*. Chapter 1 recounts a career-altering clinical relationship with a troubled and intimidating youth that ultimately provoked my decision to abandon my work and continue the search for ethical answers. The narrative traces this clinician's stark confrontation of clinical reduction, illuminating her moral distress and culpability while reflecting on James' profound vulnerability and isolation within the dehumanising institution.

Obstacles interfering with the hospitality of the vulnerable help seeker and the integrity of the clinician are entwined and normalised within praxis and the authorising institution. There are many ethical obstacles, and we focus on three in Chapter 2, "Three opponents of wonder". The first, *medicalisation*, describes the eroding boundaries of psychological normalcy and well-being threatening the spectrum of human emotion and the richness of its expression through the systematic production of mental illness. Medicalisation drives an ever-expanding and medically authorised economy, decried by many, now narrowing the bandwidth of "normal" in our increasingly psychiatrised culture. Our analysis also examines the "thesis of medical imperialism" generated by sociologist Philip Strong in 1979, which speaks—as relevantly now as then—to the "business" of mental illness as a highly profitable social-economic construct.

Another opponent, *asymmetry*, refers to the authorised inequality of the clinical relationship transacted within a professional hierarchy that subordinates the vulnerable help seeker to the clinician and the institution itself. We examine this structural discrimination, in part through Miranda Fricker's work on epistemic injustice, to show how injustice is rendered virtually invisible—and consequently non-existent—to our collective social awareness when it remains unlanguaged. The final opponent, *dehumanisation*, undermines both the help seeker *and* the clinician. We will discuss its theoretical underpinnings through Gordon Allport's early work on prejudice and an emerging strand of research on *infra-humanisation* that is virtually indiscernible. The impact of such subtle social processes, together with the problem of stigma, illustrates how the clinician colludes to create the *heartsink patient*.

These "opponents" contributed to my preference for the term "vulnerable help seeker" to define, more accurately and humanely, the person variously described as the patient, the client, the service user, the mental health consumer or even the stakeholder. The term acknowledges theorist Frank Reissman, who argued for a reconfiguration of the services paradigm to address the problem of asymmetry and its "sequelae", including "iatrogenic difficulties".[5] Reissman recognised the resistance to change in the mental health industry, with its "systemic knowledge and scientific methodology", that shapes the professional help it offers into *"a commodity to be bought, sold, promoted and marketed"*. But while this problem is all too evident, it is also largely ignored.[6]

In Chapter 3, "From behind the mask: Writing autoethnography", we discuss this emergent and challenging approach to "moral" research found first in Chapter 1, "James' Story", and in epiphanic vignettes included in each chapter thereafter. I use autoethnography to illuminate the theory and evoke the sometimes horrifying, always relational, imperative of our ethical quest. The transparent, emotionally charged nature of autoethnography also puts the researcher's personal and professional reputation in the direct line of fire of legitimate research, so-called. Most vitally, autoethnography problematises institutional injustice and the complexities of power in the clinical relationship by championing the help seeker and confronting the evidence of the clinician's ethical obligation—and ambivalence. This is a narrative approach that opens the writer—and reader—to wonder and the epiphanic that can subvert the hold of the dominant discourse. As method and process, it confirms the extremity of the help seeker's plight and the clinician's moral injury.

Chapter 4, "Wonder: A turn towards the divine", considers the trajectory of "wonder" from the origins of Western philosophy to its domination by science that, some would argue, has reduced "wonder" to a meaningless word in our vernacular. Yet, a renaissance of wonder has introduced the notion into clinical discourse. This chapter examines wonder and its ethical potential in refreshing or possibly *transforming* the perspective of the de-moralised mental health clinician overwhelmed by the demands of the dehumanising clinical environment. Wonder has fascinating implications for the therapeutic relationship, which may enable the clinician to respond more reverently and *justly* to the vulnerable help seeker.

We will analyse wonder's genealogy and etymology to explore their congruence to the therapeutic relationship. Several definitions by contemporary scholars attempting to revive our understanding of wonder are also examined. The chapter concludes with a "clinical" definition of wonder that engages with the work of Martyn Evans and Carl Rogers' idea of reciprocity. We will see how the "approach"[7] of wonder confronts the clinician with evidence of her engagement in an ethically compromising enterprise, underscored by legal authority and its privileges.

In Chapter 5, "Levinas and the wholly/holy other", Levinas' vision is focused on the problem of clinical dehumanisation to show how far from the "ethical" a clinician can stray, despite exemplary adherence to the ethics of the workplace. Levinas' work offers an antidote to institutional indifference and dehumanisation that is both epiphanic and unequivocal. A snapshot of his life and Husserl and Heidegger's influence on his work is discussed, together with his revolutionary configuration of ethics that placed the *relational* prior to ontology—to being—to thinking and the conceptual. We explore the "Face of the Other" and its excessive demand that calls for "disinterest" in our self-project and challenges institutional reduction. An autoethnography and case study illustrate how Levinas' work can guide the clinician to higher moral ground or help her recognise where she *ought* to be. His vision is neither easily translated nor fulfilled, but his formulation is astonishing in its evocation of the help seeker's exquisite welcome to the clinician. Our chapter concludes with a brief critique of the challenges Levinas' work still poses his adherents and interpreters.

Chapter 6, "Beyond clinical application: The function of the Holy", discusses the emergence of Levinas' work in praxis which is now firing the imaginations of clinicians, researchers, therapists and ethicists. His ethical vision has raised the call for the re-moralising of psychology that might open to the untamed and *irreducible* for its moral direction, and reorient the help seeker towards the *other* and the world beyond. We review the "function" of the "holy" in light of the help seeker's dehumanisation and the clinician's demoralisation. We also consider Levinas' use of language and the influence of the early mystics on the paradoxical excesses and evocations he employed in his writing to point towards the holy. The last half of the chapter focuses on the "possible/impossible" of clinical application, beginning on a cautionary note with disgraced Canadian humanitarian Jean Vanier. The chapter concludes with a discussion of the work of several clinicians, researchers and therapists attempting to "apply" Levinas' vision to highlight the challenges inherent in our re-humanising project.

In Chapter 7, "The politics of need and desire", we cast back through our inquiry to discover the presence of a fascinating artefact. This is one that attests to the indomitable resilience of clinical reduction that ethicists and researchers continue to oppose and subvert, although still unsuccessfully. This artefact is discovered in the conflation of abuse with even the possibility of intimacy, which leaves the clinician thwarted and the help seeker forever reduced and dehumanised. As we shall see, even the culture of community mental health care that argues so fluently for the ethical protection of the vulnerable help seeker must, and will, inevitably put its own considerable interests first.

Notes

1 The links to these four organisations: [accessed 16 September 2020].
2 R. Kearney, *The God Who May Be: A Hermeneutics of Religion* (Bloomington, IN: Indiana University Press, 2001), p. 7.

3 C. Racine, 'Mystical Experience of a Counsellor: An Autobiographical Journey' (unpublished master's thesis, University of British Columbia, 1996).
4 G. Jantzen, *Becoming Divine: Towards a Feminist Philosophy of Religion* (Bloomington; Indianapolis: Indiana University Press, 1999), p. 98.
5 F. Riessman, 'Restructuring Help: A Human Services Paradigm for the 1990s', *American Journal of Community Psychology*, 18 (1990), p. 222.
6 Ibid. p. 226.
7 The term "approach" is used throughout the work of Emmanuel Levinas to qualify his notion of the Face and the Other. I use it here to allude to the Levinasian definition of wonder I discuss in Chapter 5.

References

Jantzen, G., *Becoming Divine: Towards a Feminist Philosophy of Religion* (Bloomington; Indianapolis: Indiana University Press, 1999).

Kearney, R., *The God Who May Be: A Hermeneutics of Religion* (Bloomington, IN: Indiana University Press, 2001).

Racine, C.A., *Mystical Experience of a Counsellor: An Autobiographical Journey* (unpublished master's thesis, University of British Columbia, 1996).

Riessman, F., 'Restructuring Help: A Human Services Paradigm for the 1990s', *American Journal of Community Psychology*, 18 (1990), 221–30. https://doi.org/10.1007/BF00931302

1   James' Story

When we met, James was almost 19 and profoundly suicidal.[1] He had been hospitalised when he told his father his fantasy of killing both his parents and then himself. He watched violent films, played violent video games with his friends, slept half the day and abused marijuana. Unable to concentrate or cope, he dropped out of a computer program at a local technical college and was unemployed and living at home with his father and brother. By the time our work began, he had spent 20 days in the adult psychiatric ward of a large local hospital. This is a long time for a young man to spend watching adults play out the dark consequences of the kind of future one might prefer to avoid. He had also experienced his first coercive treatment when he was sedated and placed in isolation at the beginning of his hospital stay.[2]

I remembered the room well from a visit to the emergency psychiatric department of the same hospital. A colleague had taken me to meet one of the referring psychiatrists as part of my orientation when I started working in community mental health. The psychiatrist had shown me the "quiet room" with a single hospital bed mattress lying forlornly on the bare floor of a small, dim, windowless room that locked. Not long after our tour began, it was apparent that the "quiet room" was now occupied by a distressed woman, and she screamed for the duration of our interview. She screamed as though she was being tortured. I startled slightly in my chair with each fresh explosion of harrowing sound that filtered through the door of the office where we sat, while the psychiatrist continued talking as though nothing was happening and my colleague suppressed a small smile. It was a whiff of bedlam I will never forget. Not infrequently, people I worked with who had spent time in that room expressed such horror at the possibility of being sent back there that they would refuse hospital assistance.[3] Of course, patients didn't always have a choice.

Clinical files were doled out at team meetings twice a week. Cases were presented by intake nurses and assigned, sometimes under duress, to clinical staff already staggering under caseloads beyond their capacity.[4] I had established a modest reputation for taking cases no one else wanted and offered to take James' following the long silence in the room after his file was presented. It was a difficult file, but there were reasons for my magnanimity. After several years on intake, I had finally claimed my role as a therapist and was very willing to work with the least favoured in clinical practice.[5]

My first job in this community mental health centre had been on intake. It was demanding work and essentially a triaging position that required me to separate those who qualified for service from those who didn't. The reality was much more complicated and fraught because the primary task of intake was mainly that of gatekeeper. The intake clinician stood between those desperate souls trying to access service and the often fluid "mandates" of the various teams within the Centre that we were constantly negotiating.

Further complicating the picture was the priority given those discharged from hospital to our Centre. The demand for care far exceeded our capacity. My intake colleague and I were refusing up to seventy percent, and more, of all requests for service while attempting to support those we turned away, either by counselling them on the phone or seeing them if they showed up in person at our door. Suggestions would be given, resources and phone numbers offered and some kind of plan suggested, which was carefully documented. If the individual showed up again or deteriorated and came back through their physician's office or the hospital, or if they complained to the manager about being refused service, there had to be a paper trail. We had to confirm that the institution and clinician were not responsible, or irresponsible, and *had* done what was legally defensible despite the refusal of service.

Intake was traditionally a nursing stronghold that had been challenged by a maverick manager at our Centre who believed a change of the old guard was needed. He had hired me as clinical counsellor along with a social worker to take over the two intake positions shortly before his retirement. The backlash was brutal, and the rift between nursing staff and other clinical professionals became ever more acrimonious. My intake colleague and I were scapegoated for being in positions we—apparently—had no right to hold.[6]

Three months later, the day my probation period was over, I wanted to bring a cake to work to celebrate with my new colleagues but thankfully never did. That was the day I read with incredulity an email the nurses had circulated to every staff member concerning a meeting to discuss their collective outrage about the recent intake hires—my social worker colleague and myself—to which they had invited the head of their nursing union. We didn't go, why would we? The whole staff jammed into the meeting room that afternoon behind closed doors, and with the halls empty and silent, the two-woman intake team got on with their job. Later we learned that the cries of incompetence about the non-nursing intake team had failed to move the manager and he'd dug in his heels. Some nurses suggested he was so out of touch he was likely dementing. Dementing? What were they saying about me? I knew what some of them were saying about the patients I presented at intake meetings, and not only the nurses, other clinical staff as well.

Coming into a government-paid job from the non-profit sector had almost doubled my salary overnight, but the price was steep. I ruefully remembered my joy a few weeks in when I approached the manager to express my pleasure with the work and the fascinating challenges it provided. His measured smile and quizzical response, "Wait a while", proved all too prophetic. Several years later, I was finally given a counselling job on the ASTAT team, and two nurses were moved back into their "rightful" positions on intake.[7] My social worker colleague had long since moved on to safer pastures in another team within our Centre. It was an immense relief for me and a reclamation victory for the nurses. Even the messiest cases failed to daunt me after that, and I may well have aligned myself with the most unwanted, having made it through the fire of my professional ostracisation. James himself was nothing if not an outsider.

During his hospitalisation, James had been assessed by a psychiatrist, tested by a psychologist and been later referred to the outpatient Early Psychosis Intervention (EPI) program, for yet another psychiatric assessment with a specialist in psychotic illness. James met the mandate for the program, having never been prescribed antipsychotic medication, and was sent for follow-up with the EPI social worker who worked on our team. The hospital workup he had received was intensive and extensive but ultimately vague. The sheer volume of documentation filled with conflicting assessments and narratives speculating about an 18-year-old young man with no previous history of mental illness was bewildering. This psychiatric hash would follow him the rest of his life and be damning should he ever need to defend himself legally or find himself dealing with any number of situations requiring evidence of his mental health history. Beyond that, what would it do to his sense of self?[8]

When James was discharged from hospital, he was advised to go home and monitor himself for signs of psychosis, which is remarkable advice for a labile 18-year-old who was using recreational drugs and suicidal. How could he adequately determine such symptoms, let alone respond to them responsibly? When we met, James still had no idea what he should be looking for, and I saw the shadow of fear on his face when he asked me to tell him. I outlined my understanding of psychosis, especially its connection to marijuana abuse in youth.[9]

The combined diagnoses from the three respected specialists who had assessed him were all but meaningless. They ranged widely from major depression and anxiety to prodromal or early psychosis through to borderline or possibly antisocial personality disorder or features, complicated by marijuana abuse. His interest in speaking about philosophical matters had also been duly noted, and patronised as intellectual posturing. Following his hospital stay, James never did follow up with the EPI clinician on our team. Instead, he stopped his medications and dropped out of a system too overwhelmed to notice or care, only to re-emerge three months later when he became suicidal once again. James returned to the hospital, was sent back to our mental health centre once again and assigned to me. By then he had also started to use LSD regularly with his girlfriend, a fact he willingly shared to my enormous chagrin, which added more risk to this already suicidal youth and his predisposition to psychosis.

James intimidated me from our first handshake. He was tall, rawboned, ashen, unkempt. He was aloof, emotionally flat and answered questions in monosyllables with a fixed gaze and glacial disdain. James had felt neither understood nor valued from his first encounter with the mental health system. Our initial meeting was another opportunity for him to confirm what he already knew about a chaotic and ineffective service. He'd been asked the same questions too often by too many people and invaded, observed, assessed, judged, labelled and incarcerated with too few results. He scoffed at questions about how homicidal he might be and denied a history of self-harm but admitted spending time as a boy tearing the wings off bees to watch their behaviour. He blandly claimed his suicidality was insignificant, which alarmed me given the deadly statistics.[10] I hoped he was bluffing.

Halfway through our first session, I knew beyond all doubt that I did not want to work with James. He scared me half to death but finding someone else to work with him would be tricky. He was a hot potato given the lack of follow-up he'd received that had enabled him to slip away only to be brought back through our doors via the hospital for a second time, and now he was high profile. Not just because he was at such high risk, but because our Centre had failed to keep tabs on him and there was no more margin for error—we would be liable if anything happened to this kid.

A community mental health centre is comparable to a MASH unit, with limited resources and staffing and incoming wounded attended by whoever can handle the next casualty.[11] If a help seeker didn't like the clinician assigned to her case, she would likely be pathologised, viewed as demanding or shown the door but never offered the luxury of another choice. Nor could a clinician easily pass on a file. It just wasn't done, and I had never attempted to negotiate such a manoeuvre, but this was different. Being afraid of a patient would be a frank admission of professional inadequacy, although the "danger card" could be played, but not easily in this case as James had not done anything, yet.

There was little love lost between the line manager and a great many of us who reported to her. She was in over her head and not suited to her job in this pressure cooker, and she managed her anxiety by micromanaging the rest of us. I approached her and casually explained my wish to transfer the file. Without missing a beat, she looked up coolly from her desk and told me I was welcome to trade the file with whoever on the team might be willing to pick it up. Checkmate. I tried half-heartedly to talk to a couple of colleagues about a trade but knew it wouldn't fly. Everyone was maxed out and nobody was going to pick up a file like this. I talked to two trusted colleagues about the matter and decided to try again. There remained one faint hope.

Typically, psychiatric nurses were assigned people with a history of schizophrenia or bipolar disorder with mania—those who were or had been floridly psychotic. Such patients were higher up the ladder of pathological legitimacy as opposed to those dealing with "acute situational stressors" who were generally seen by the counsellors.[12] I pressed my advantage and informed my line manager that James' case was not a good fit because it meant "working outside of my scope of practice". This doublespeak was to remind her of those professional limitations of the institutional hierarchy from which she benefited more as "medical" staff than I did, and that was to my ethical credit to respect. To disregard them placed her in an ethically compromising bind.

I stood in my line manager's office, looking over her shoulder while she flipped through James' file. "It's a dog's breakfast", she said, and grudgingly agreed to pass the file on to a nurse who unexpectedly left the following week for another position. The file bounced back to me; there was nothing to be done, but psychosis was the least of my worries. Here was an unknown teenager with no previous psychiatric history and an inconclusive diagnosis following a lengthy stay in hospital. Against his will, James had been certified and hospitalised for expressing an interest in killing his family and himself and, according to one assessment, might have an "antisocial or borderline personality disorder".[13]

James was now using LSD in addition to having a long-standing marijuana habit and could deadpan a seasoned professional for an hour with spine-tingling effect. He knew exactly how to express in few words a brooding ambivalence towards a system of care that, far from helping, had wasted his time and diminished him as a human being. He was a loose cannon I had done everything possible to avoid for fear that he might be a danger to me, find out where I lived, come to my home or kill himself on my watch.[14] There was no choice but to confront this spooky kid who was young enough to be my grandson.

James had no good reason to like me, given my failed attempt to have his file transferred. I soft-pedalled my embarrassment the day I invited him into my office for our second meeting to explain that the nurse who was to have taken over his case had left our Centre. James eyed me levelly, silently. He had been passed around from one professional to another since his first contact with the system. Everyone had listened, for there is nothing quite like a homicidal and suicidal youth to capture professional attention, but no one had heard him. He stonewalled for the first several sessions and resisted my every attempt to leverage a connection. It was a standoff, and the tension was palpable.

The day I dropped all pretence of professional equanimity and reached out to James to reveal myself, I felt utterly reckless. I acknowledged my part in the mismanagement of his case as someone who represented the gross inadequacy of a system that sustained me at his expense. I confirmed his experience and apologised sincerely for what he had been through and confessed I was deeply concerned he would kill himself. I admitted I had no idea how to proceed in the face of his impassive defence. I appealed to him to tell me what he needed, or thought he needed, and talked for a long time until I felt he could see me.

My attempt had the desired effect of thawing his façade. But what had I invited him to do? Trust me? To what end, and for whose purpose? Almost immediately, his flat-eyed impassivity fell away. I was unprepared for the speed with which he met my appeal in his eagerness to get on with the project he wanted to share so badly. Soon James' sessions were saturated with references to his search for the ultimate meaning or essence of life, his growing interest in Buddhist practice and his aspirations to greatness. He wanted to be a philosopher, a mathematician, a physicist, a linguist, a musician, but could hardly get out of bed in the afternoon. His journals revealed his thoughts at that time.

> I think the reason everything is so visually appealing is because I'm seeing everything in my patterns. Life is an infinite amount of continuous patterns being projected onto our brains at the speed of light. Is there a negative infinity? If I stay alive I will eventually discover the secret of the universe because I see the patterns.

He also documented his self-loathing, rage, terror and his desire to share his unique perspective with someone who could understand. "Is it too late for me. . . [w]ill uncertainty claim my mind as it has the uncertain world?"

James wasn't interested in talking about how he "felt" about symptoms or suicide, about what may or may not have been troubling him or even the story of how he had come to be where he was now. He was not interested in falling into line, playing the patient role or talking about his suffering, and he didn't complain, ever. When he did speak of such things, it was always in the service of his obsession to know. My appeal had not so much resulted in increasing James' trust in me as a therapist but in recognising me as a possible mentor or colleague. I was someone who presumably knew more, given my age and profession, someone who might support his quest because it was the only one of possible interest or merit. James was without pretence, undefended and unwilling to hide for any reason. His candour combined intellectual maturity with innocence and urgency. It unsettled me, for he never sought the advantage and addressed me as an equal. His transparency contrasted with the opacity of the shield behind which I hid and sometimes cowered. If he was guileless, he was also intellectually and emotionally subtle, profoundly interested in his psychological process and in sharing it with someone who might help him decode his experience.

James attended his first psychiatric interview at our Centre carrying a book by Kant, which he lacked the concentration to read. The psychiatrist was a seasoned veteran in the field. He asked James to extemporise on his reading and waited a long time for James to answer, while I witnessed the humiliation of a fragile youth who sat dumbly in his chair looking at his feet, unable to answer. Only minutes before he had been animatedly describing to me his passion for philosophy. At the end of this assessment, the psychiatrist put James on a high dose of antidepressant and a modest dose of antipsychotic.

Previous assessments from the hospital had alluded to the "pseudo-intellectuality" of this 18-year-old youth. But it was a stunning condemnation of one so young whose vocational orientation, it seemed to me, spoke through his desire. From my perspective, he was earnestly seeking answers to big questions with no immediate means of finding them, let alone the concentration to do so. No one had considered that he might be following the first inarticulate murmurings of a calling to philosophy or theology or psychology or, as Jungian therapist James Hillman might have suggested, that he was practising what he might later become.[15] James' wish to be identified as someone interested in philosophy had never been considered as a possible way out of his suffering or as an innate talent that could be productively fostered. Instead, it was interpreted as something phoney and insincere that needed to be rooted out, labelled and justifiably shamed. Within such an environment, James' attempts to connect with something greater than himself was labelled as suspicious, transitory or incidental, hardly life-affirming or transformative. No one had championed his impassioned inclination towards the transcendent, but it seemed to me that his relentless pursuit of something beyond himself, or its pursuit of him, had been his saving grace.

I sat and witnessed James' humiliation by the psychiatrist that day without a murmur, watched his intellectual and spiritual blistering at the hands of a man three times his age. After the consultation, we walked back to my office to finish the session. I did not tell him the psychiatrist had been wrong, disgraceful, to treat him that way. I smoothed it over, only implying as much without actually holding the psychiatrist accountable in the name of professionalism, lest James should tell him sometime later what I had said.

While intrigued by James' outpouring, I was also guarded. Was he expressing grandiose ideas, experiencing psychotic delusions, or was this the spiritual outpouring of a troubled youth on a spiritual quest? James ardently sought an answer in Buddhism and, early in our work together, told me that he had gone to a Buddhist temple close to my home to explore meditation. I fervently hoped he did not know this temple was in my neighbourhood or that I lived in a ground-floor apartment and slept with the window open. Yet I could not discount that this grey-faced youth, so incapacitated by "mental illness", was prepared to spend five hours alone on a return bus trip to engage in conversations about consciousness and meditation with Buddhist monks he had never met.

James had discovered something revelatory and vital in the repeating patterns of his life, in his thought processes, his engagement with complex forms of music and what he described as the "thrill of math". He was also able to create this marvellous experience when talking on the phone to the only friend who seemed to understand him. Before using cannabis and LSD, he had not seen the world this way. James had no formal religious background but knew that what he was pursuing involved an ultimate revelation of love. He called it by many names—cosmology, metaphysical passion, the essence of life, God—and preferred not to label it too precisely. I wondered if his experience met the criteria for extrovertive mystical experience[16] or something similar, but his obsession drove him and gave his life direction and purpose.[17] Burdened as he was, James also seemed remarkably free, immune to the cultural and symptomatic evidence of his pathology in his flight towards something greater than himself. It was as if he had walked through the wrong door looking for help with something else but having nowhere else to go, and finding something of possible benefit to forward his project, had stayed and asked for further direction.

8 James' Story

James asked pointed, and personal questions about my spiritual practice, experience, reading and beliefs for clues to his next step. I felt self-conscious responding to his queries, afraid of influencing him and of revealing my ragged spiritual history. It was a two-faced timidity, given my clinical carte blanche to interrogate him on the most intimate details of his life—his past, his thoughts and habits—and to influence him unequivocally in staying the course on a "treatment plan" over which he could have very little say. That plan, however, was to guide him on issues related to symptom management and future "functionality", not the possibility of a spiritual awakening. I evaded James' forthright questions, counselling him instead to look for spiritual mentors and communities of practice. I printed out a long list of Buddhist communities in the city and gave it to him. I urged him to move in the direction of higher education, believing, as I still do, that he was gifted and would excel academically despite his problems with concentration and his vocational moratorium. But, moving too closely towards his spiritual search, immersing myself in his quest made me uneasy. Why? It would mean stepping beyond the boundaries of my professional role, although I was well aware of the emerging literature on spirituality, religion and mental health and the benefits it was claiming,[18] the questions it was raising and the controversies it was igniting.[19] Yet, I doubted my ability or my right to engage with James honestly and deeply about spiritual matters. Beyond that, how could I even be sure I would not be feeding into his illness[20] or engaging with some darkness knit permanently into his psychological makeup that he might be using to manipulate me?[21] He was enigmatic, difficult to read despite his candour and had a very particular way of expressing himself verbally.

Within my work, I constantly baulked at the pathologising machine of the institution that defeated unusual or untypical ways of being or perceiving. Yet this machine mesmerised me, authorised me and justified my vigilance, given the possibility of danger which I could never entirely discount. This machine justified my collusion with medical protocols that not infrequently appalled me and endorsed a professional façade meant to reassure and support but that hid my vulnerability and outrage. The system in which James was caught also protected me, safeguarded my position and hid my private self.[22]

James' process intrigued me at first, but eventually it thrilled me. The profundity of his insight mirrored my fascination with the clinical implications of mysticism—of actually "seeing" the help seeker in ways James appeared to be apprehending his world. It felt exploitative to mine his perspective. Yet to ignore, downplay or pathologise his process denied the most life-affirming theme in his story that I also counted on to help keep him alive. Caught as he was within the machine of mental health care, James' plight confirmed what I had long believed was the brutalising and assimilating folly of our institutional approach to emotional suffering. More distressingly, it denied James' wonderful *vision* and the implications of what I was then calling "mystical experience" as a more life-affirming possibility for our approach to psychological distress.

With our work now underway, James agreed to take the prescribed medication[23] and attended his appointments with me promptly, if not eagerly, as if what was on offer might actually help him in his quest of spiritual discernment. "Yes, and the sooner the better", was his standard reply to my inquiry about his interest in coming back the following week to talk some more. I experienced that answer with a sting of shame because he was offering so much more than I could return. He was ablaze, and I was warming my bloodless hands at his fire.

I asked him to report on his suicidal feelings each time we met which, to my chronic apprehension, did not abate for several months. "Are you suicidal James? Is it better or worse than last week? Please tell me. Have you got a plan? Come on James, give. A place? A time? Don't look at me like that. This is serious. Do you know the risk of using LSD and being suicidal and mildly psychotic? Do you? Are you taking the antidepressants? Do you think they're helping? What about the antipsychotics? No, stay on them, don't mess with them. This is not funny. Yes, it does matter. On a scale of one to ten, tell me James tell me". It was the same mantra I repeated for weeks. "If you think you're getting close you can tell your dad, or call your mom, or call me, or go to Emergency, or call Afterhours, or call 911 or just get in a cab and get to the hospital. Ok? Promise me. PROMISE me!"

I wanted to be there to catch him should he ever fall out of that tree, but there was no guarantee. He would not die, I hoped. I worried about the medication hurting him, worsening his suicidal feelings, numbing him, contributing to his suffering, but said nothing.[24] How could I? These were a doctor's orders. My self-protective fear also drove my ambivalence about James' medication. I really couldn't tell if I wanted him to live as much—or more—for my sake as for his. If the drugs kept him alive, even if everything else about them was wrong, they could be justified.

As our relationship developed, it became apparent that James had found a place where he could discuss his "metaphysical passion" and be himself. This situation rewarded me but also haunted me because James felt so isolated. Though socially well connected to a group of childhood friends, he felt his consuming interest in "cosmology" contributed to his loneliness and his inability to connect meaningfully with others his age. James could not speak easily about his inner world to his contemporaries who lacked his perspective and did not share his values. He played along wishing to belong but saw through the game and had little heart for it. He was comfortable talking to adults and described himself as a freak, as someone who needed to hide to fit in, which seemed manipulative and troubled him.

While relieved and somewhat puzzled to witness James' imperviousness to clinical indoctrination, I was discomfited by his lack of guile that made him look like an innocent treading trustingly through an institutional minefield about which he had no understanding. Protecting him from this environment was no simple matter. While attempting to straddle the diverging mandates of professional and personal ethics, I found small comfort in recognising I could do neither well. It was confusing to feel so ethically compromised by stepping even slightly outside my professional role. I resisted the constant urge to tell him to trust no one, including me. But as our conversations evolved, I became increasingly aware of the disquieting joy I felt in my growing recognition of James as a spiritual friend on a journey not dissimilar to my own.

The day James arrived in my office with religious tracts given to him by one of the monks at the Buddhist temple, my wariness of this young seeker suddenly seemed grotesque. He handed the literature over for me to look at and solicit my advice. James' fragility and terrifying proximity to suicide contrasted with the immensity of his wholeheartedness, raw courage and determination to find answers he knew must be out there. His defencelessness was flawless: a deep mirror that finally, that day, captured and exposed my fraudulence as I confronted what appeared to be the superior moral integrity of this boy.

Clumsily, fearfully, I began to share what knowledge I had of spirituality and mental health, of Buddhism, of my fragmented meditation practice and religious uncertainty, knowing I was leaving behind a familiar approach to therapy that left me sitting on the edge of my chair. It was a tipping point that stripped away the final vestiges of a professional identity I had questioned for years and would never reclaim. There was no sense of elation, freedom or even appropriateness in this choice that felt more like letting go than a decision. I could not do it anymore. If this move intended, even partially, to shield James from the risk of harm by the system, it also shifted the risk to me alone. I was still afraid for him and myself, only now I was the main threat.

From then on, we focused on his pursuit of the mystical, the wonder-full, God, while I attempted to remove any impediments from his trajectory. I sought to help him plan his future and encouraged him to explore his experience and purpose during our sessions. I continually urged him to think about higher education. I also appealed to him to join a meditation community rather than practice on his own, concerned as I was that solo practice could put him at further emotional risk,[25] but he disregarded my direction. Soon after, I decided that the benefits of introducing him to the Buddhist community to which I belonged outweighed the dangers of the professional boundary violation.[26] I spoke to him about attending a weekend retreat with me and ensured his father knew where he would be. We exchanged home phone numbers, another taboo.

The night I drove James to his first Buddhist meditation retreat at the local university in the hopes of helping him find a spiritual community, I crossed another significant professional boundary. His pallor and the flatness of his affect worried me. He asked if he could put the car seat back so he could rest. He was exhausted for reasons I didn't understand. He looked so unwell. I reflected on the legal implications of transporting a "patient" in a vehicle uninsured for such purposes and drove with not a little fear. We arrived at the meditation hall, where I shepherded him through the registration process before we settled for the evening into the cavernous space of the University of British Columbia's Asian Centre. Meditators sitting on the floor or in chairs, some already with their eyes closed, surrounded us. James sat down beside me in a lotus position with the ease of a skilled practitioner. When the meditation teacher walked by the following day, I eagerly introduced James to him, explaining that I had brought James to connect with the community, hoping this world-renowned teacher[27] would confirm the importance of James practising with others. Meditators as young as James are valued and supported in this community. Instead of agreeing with me, this man smiled kindly at James and assured him that he had much to gain by meditating alone.

As we left the retreat, I asked James if he was hallucinating, and he calmly described how the sidewalk seemed to undulate and break up before him as he walked. It was not what I wanted to hear. Months later, he explained how the meditation had helped him learn to observe and recognise his delusional thinking, which reduced his fear when he had these experiences. He also believed the marijuana and LSD had been responsible for altering his mind and for opening it to a source of understanding and connection he now craved.

Throughout that weekend, I was vigilant and unsettled about my decision, about James' well-being and how far beyond the boundaries of my institution I had strayed. I felt awkward engaging with James outside the confines of my professional role, which left me feeling alienated from him. Who was this young man to me outside my counselling cell? What did I owe him? Why was I doing this? How could I see him, adequately or at all, beyond the organising principle of our therapeutic relationship? What was the benefit to me? I was risking so much for what? I felt more like an anxious parent than a seasoned therapist. I wanted to protect him and help him. I saw the awe-full beauty of his quest, his pursuit of the transcendent, his transparent nature, his physical being and goodness. In that seeing was such love and a wrenching sense of responsibility that I owed this young man, this boy, something that I could neither fully determine nor pay.

Despite our rocky start, James made astonishing progress in the first several months of our work together. He stopped using cannabis and LSD. He stopped watching violent videos and began spending more time outside on his bicycle. He was amenable to participating for a while in a college preparation course. He began to change physically, the colour in his face returned, his skin took on a youthful lustre, his interest in killing himself eased and he found part-time work. Wanting to be sure he was experiencing no further thought disorder, I had him assessed by the staff psychologist who agreed that while James had a unique perspective and way of expressing himself verbally, there appeared to be no evidence of any psychotic process. During that time, James also maintained a meditation practice but preferred to meditate alone.

Remarkably, the significant gains James made in such a short time were never lost. There is no way of knowing how the many variables involved contributed to his rapid improvement. His recovery was even more astonishing, given the stolid reality of the institutional environment and the truth of Hillman's observation, that "[o]f all of psychology's sins, the most mortal is its neglect of beauty".[28] Nonetheless, James' relentless search flourished and with it the many decisions he made to turn his life around. Through his struggle, he emerged like a young Atlas carrying the weight of his addicted, disconnected, materialistic culture; his parents' broken marriage, his vocational uncertainty and profound loneliness not easily understood or addressed within our community-riven culture. He stood in my doorway illuminating the destitution of my professional world, revealing the enormity of my privilege, including my relationship with him, and the paucity of what I had to offer within my professional role.

Ultimately, it seemed to me that my most important task was to help James recognise and reclaim his place in the human community. I wanted him to grasp that we—the world around him—needed him to join us for his benefit, yes, but even more pressingly for *ours*. In one of our final meetings, logic spun on its head the day I carefully explained to James that the very system he had approached for help was the same one that created and maintained his sense of exile—both inside and outside institutional walls. He listened carefully, quietly, the day I played that card, placed the final revelation of institutional complicity in his hand. "Do you understand me, James? Do you understand what I'm saying?" He was so young. Yet my confession could not sidestep my role in his alienation despite my best intentions and many attempts to subvert and resist the institution. Paradoxically and painfully, my sense of guilt was further complicated by the very love that had emerged and driven my desire to keep him safe and help him understand and touch the transcendence he sought.

I had walked—or tried to walk—a tightrope between my fear of oppressing him professionally or exploiting him personally. The joy of witnessing the lovely arc of this young man's repeated attempts at flight towards something beyond—from which I profoundly benefitted—had called forth my love, the fierce desire to protect him and the stinging recognition of my loneliness. It was only much later that I would grieve, turning to a mentor to help me unpack this thing. I had done nothing wrong, had I? Had I? I was not comforted by the reassuring words. I know what the path to hell is paved with and that within my institutional and professional roles I would always be culpable of keeping the best for myself, no matter what I did. How could it be otherwise? From whatever angle I tried to "protect" James, I would always come out on top.

About a year after our initial meeting, I transferred to another community mental health centre to work part time while I grieved the death of my mother and began preparations to pursue PhD studies in England. I asked a trusted colleague on my team to work with James in my absence. When I returned to my position months later, I resumed my connection with James for another few months. My colleague informed me that James had approached a Buddhist community and requested admission to train as a monk but had been refused by temple staff because he was still under the care of mental health and on medication.

James was transformed. He had matured and bore himself with immense dignity and was even more articulate than the last time we had met. I could see how well he was. James was now 21 years old. His suicidality had resolved but remained, in his words, "ideologically interesting". The diagnosis of early psychosis never manifested into schizophrenia. When he was finally weaned off his medications and his file closed, the psychiatrist who had first treated James with such disdain was impressed with James' quiet confidence during the final consultation. He later commented with amazement that James appeared to have the poise of a man twice his age. By then, James was well enough to move out of his father's home and was living for the first time on his own. He was eager "to be of value to his employer", he said, despite the superficiality of his work environment in a restaurant and the indifference of his manager. James was "practising confidence", working on his anger and trying to learn gratitude. He explained he wanted to stay open and undefended when someone was mean to him. He was intentional in cultivating himself and presented with the equanimity of a Buddhist monk, relaxed, easily moved to laughter and quick-witted.

James also talked about his loneliness, how it embarrassed him and his wish to understand it better. As for his future, he explained that "the essence of life" that he pursued so ardently was all he wanted to do with his life. But he had no idea how to translate this into practical action or a career path, and he still struggled with what he perceived as the freakishness of this passion. "No James, you're wrong", I countered. "This is a great gift, and you must cultivate it, there are many things you can and must do with this. Many people have built their lives writing and teaching about this very thing. Go to school and study anything—math, philosophy, physics, music, languages. Any of those paths can get you there, but you must study".

I told him that keeping this passion for himself was like hiding his light under a bushel. He had no real sense that his knowledge, his courage and his quest might be of benefit to someone else or that it had already been a tremendous gift to me, although I had told him so more than once. He also knew that I had written a paper about him and presented it at Durham University shortly before my final departure to the United Kingdom to begin my studies. After the conference and my return to Canada, we sat in my office and I read the paper aloud to him while he listened. It was not enough but it was something. I was overjoyed to give it to him, and I think he understood the homage.

Whether James might be described as a mystical visionary or simply a young man whose porous nature and experimentation with drugs facilitated his profound apprehensions of something beyond, his emergence within my Centre and practice was epic. James' overwhelming desire to know and to love and his keen sense of being onto something of great import had immunised him against the influences that entrap individuals connected with community mental health care and draw them away from their agency and potential. Equally, his vision and courage in reaching for the transcendent had illuminated how far I had strayed from my most cherished values as someone who had wanted to be a healer.

When we met again for the first time after my year's absence from the Centre, shortly before his final discharge, I teasingly asked James if he was still passionately committed to finding the essence of life. He looked at me with some impatience and said with utter conviction, "C'mon Catherine, we're all looking for that".

> *I have recently met again with James after many years. At the age of thirty, he is blooming, interested in life, an independent thinker. He is a self-aware, self-contained young man who tells me he wants to increase his emotional availability to his immediate family. He hopes to make a long-term commitment with a partner and have a family of his own. Perhaps. He works in the government, contentedly enough for now, and tells me he is studying calculus on his own but still has thoughts of becoming a counsellor. He knows this is not what I want to hear, although he has reassured me that our professional relationship was of real value at a time in his life when he needed help. I want to believe that his endorsement and future plans speak of how very little a fragile mortal may really need from another in order to right themselves and move on—if the listener is sincere enough, the message clear enough, and the timing is right. I encourage him to get serious about calculus and go back to school.*

Notes

1 A section of this narrative is reprinted by permission of the publisher. (Taylor & Francis Ltd, www.tandfonline.com). From: C. Racine, 'Loving in the Context of Community Mental Health Practice: A Clinical Case Study and Reflection on Mystical Experience', *Mental Health, Religion & Culture*, 17 (2014), pp. 116–19.
2 The human rights of the "mentally ill" are routinely violated, according to some, through the use of forced hospitalisation, isolation and physical or chemical restraint. For arguments supporting these practices, see: S. Klag, F. O'Callaghan, and P. Creed, 'The Use of Legal Coercion in the Treatment of Substance Abusers: An Overview and Critical Analysis of Thirty Years of Research', *Substance Use & Misuse*, 40 (2005). For arguments opposing these practices, see: M. Sjöstrand and G. Helgesson, 'Coercive Treatment and Autonomy in Psychiatry', *Bioethics*, 22 (2008).
3 Many more were discharged directly from psychiatric emergency to our Centre than were admitted for hospitalisation. Not infrequently, clinicians urged patients to return to the hospital if, in the opinion of the clinician, they'd been prematurely discharged.
4 For an analysis of the response of health workers to trauma, see: S. Collins and A. Long, 'Too Tired to Care? The Psychological Effects of Working with Trauma', *Journal of Psychiatric and Mental Health Nursing*, 10 (2003). Two types of burn-out are identified as emotional exhaustion and depersonalisation, the latter being related to "feeling cynical about clients' success". See: S.W. Kraus and C.H. Stein, 'Recovery-Oriented Services for Individuals with Mental Illness and Case Managers' Experience of Professional Burnout', *Community Mental Health Journal*, 49 (2013), p. 8. Also: C.H. Stein and S.A. Craft, 'Case Managers' Experiences of Personal Growth: Learning from Consumers', *Community Mental Health Journal*, 43 (2007), p. 184.
5 See: D. Markham, 'Attitudes Towards Patients with a Diagnosis of Borderline Personality Disorder: Social Rejection and Dangerousness', *Journal of Mental Health*, 12 (2003). For a brief description of epidemiology, diagnosis and causal factors,

see: K. Lieb and others, 'Borderline Personality Disorder', *The Lancet*, 364 (2004), pp. 453–55.
6 Literature investigating conflict within multidisciplinary teams shows how professional groups assert and protect their professional identities and theoretical approaches. See: B. Brown, P. Crawford, and J. Darongkamas, 'Blurred Roles and Permeable Boundaries: The Experience of Multidisciplinary Working in Community Mental Health', *Health & Social Care in the Community*, 8 (2000). Given the preponderance of nursing staff in mental health teams, other professionals may report feeling isolated or silenced because they are outnumbered. According to one study: "An intriguing finding is the readiness for some clinicians to establish for themselves a mandate to critique their colleagues. . . by exploiting a perceived position of power to expose these perceived faults in practice". See: A. Jones, 'Multidisciplinary Team Working: Collaboration and Conflict', *International Journal of Mental Health Nursing*, 15 (2006), p. 26.
7 ASTAT: Adult Short Term Assessment and Treatment (Team). See: fraserhealth.ca/Service-Directory/Services/mental-health-and-substance-use/mental-health-community-services/adult-short-term-assessment-and-treatment-program#.X8hR49hKjD4
8 The mental health consumer/survivor movement identifies the traumatic impact of being "treated" as a mental health patient as so damaging that there can be no "return to a pre-illness state". L. Davidson and others, 'Recovery in Serious Mental Illness: A New Wine or Just a New Bottle?', *Professional Psychology: Research and Practice*, 36 (2005), p. 481.
9 A meta-analysis of research on cannabis as a risk factor for schizophrenia, or schizophrenia-like symptoms, indicates a "three-fold" increase in pathology. See: D.M. Semple, A.M. McIntosh, and S.M. Lawrie, 'Cannabis as a Risk Factor for Psychosis: Systematic Review', *Journal of Psychopharmacology*, 19 (2005), p. 191. One study of 216 people showed that three months following discharge from hospital for psychotic illness, one-fifth of the cohort was non-compliant with medication, the strongest predictor being substance misuse. See: M. Olfson and others, 'Predicting Medication Noncompliance after Hospital Discharge among Patients with Schizophrenia', *Psychiatric Services*, 51 (2000), p. 221.
10 Following accidental death, suicide is the leading cause of death among young men worldwide, the numbers being likely "substantially underestimated". See: A. Pitman and others, 'Suicide in Young Men', *The Lancet*, 379 (2012), pp. 2383–84. Other research notes that, "psychiatric diagnosis is a weak predictor of suicide", although attempts by psychiatric patients are generally "interpreted as irrational" and related to their clinical profile. Attempts in non-clinical populations are differently interpreted; a "temporary imbalance of mind" is only one of many possibilities. These authors suggest "psychiatric patients might, for very good (rational) reasons, feel devalued and disabled". They also claim that attributing suicide to mental illness hides the more significant social issues and responsibility for "a range of public policy factors. . . in relation to primary prevention". Included is the need to address "the lax prescribing of psychiatric drugs by the medical profession [that] increases suicide rates". See: A. Rogers and D. Pilgrim, *A Sociology of Mental Health and Illness* (Maidenhead, England: Open University Press, 2010), p. 208. Suicide among borderline patients may be as much as 50% higher than in the general population. See: K. Lieb and others, 'Borderline Personality Disorder', p. 453.
11 "MASH", the acronym for Mobile Army Surgical Hospital, is an allusion to the film and television series based on the novel by R. Hooker, *Mash: A Novel About Three Army Doctors* (New York: HarperCollins, 1997).

16 *James' Story*

12 The ranking of mental illness in order of importance and legitimacy is complex, and a key issue is personal control. Psychosis is typically viewed as beyond an individual's control and more legitimate—it might be argued—than the emotional response caused by acute situational stressors, including historical trauma and loss. This legitimacy is additionally supported by the "medical" nature of "serious and persistent mental illness" (SPMI) and the use of antipsychotic medication and mood stabilizers.

13 Antisocial personality disorder is one of the best predictors of violence, particularly when diagnosed with substance abuse. Even then, "accurate prediction is impossible", especially in the case of a poorly defined diagnosis likes James', while psychosis itself is *not* a strong predictor of violence. These authors also note the spectacular inaccuracy of mental health professionals in predicting dangerousness. The possibility of human rights infringement is a given with such predictions along with the implications of social control and policing that "some professionals worry. . . is incompatible with a caring and therapeutic role". See: Rogers and Pilgrim, 'A Sociology of Mental Health and Illness', pp. 205–12.

14 The death of a counsellor murdered in the parking lot of his workplace by a former client in the Vancouver area in 2005 shocked the clinical community. While such incidents are rare, they stoke the historical, still widespread, fear of people with mental illness, especially psychotic illness, as dangerous, even among clinicians. See: www.cbc.ca/news/canada/british-columbia/mental-health-worker-killed-1.532535. More disturbing is the high number of people with mental health issues who die when attended by the police. See, for example: www.cbc.ca/news/canada/british-columbia/police-bc-mental-health-report-1.5161557.

15 J. Hillman, *The Soul's Code: In Search of Character and Calling* (New York: Warner Books, 1997), p. 35.

16 The extrovertive and introvertive types of mystical experience defined by Stace generally conform to kataphatic and apophatic mysticism, respectively. The former refers to an emotional or spontaneous and embodied type, the latter to an intellectual or cultivated type. See: W.T. Stace, *Mysticism and Philosophy* (London: Macmillan, 1961), pp. 44–65.

17 These authors examine the positive impact of mysticism that arguably fits into the much larger body of research on spirituality, religion and mental health. See: K.R. Byrd, D. Lear, and S. Schwenka, 'Mysticism as a Predictor of Subjective Wellbeing', *The International Journal for the Psychology of Religion*, 10 (2000).

18 Harold Koenig highlights the strong positive correlation between "religiosity and spirituality" and mental health regarding the many emotional benefits suggested by such research. See: H.G. Koenig, 'Research on Religion, Spirituality, and Mental Health: A Review', *Canadian Journal of Psychiatry*, 54 (2009). A contentious debate, initiated by Koenig, suggests it is appropriate and desirable for a psychiatrist to pray with his patients if requested to do so. H.G. Koenig, 'Religion and Mental Health: What Should Psychiatrists Do?', *Psychiatric Bulletin*, 32 (2008), p. 203.

19 My reticence was informed by many factors, including the ethical issues raised in the prayer debate, and the fear of transgressing professional boundaries. Nonetheless, the humanist focus of my counselling education emphasised the almost sacred intimacy of the client-counsellor relationship and examined ideas about the transcendent. See: G. Egan, *The Skilled Helper: A Systematic Approach to Effective Helping*, 4th edn (Belmont, CA: Thomson Brooks/Cole Publishing, 1990). See also: A.H. Maslow, *Religions, Values, and Peak-Experiences*, Vol. 35 (Columbus: Ohio State University Press, 1964).

20 The presence of spiritual and religious content in psychotic delusions is well established and of interest to researchers attempting to differentiate between legitimate religious or mystical experience and pathology.

21 See: M. Zimmerman, L. Rothschild, and I. Chelminski, 'The Prevalence of DSM-IV Personality Disorders in Psychiatric Outpatients', *American Journal of Psychiatry*, 162 (2005).
22 The need for greater mutuality and honesty on the part of clinicians regarding their own "roadblocks to change" is discussed in: S. Mead and M.E. Copeland, 'What Recovery Means to Us: Consumers' Perspectives', *Community Mental Health Journal*, 36 (2000), pp. 320–21. The issue of mutuality is not easily resolved within an unequal power structure despite Rogers' claim to the contrary. See: Chapter 4, "Reciprocity and mutuality", pp. 94–95. See also: Racine, 'Loving in the Context of Community Mental Health', p. 116.
23 Patients with a good "therapeutic alliance" with their clinician are much more likely to remain medication compliant, which ironically may compromise a person's health and well-being. See: M. Olfson and others, 'Relationship Between Antidepressant Medication Treatment and Suicide in Adolescents', *Archives of General Psychiatry*, 60 (2003), p. 219.
24 The question of SSRIs (Selective Serotonin Reuptake Inhibitors) contributing to an increase in completed suicides among youth remains contentious and inconclusive. One study found "there was no statistical difference in crude suicide rates among patients assigned to SSRIs, other antidepressants, or placebo". See: A. Khan and others, 'Suicide Rates in Clinical Trials of SSRIs, Other Antidepressants, and Placebo: Analysis of FDA Reports', *American Journal of Psychiatry*, 160 (2003), p. 791. Another study looking exclusively at youth, funded by major pharmaceutical companies, highlights the difficulty of determining to what extent antidepressant medications can even reduce suicidality. See: M. Olfson and others, 'Relationship between Antidepressant Medication Treatment and Suicide in Adolescents', p. 980.
25 The literature examining the benefits of mindfulness meditation as an adjunct treatment for physical and psychological dis-ease is extensive and well established. See: J. Kabat-Zinn, 'Mindfulness-Based Interventions in Context: Past, Present, and Future', *Clinical Psychology: Science and Practice*, 10 (2003); J. Kabat-Zinn, *Full Catastrophe Living: Using the Wisdom of Your Body and Mind to Face Stress, Pain, and Illness* (New York: Dell, 1990). Two studies suggest evidence supporting the therapeutic use of mindfulness training with people dealing with psychosis. See: P. Chadwick and others, 'Mindfulness Groups for Distressing Voices and Paranoia: A Replication and Randomised Feasibility Trial', *Behavioural and Cognitive Psychotherapy*, 37 (2009); P. Chadwick and others, 'Mindfulness Groups for People with Psychosis', *Behavioural and Cognitive Psychotherapy*, 33 (2005).
26 A.A. Lazarus, 'How Certain Boundaries and Ethics Diminish Therapeutic Effectiveness', *Ethics & Behavior*, 4 (1994). A thoughtful argument on the difference between dual relationships and exploitation is found in: K. Tomm, 'The Ethics of Dual Relationships', *The California Therapist*, 5 (1993). A literature review on the subject of dual relationships examined the complexity and ambiguity of this issue and concluded that "[w]hat one professional may deem as appropriate behaviour, another professional may view as a boundary violation". See: S.M. Moleski and M.S. Kiselica, 'Dual Relationships: A Continuum Ranging from the Destructive to the Therapeutic', *Journal of Counseling & Development*, 83 (2005), p. 8.
27 Joseph Goldstein is one of the founders of the influential Buddhist teaching centre, the Insight Meditation Society, which operates out of Barre, Massachusetts. See: <www.dharma.org/meditation-retreats/retreat-center> [accessed 2 Dec. 2020].
28 Hillman, *The Soul's Code: In Search of Character and Calling*, p. 35.

References

Brown, B., Crawford, P., and Darongkamas, J., 'Blurred Roles and Permeable Boundaries: The Experience of Multidisciplinary Working in Community Mental Health', *Health & Social Care in the Community*, 8 (2000), 425–35. https://doi.org/10.1046/j.1365-2524.2000.00268.x

Byrd, K.R., Lear, D., and Schwenka, S., 'Mysticism as a Predictor of Subjective Well-Being', *The International Journal for the Psychology of Religion*, 10 (2000), 259–69. https://doi.org/10.1207/S15327582IJPR1004_04

Chadwick, P., Hughes, S., Russell, D., Russell, I., and Dagnan, D., 'Mindfulness Groups for Distressing Voices and Paranoia: A Replication and Randomized Feasibility Trial', *Behavioural and Cognitive Psychotherapy*, 37 (2009), 403–12. https://doi.org/10.1017/S1352465809990166

Chadwick, P., Taylor, K.N., and Abba, N., 'Mindfulness Groups for People with Psychosis', *Behavioural and Cognitive Psychotherapy*, 33 (2005), 351–59. https://doi.org/10.1017/S1352465805002158

Collins, S., and Long, A., 'Too Tired to Care? The Psychological Effects of Working with Trauma', *Journal of Psychiatric and Mental Health Nursing*, 10 (2003), 17–27. https://doi.org/10.1046/j.1365-2850.2003.00526.x

Davidson, L., O'Connell, M., Tondora, J., Lawless, M., and Evans, A.C., 'Recovery in Serious Mental Illness: A New Wine or Just a New Bottle?', *Professional Psychology: Research and Practice*, 36 (2005), 480–87. https://doi.org/10.1037/0735-7028.36.5.480

Egan, G., *The Skilled Helper: A Systematic Approach to Effective Helping*, 4th edn (Belmont, CA: Thomson Brooks/Cole Publishing, 1990).

Hillman, J., *The Soul's Code: In Search of Character and Calling* (New York: Warner Books, 1997).

Hooker, R., *Mash: A Novel About Three Army Doctors* (New York: HarperCollins, 1997).

Jones, A., 'Multidisciplinary Team Working: Collaboration and Conflict', *International Journal of Mental Health Nursing*, 15 (2006), 19–28. https://doi.org/10.1111/j.1447-0349.2006.00400.x

Kabat-Zinn, J., *Full Catastrophe Living: Using the Wisdom of Your Body and Mind to Face Stress, Pain, and Illness* (New York: Dell, 1990).

——, 'Mindfulness-Based Interventions in Context: Past, Present, and Future', *Clinical Psychology: Science and Practice*, 10 (2003), 144–56. https://doi.org/10.1093/clipsy.bpg016

Khan, A., Khan, S., Kolts, R., and Brown, W.A., 'Suicide Rates in Clinical Trials of SSRIS, Other Antidepressants, and Placebo: Analysis of FDA Reports', *American Journal of Psychiatry*, 160 (2003), 790–92. https://doi.org/10.1176/appi.ajp.160.4.790

Klag, S., O'Callaghan, F., and Creed, P., 'The Use of Legal Coercion in the Treatment of Substance Abusers: An Overview and Critical Analysis of Thirty Years of Research', *Substance Use & Misuse*, 40 (2005), 1777–95. https://doi.org/10.1080/10826080500260891

Koenig, H.G., 'Religion and Mental Health: What Should Psychiatrists Do?', *Psychiatric Bulletin*, 32 (2008), 201–3. https://doi.org/10.1192/pb.bp.108.019430

——, 'Research on Religion, Spirituality, and Mental Health: A Review', *Canadian Journal of Psychiatry*, 54 (2009), 283–91. https://doi.org/10.1177/070674370905400502

Kraus, S.W., and Stein, C.H., 'Recovery-Oriented Services for Individuals with Mental Illness and Case Managers' Experience of Professional Burnout', *Community Mental Health Journal*, 49 (2013), 7–13. https://doi.org/10.1007/s10597-012-9505-2

Lazarus, A.A., 'How Certain Boundaries and Ethics Diminish Therapeutic Effectiveness', *Ethics & Behavior*, 4 (1994), 255–61. https://doi.org/10.1207/s15327019eb0403_10

Lieb, K., Zanarini, M.C., Schmahl, C., Linehan, M.M., and Bohus, M., 'Borderline Personality Disorder', *The Lancet*, 364 (2004), 453–61. https://doi.org/10.1016/S0140-6736(04)16770-6

Markham, D., 'Attitudes Towards Patients with a Diagnosis of Borderline Personality Disorder: Social Rejection and Dangerousness', *Journal of Mental Health*, 12 (2003), 595–612. https://doi.org/10.1080/09638230310001627955

Maslow, A.H., *Religions, Values, and Peak-Experiences*, Vol. 35 (Columbus: Ohio State University Press, 1964).

Mead, S., and Copeland, M.E., 'What Recovery Means to Us: Consumers' Perspectives', *Community Mental Health Journal*, 36 (2000), 315–28. https://doi.org/10.1023/A:1001917516869

Moleski, S.M., and Kiselica, M.S., 'Dual Relationships: A Continuum Ranging from the Destructive to the Therapeutic', *Journal of Counseling & Development*, 83 (2005), 3–11. https://doi.org/10.1002/j.1556-6678.2005.tb00574.x

Olfson, M., Mechanic, D., Hansell, S., Boyer, C.A., Walkup, J., and Weiden, P.J., 'Predicting Medication Noncompliance After Hospital Discharge Among Patients with Schizophrenia', *Psychiatric Services*, 51 (2000), 216–22. https://doi.org/10.1176/appi.ps.51.2.216

Olfson, M., Shaffer, D., Marcus, S.C., and Greenberg, T., 'Relationship Between Antidepressant Medication Treatment and Suicide in Adolescents', *Archives of General Psychiatry*, 60 (2003), 978–81. https://doi.org/10.1001/archpsyc.60.9.978

Pitman, A., Krysinska, K., Osborn, D., and King, M., 'Suicide in Young Men', *The Lancet*, 379 (2012), 2383–92. https://doi.org/10.1016/S0140-6736(12)60731-4

Racine, C., 'Loving in the Context of Community Mental Health Practice: A Clinical Case Study and Reflection on Mystical Experience', *Mental Health, Religion & Culture*, 17 (2014), 109–21. https://doi.org/10.1080/13674676.2012.749849

Rogers, A., and Pilgrim, D., *A Sociology of Mental Health and Illness* (Maidenhead, England: Open University Press, 2010).

Semple, D.M., McIntosh, A.M., and Lawrie, S.M., 'Cannabis as a Risk Factor for Psychosis: Systematic Review', *Journal of Psychopharmacology*, 19 (2005), 187–94. https://doi.org/10.1177/0269881105049040

Sjöstrand, M., and Helgesson, G., 'Coercive Treatment and Autonomy in Psychiatry', *Bioethics*, 22 (2008), 113–20. https://doi.org/10.1111/j.1467-8519.2007.00610.x

Stace, W.T., *Mysticism and Philosophy* (London: Macmillan, 1961).

Stein, C.H., and Craft, S.A., 'Case Managers' Experiences of Personal Growth: Learning from Consumers', *Community Mental Health Journal*, 43 (2007), 183–95. https://doi.org/10.1007/s10597-006-9068-1

Tomm, K., 'The Ethics of Dual Relationships', *The California Therapist*, 5 (1993), 7–19.

Zimmerman, M., Rothschild, L., and Chelminski, I., 'The Prevalence of DSM-IV Personality Disorders in Psychiatric Outpatients', *American Journal of Psychiatry*, 162 (2005), 1911–18. https://doi.org/10.1176/appi.ajp.162.10.1911

2 Three opponents of wonder

The importance of reverencing the vulnerable help seeker who reaches out to community mental health care for help in understanding and healing the chaos and anguish of her or his life is indisputable. But what does this comprise, and can reverence be refreshed or restored? Reverence is not easily found or expressed in the climate of a large community mental health centre with its relentless pressures, tight economies and competing ethical demands.

> *[T]he doctor's ten-thousandth patient needs and deserves the same recognition of his common humanity and the same hushed acknowledgement of his tender fragility as does her first patient. These needs inhere in all patients equally, regardless of their personal qualities.*[1]

In this chapter, three impediments—opponents—to ethical care are examined narratively and theoretically to analyse how they shape the assumptions and behaviours of clinicians. We wish to understand their contribution to the de-moralisation of the clinician; to the proliferation, misunderstanding and mismanagement of "mental illness"; and, most importantly, to the global dehumanisation of the person labelled in this way.

We begin with an examination of *medicalisation* and the provocative debate on "medical imperialism" forwarded by sociologist Philip Strong, who took his own field to task for speaking out of both sides of its mouth by criticising medicine while still enjoying the status that medicine conferred. This debate has implications for all professionals in the "allied health field"—including my field, counselling psychology—given its connection to the medical model within community mental health care. Another opponent, *asymmetry*, describes the unresolved problem of institutional hierarchy found in the imbalance of power between the clinician and the vulnerable help seeker and also *among* professionals within the mental health team. We will also consider the prevalence, and meaning, of *dehumanisation* with a brief account of the scholarship on prejudice from the field of social psychology and the pioneering work of Gordon Allport. This evolving science is refining our understanding of how dehumanisation is predicated on the complex relationship between the individual and the in-group, or out-group, to which she or he belongs. Social psychology is showing how the group dynamics that can influence and inflame prejudice *are the same* as those that can extinguish it. Emerging from this research is an especially subtle form of discrimination called infra-humanisation, which will be discussed, along with the problem of stigmatisation and the "heartsink" patient. The chapter concludes with a reflection on the dehumanised clinician.

We begin, however, with an examination of the system of community mental health care and the influences that have helped move psychiatric care from the asylum to the community.

Community mental health care: An introduction

In British Columbia, Canada, community mental health care is a provincial service—covered under the province's medical services plan—that employs a case management model within freestanding day clinics, or outpatient clinics attached to hospitals.[2] Case management has been described as "an attempt to overcome deficiencies in community care. . . due to fragmented service systems and lack of continuity of care".[3] People attending community mental health services are often multiply disadvantaged and in need of many services, from life-skills coaching and dentistry to housing and employment, all of which extend far beyond the treatment of their psychological issues. Others are referred directly from the hospital psychiatric ward, and a primary function of community mental health centres is to keep people *out* of hospital. While there are various types and styles of case management, what they typically share in common is a multidisciplinary team approach.[4] According to one dated account, this approach bears no small resemblance to current practice, although there has been a significant increase in para-medical staff and specialised services.[5] In contemporary community mental health settings, psychiatrists, general practitioners, psychologists, clinical counsellors, social workers, occupational therapists, psychiatric nurses, mental health support staff, administrative staff and others typically work as a "team" under one roof.

The "case manager" is the clinician who oversees and manages the care of any given individual receiving service. Typically, this is a psychologist, a clinical counsellor, a social worker or a psychiatric nurse, as was the case in my community mental health centre. Case managers are responsible for assessing the help seeker's psychosocial needs, for providing individual care plans and for making referrals and linking the help seeker to appropriate services or supports. Their work includes monitoring the help seeker's progress regarding the established care plan, her mental state and her compliance with medication and its side effects. The case manager is also responsible for advocacy, for establishing and maintaining the therapeutic relationship and, depending on her education, for offering therapy.[6]

Although caseloads may vary from one community mental health centre to the next, case managers in my Centre carried caseloads of 30–40 files or more varying in acuity and complexity. Often, help seekers were already connected to multiple services within the community. Depending on her education and role within the team, a case manager might also provide one-on-one or group therapy, psychiatric follow-up and community outreach. Mental health centres provide services including adult community support, adult short-term assessment and treatment, community residential programs, geriatric programs, crisis intervention, day and outpatient programs, addictions counselling, concurrent disorders services,[7] group therapy, peer support, and after-hours mental health support and more.[8]

Community mental health care employs a medical, psychiatrically informed perspective focused primarily, although not exclusively, on underlying pathology.[9] The pathologising of mental distress also gives primacy to the function of the doctor, the psychiatric "team" and psychiatric medicine itself. Every person accepted for care, for example, was assessed by a psychiatrist or general practitioner, diagnosed, prescribed medication and followed up.[10] *Only* doctors prescribe, while nurses manage and monitor the effects of medication and give injections, which is why psychiatric nurses are near the apex of the team hierarchy. Psychiatric nurses also have considerably fewer years of education than colleagues with master's degrees in social work, counselling and occupational therapy. The difference in education, training and professional orientation between medical staff and allied health team members also creates inter-team conflict and alienation, but the primacy of medicine and medication is unequivocal.

The rise of para-professionals—allied health professionals—in community mental health care over time has enabled doctors to "expand their empire while. . . severely restricting the production of new doctors". Indeed, this was confirmed by the chronic shortage of psychiatric hours available in my institution.[11] Severe doctor shortages in the community also meant it was difficult to find general practitioners to accept people labelled with mental illness as new patients or to find private psychiatrists for those who were refused service by our Centre. While it may be true that para-professionals now fulfil tasks formerly under the jurisdiction of the doctor, they also remain "firmly under medical control".[12] This control, along with the physical containment of patients, was significantly greater inside the asylums that preceded the establishment of today's community-run clinics.

The shift from the asylum

The closure of mental institutions occurred with the emergence of the antipsychiatry movement. Its chief proponents were vocal, prolific and political in their ambitions to reform psychiatric health care. This movement was represented among others by critic Thomas Szasz, an indefatigable intellectual who denied the existence of mental illness for over five decades.[13] Although Szasz has been criticised for his provocative and flamboyant argumentation, his staying power continues to influence contemporary critics of psychiatry.[14] R. D. Laing, another psychiatrist, distinguished himself by challenging the roots of mental illness and famously arguing that "paranoid delusions were not signs of illness but an understandable reaction to an inescapable and persecutory social order".[15] Both Szasz and Laing spoke out against psychiatry, the medicalisation of social issues and the abuse of professional power, although from different perspectives.[16]

A third psychiatrist and social reformer, Franco Basaglia, was enormously influential in changing the culture of the mental institution.[17] Basaglia's work led to the passing of the Italian National Reform Bill of 1978, which resulted in the dismantling of psychiatric hospitals and the rise of community mental health services in Italy. At the same time, hundreds of psychiatric institutions closed "throughout Europe, New Zealand, and Australia, including many in Ireland and Finland where the highest number of asylum beds were located".[18] Another major critic, Michel Foucault,[19] was the only non-psychiatrist whose work still drives the arguments of the most recent wave of psychiatric critics in the Critical Psychiatry Network.[20] All four critics "championed the notion that personal reality was independent from any hegemonic definition of normalcy imposed by organised psychiatry".[21] However, hegemony prevails.

Psychiatry is still being challenged by its own and is unique among medical specialities for this reason. Its internal dissenters underscore the irony and implausibility of finding comparable ethical vigilance in an "anti-paediatrics" or "anti-anaesthetics" movement. Encouragingly, the ongoing influences of the anti-psychiatry and critical psychiatry movements, as well as the move towards post-psychiatry and justice in psychiatry, continue to assert themselves[22] and are growing.[23]

High-profile professionals, like psychiatrist Joanna Moncrieff, further endorse the validity of some claims against psychiatry, in particular the prescription of medications. Moncrieff, who is a professor of critical and social psychiatry at the University College of London, founded the Critical Psychiatry Network. She continues to speak out and has published widely on the "myth" of a chemical cure for psychiatric symptoms, warning of the limitations and dangers of psychotropic medication.[24] She is but one in an impressive line of psychiatrists who have challenged the institution over many decades. Moncrieff and those who have preceded her may not have eliminated a role for psychiatry, but they have strenuously called its practices into question.

> [A]cademic psychiatry has helped the industry to colonise more and more areas of modern life. . . . Persuading people to understand their problems as biological deficiencies obscures the social origin and context of distress and prevents people from seeking social or political solutions. . . . Psychiatry with its medical credentials and associated respectability, and the financial power of the industry represents a formidable combination.[25]

Medicalisation

The alarm raised about escalating mental illness and inadequate services for the "mentally ill" and the ever-increasing range of activities recommended as "therapeutic"—from walking in the forest[26] to visiting the art gallery[27]—points to medicalisation as a form of socio-cultural entrancement. Sociologist Peter Conrad describes it as "a process by which non-medical problems become defined and treated as medical problems, usually in terms of illness or disorders",[28] which shows "strong evidence for expansion rather than contraction of medical jurisdiction".[29] But due to "complex social forces" and "market interests", medicalisation is worryingly less influenced by the censure of medical imperialism or the control of physicians than it was in the 1970s.[30] These forces and interests represent aggressive strategies used by drug manufacturers to increase profits and influence the rise of individual consumerism. The latter is enhanced by the presence of social media where people can now diagnose themselves, communicate with others on chat lines and instruct their doctors on what medications to prescribe. Medicalisation goes "far beyond psychiatry".[31]

> Marketing diseases, and selling drugs to treat those diseases, is now common in the "post-Prozac era" . . . GlaxoSmithKline has spent millions to raise the public visibility of SAD (social anxiety disorder) and GAD (generalised anxiety disorder) through sophisticated marketing campaigns. . . . The tag line was "Imagine being allergic to people". . . . Paxil internet sites offer consumers self-tests to assess if they have SAD or GAD (*www.paxil.com*). The campaign successfully defined these diagnostic categories as both common and abnormal, thus needing treatment.[32]

One contentious example is the medicalisation of grief, which almost found its way into the newest and fifth edition of the *Diagnostic and Statistical Manual of Mental Disorders (DSM V)*; the primary tool used in psychiatric diagnosis.[33] Described as "complicated grief", or "CG", the anticipation of this diagnosis provoked criticism and concern.[34] Clinical supporters claimed that CG's inclusion in the *DSM V* would help many who are crippled by its debilitating symptoms. Not surprisingly, the "hallmark" of CG is sadness and yearning. According to one source, the *only* potential harm for this diagnosis would have been primarily related to labelling and stigma, which the authors nonetheless felt was outweighed by the benefits, "as long as the diagnosis was applied appropriately".[35] Given the ease with which bereavement *could* be misdiagnosed and treated as depression, it might reasonably be assumed this diagnosis would be all too likely misapplied. Indeed, the level of medicalisation within our cultural consciousness could propel *anyone* dealing with the wrenching anguish of bereavement to believe they *needed* clinical help. A brief extract from an article that supported the recognition of CG as a distinct mental illness illustrates how yearning is pathologised:

> Intense yearning or longing for the deceased is common in CG. There are strong feelings of wanting to be reunited with the lost loved one, associated with behaviours to feel close to the deceased, frequent intrusive or preoccupying thoughts of the deceased and efforts to avoid experiences that trigger reminders of the loss. . . . [W]ell studied treatment for depression and medication studies suggest that improvement in depression can occur with only modest changes in CG symptoms. Overall, while symptoms can overlap, there is strong evidence that CG is distinct from major depression.[36]

The construal of bereavement and yearning as an "illness" is anathema to those who oppose such reduction, given the concern about misdiagnoses and the implication of untapped markets waiting to be developed and exploited. Such is the tide of medicalisation that washes over scholars and clinicians, past and present, who are challenging the progress of medicalisation while witnessing the spectrum of "normalcy" slowly dwindle. For now, the diagnosis of CG appears in the appendix of the *DSM V*, as a condition for further study described as "persistent complex bereavement disorder".[37]

Medical imperialism and medicalisation

Medicalisation is closely tied to the issue of medical imperialism, a term coined by Schreier and Berger in 1974.[38] The thesis of medical imperialism prompted debate over two decades following a provocative essay on the subject by sociologist Philip Strong. While disturbed by the implications of medical imperialism, Strong claimed it was *rivalled* by the imperialism of medical sociology for which he lampooned his own field. The tenets of this thesis are arguably familiar, even banal, but the massive sweep of their dominion and ongoing potential is impressive and hides in plain sight through the entrancement of medicalisation. For brevity and clarity, the following list provides an overview of the attributes of medical imperialism, which:

(i)   has led to social problems being "professionalised" and, in turn, has increased the number of professions, professionals and bureaucracies who stand to benefit
(ii) has promoted a monopoly in service provision that generally excludes the involvement, or the legitimacy of involvement, by other types of professionals or laypeople
(iii) has resulted in "services" and their criteria that are almost entirely controlled by the professional rather than by the vulnerable help seeker

Three opponents of wonder 27

(iv) has led to "empire building" and the redefinition of existing problems as well as the discovery of wholly new ones that medicalisation would have us believe is the job of medicine to solve
(v) has created a seemingly indefinite expansion of needs and problems based on manufactured definitions and a growing awareness that illness has *not*, in fact, been conquered by the creation of a national health service. On the contrary, the very agencies dealing with these problems have played, and still play, a central role in their discovery and development
(vi) has contributed to the possibility of the limitless expansion of any one profession, given the relative nature of need and the flexible nature of professions
(vii) has informed the perception of aetiology as something to be understood in individualistic terms rather than something related to a social problem. Hence, "symptoms" are separated from the culture in which they emerge, which consequently leads to the "depoliticisation" of social problems
(viii) has resulted in such problems being primarily expressed in medical terms, with the emphasis being placed on science and those professionals dealing with matters related to the sciences, including psychologists, psychiatrists, biologists and doctors. Even where such professionals do not directly manage or "treat" the help seeker, their doctrines inform the professions that do
(ix) has ultimately resulted in the construal and handling of contemporary social problems in predominantly "medical" terms
(x) has contributed to the belief that effective prevention of disease must necessarily involve major social change rather than professional "tinkering" at the individual level
(xi) has developed the perception of the help seeker as someone who is ultimately "addicted" to and "dependent" on professionals, medical or otherwise.[39]

In his argument, Strong does not discount the "illegitimate medicalization of the social world", which Simon Williams agrees is a well-rehearsed issue. But he uses the thesis of medical imperialism to excoriate sociology's covetousness of medicine's power and territory. Strong claims, for example, that sociology has only prospered through its critique of medicine while attempting to capture some of its status in the process. "Sociologists may be said to play a double game, seeking the support of the less powerful on occasion but in turn using this alliance to foster its other alliances with those in power".[40] Such an accusation might seem to hobble even the most legitimate sociological critique of medicine, psychiatry or any other area of human concern, leaving the most vulnerable at even greater risk of exploitation. Yet Strong's claim has merit, even (or perhaps especially) for those para-professionals like myself who find themselves embroiled to their benefit and ethical discomfiture in the cachet and trap of "the medical". His coup de grace makes clear that sociology might ultimately create even greater problems than the ones it seeks to challenge.

> The critics of the "medical model" tend to forget that its use, however barbarous on some occasions, has been liberating in others. In an alienated world, the sick role, far from having the entirely conservative implications which some ascribe to it may serve as an individual defence and refuge. A fully social model, because it reintroduces human agency into health and illness, can serve, in a context where the state has still to wither away, as a means for an even more systematic oppression than is offered by organic medicine.[41]

This argument is compelling in the face of those inevitable losses, traumas and extremes of emotional human suffering, incapacity and instability that demand respite, time, shelter, care and professional attention. But the acceptance of *any* barbarity in exchange for the "luxury" of being identified as "mentally ill" seems to have little to recommend it. That said, Strong never entirely discounted the thesis of medical imperialism despite cautioning sociology against its own naivety and hubris. He recognised medicine's "complex, multi-dimensional, multi-factorial knowledge base and its heterogeneous, if not faction riven, nature and internally contested boundaries". Strong also saw "the positive (as well as negative) contribution which modern medicine makes".[42]

Strong's challenge to his field of medical sociology has resonance for *all* allied health professionals working under the jurisdiction and protection of medical authority in community mental health care. This authority keeps clinicians compliant and morally disengaged—or at least stretched and silent—in the face of questionable praxis, assumptions and behaviours in exchange for a cut of the action that medicine has to offer.

> It is power and authority over individuals under care with which mental health should be concerned. These are the tools used to legitimise assessments, diagnoses, prescriptions, and hospitalisations. These tools... allow clinicians to medicalize human emotion, facilitate the removal of children from family homes, and report at their discretion to the full roster of professionals including police, probation officers, social workers, and family doctors who are similarly endowed.[43]

Medicalisation is a complex mix with no "one" to hold responsible, yet the threat to the help seeker in community mental health care is no less real on that account. Regardless of where she is within the hierarchy, every clinician holds remarkable power over every vulnerable help seeker she encounters within this system through the privilege of an asymmetrical relationship.

Asymmetry

Medical asymmetry refers to the inevitable imbalance of power between the clinician and the vulnerable help seeker in a hierarchy of care to which the help seeker must submit. Asymmetry describes the "knowledge and authority that allows doctors to promulgate a biomedical model of disease and simultaneously undermine patients' own experience and understanding".[44] Such inequality, Douglas Maynard suggests, is negotiated and "interactively achieved" with patient consent, by using "ordinary talk" to enlist the opinion of the patient and over-ride her opinion, experience and knowledge. Its dynamic ostensibly forwards legitimate evidence based on tests, assessments and their objective findings. But the "evidence" presented to the help seeker in specialist language is loaded with larger social and economic implications related to treatment options, privileges and services. Asymmetry is not only weighted in terms of power differentials but also in terms of the biomedical model *and* the opinion of the professional supporting it.[45]

> The prototypical example is of a patient who arrives at a doctor's office and presents a complaint. The doctor, mainly by way of questioning strategies that require delimited responses, works the complaint into biomedical categories that lack sensitivity to the patient's psychosocial concerns, life world, and folk understandings.[46]

Maynard describes this kind of transaction as the "Perspective Display Sequence", which involves the affiliative move of the clinician making an inquiry by appearing to solicit an opinion.[47] This process is not merely to gain information but to gain an advantage, albeit collaboratively, that enables the medical professional to *endorse* and *trump* the patient's experience. To show how it works, Maynard analysed this particular manoeuvre in verbal exchanges between a diagnosing physician and a cohort of parents and guardians whose infants and children were referred to a clinic for developmental delays. The physician's strategy is to confirm the patient's point of view while essentially exploiting it "to reinforce or affirm the position in the inviter's response".[48] This sequence is used where caution is needed, for example, in the delivery of "highly charged diagnoses". A developmental delay would surely qualify, considering the repercussions of such a diagnosis on every aspect of that child's life for the rest of her life, and the life of her family. Interestingly, such verbal manipulation helps sell an idea that is not only outside the help seeker's experience but may *deny* it.

Reformulating the problem to diminish or selectively ignore the content of the help seeker's experience "permeates [the] doctor-patient interaction" and is a well-established phenomenon, although the reasons are less clear. Maynard suggests several possibilities, including technology itself, by which he presumably means the technology of assessment and diagnosis,[49] which shapes and delimits human experience into proscribed categories. Asymmetry is also underscored by the "surveillance" of computerised documentation, which must at least appear to uphold institutional norms and, importantly, their unassailability.

A complex, layered picture emerges when we consider how embedded the clinician is in a web of corporate accountability to "schools, school systems [and] government agencies". The "orientation to social structure" is exceptionally "clear and concrete" when the clinician is accountable to every member of the immediate and extended clinical team.[50] The clinician is also accountable to the help seeker's employers, medical insurers, physician, lawyer, probation officer and financial worker as well as the police, the Ministry of Children and Family Development and the welfare office, among others. Within this "social safety net", the help seeker becomes, to some extent, the common property of every professional within and beyond the walls of community mental health. There are checks and balances, benefits and liabilities in this safety net, for both the clinician and the individual seeking help. But within this corporate structure, the clinician must manoeuvre skilfully when she, or he, confronts the ruling structure of the hierarchy that keeps workers firmly in line.

Tread lightly!

> *I am in my office when two team managers come in looking very serious and shut the door without asking my permission. All clinical staff members are being subjected to this process—the auditing of their clinical files—and I am prepared but suddenly feel invaded and wary. All clinical notes are computerised, and mine have already been accessed and examined. My notes tend to be extensive, neutral, observational and itemised with tasks to which I must attend on the client's behalf or that need to be fulfilled by the client.*
>
> *The issue of confidentiality is discussed with each help seeker. At the beginning of "treatment", a signature is requested as "proof" of the clinician's due diligence, and the help seeker's agreement to the "ethical" and "confidential" contract into which she is entering with the institution. But confidentiality is arguably an invention when every word documented about a given individual is stored within a computerised file. These can be accessed by employees from other hospitals and other community mental health centres operating within an enormous jurisdiction, although admittedly, with some restrictions. Interestingly, the penalty for going into the system to look at one's own medical file is immediate dismissal.*
>
> *Something is wrong with my work. Without much preamble, one of the managers who is now sitting beside me in front of the computer monitor asks me to go into a particular file to access a note and read it as proof of my transgression. I have written something about a help seeker who, following recent surgery now breathes through a small hole in his neck. This man had learned to speak through this apparatus. He must also blow his nose and cough through it, which is unsettling to witness and embarrassing for him to do in the presence of others. He turns away when he coughs or removes phlegm from his throat with*

a Kleenex and apologises. Yet, he does so with some frequency as his condition causes him to suffer chronic lung infections. When he asks permission to put his Kleenex in my office waste paper basket, I typically pick it up and place it on the floor in front of him so he doesn't have to reach.

My apparent insurrection lies in a statement I have made about the distress he has expressed regarding his probation officer who prohibits him from putting his used Kleenex in the office wastepaper basket. Having already occurred on several occasions, it is a source of mortification and rage for my client. I have allowed myself one carefully worded sentence reporting my client's experience in neutral terms.

I am asked why I have written this. The manager sitting beside me is looking very intently at me, the arms of our chairs are touching, the file is open on the screen before us, and my mind goes completely blank. An unpleasant tingling spreads up my back from the base of my spine. The other manager, whose micromanagement I am continually attempting to deflect, is in a chair behind us and informs me I could get into trouble for writing this. I coolly ask what kind of trouble that might be, but I feel the fear. There is no answer. They want to know if I am aware of having written something that could reflect badly on the team's relationship with the probation office across the street from us and imply that my job could be at risk. I remonstrate but sound defensive. I have sinned against the hierarchy, and it will not be tolerated for here deference to the system is law and one's solidarity with a vulnerable help seeker is more wisely expressed in private or not at all.

Hermeneutic and testimonial injustice

Miranda Fricker's work on hermeneutic injustice demonstrates the significance of the dynamic that Maynard has examined. Hermeneutic injustice is "the injustice of having some significant area of one's social experience obscured from collective understanding owing to a structural prejudice in the collective hermeneutical resource".[51] Fricker suggests that in the gap of unidentified experience there is no description because the injustice is hidden, unlanguaged and consequently invisible to collective social awareness. Fricker illustrates this phenomenon in her analysis of a story from Susan Brownmiller's work on the rise of the American women's liberation movement. The story documents the discovery of "sexual harassment" and the "aha" moment that revealed a truth that was finally and collectively recognised.[52] Its "discovery" may not have eliminated the problem, but sexual harassment is now legitimised as unjust and *illegal*. The strength of Fricker's work lies in her interest in *naming* this gap and in bringing it to collective awareness by singling out its essential, undeniable injustice. "For something to be an injustice it must be harmful but also wrongful, whether. . . discriminatory or otherwise unfair".[53]

If we return to the asymmetry in Maynard's example of the diagnosing clinician, we can see that such injustice or wrongfulness is not so easily assigned. What is *wrong* after all, with a concerned and over-extended paediatrician doing his best to relay difficult news to frightened parents about the developmental delay of their child? Yet, Fricker's work suggests that even if the physician is grieved to do so, the significance of the parents' powerlessness is of more concern. *They* are the ones suffering the injustice and are consequently more disadvantaged whereas for the doctor, "there is an obvious sense in which it suits his purpose".[54] The clinician is not the one labouring to understand within this asymmetrical relationship. Nor will he have to live with the full implications of a diagnostic label, treatment plan and system of care he is recommending. Even if both parties are "cognitively handicapped by the hermeneutical lacuna", it is *only* the patient who is seriously disadvantaged.

> The cognitive disablement prevents her from understanding an important patch of her experience; that is, a patch of experience which is strongly in her interests to understand, for without that understanding she is left deeply troubled, confused, and isolated, not to mention vulnerable to continued harassment. Her hermeneutical disadvantage renders her unable to make sense of her ongoing mistreatment, and this in turn prevents her from protesting it, let alone securing effective measures to stop it.[55]

Fricker's work is coming under scrutiny by researchers examining its relevance to health care. Havi Carel and Ian Kidd use Fricker's work on testimonial injustice to explore the difficulties of communication between doctors and patients.[56] The well-known complaint of people not being or feeling heard by their physicians is borne out by the evidence.

> [T]he epistemic concerns of patients continue to be voiced through a vast body of pathographic literature, including online patient support groups, blogs, narratives, and listservs. These attest to patients' persistent experiences of being ignored, marginalised, or epistemically excluded by those professions who are charged with their care.[57]

Carel and Kidd focus their analysis on the experience of people with chronic "somatic illness", as opposed to mental illness, which, I would suggest, offers even greater opportunity for this type of injustice.

> Actual and potential testimonial injustice is endemic within mental health service delivery. For example, central to mental health legislation is the idea that some people lack the capacity to make decisions and it follows that what they might say, how they construe problems, their choices and preferences lack coherence, logic, or credibility. It is not surprising then that the testimony of all or most people who use mental health services might be considered suspect.[58]

The global implications of such injustice are immense and confirm Fricker's description of hermeneutical injustice as "a kind of structural discrimination",[59] which would suggest that testimonial injustice is part of the very framework of institutional mental health care. Carel and Kidd express the same concern a little differently.

> Since the social and epistemic practices of giving information to others and interpreting our experiences is integral to our rationality, identity, agency, and dignity, it is evident that injustice which harms our testimonial and hermeneutical capacities will be sources of very deep harm.[60]

Asymmetry's power is striking and subtle as we have seen in Maynard's work on asymmetry in action and in Fricker's work, which identifies two kinds of injustice within it. In clinical care, hermeneutic injustice identifies the help seeker's lack of understanding within the asymmetrical clinical encounter and the system of care in which her life may be subsumed and harmed. Testimonial injustice occurs when a hearer discredits, diminishes or disbelieves the testimony of another. Testimonial injustice provides additional evidence for the significance of hermeneutical injustice. These processes also describe the phenomenon underwritten in community mental health care that legitimises the flagrant abuse of the help seeker's trust. This injustice is well documented in the literature on dehumanisation, the final "opponent of wonder" for our consideration that presents another phenomenal barrier to ethical care.

Dehumanisation

> *The ethical ideals of the medical profession are often and routinely unmet. One way this happens is when subtle forms of dehumanisation enter hospital life. Specifically, care-givers may treat patients less like persons and more like objects or nonhuman animals—situations that physicians themselves often satirise.*[61]

The "essence of dehumanisation" denies the "distinctly human mind" of another person that discounts a person's experience or agency or her ability to feel the full spectrum of human emotion, including the capacity to choose and to act.[62] When we deny the experience of others, we tend to treat and see them as machines. When we deny their agency, we are more likely to treat them like animals, "dogs, pigs, rats, parasites, or insects. . . . At other times they are likened to children, their lack of rationality, shame and sophistication seen patronisingly as innocence".[63] The most sobering form of dehumanisation occurs when another human being is described as "vermin" or filth.[64] While generally tied to the horrific violence of genocide like the Holocaust or the Rwandan massacre,[65] the anathema of dirtiness and infection is not limited to such extremes.

Staff toilets only!

> Discussions about the disgust that a number of mostly female clinicians felt about having "our" toilets used by patients, routinely occurred during staff meetings and the majority of the staff was female. Reasons given were that the toilets were left in a mess; they smelled bad and were not being flushed after use. Used paper towels were not being placed in the bin but left on the sink. There was the possibility of catching something off the toilet seat or of finding the toilet seat wet or soiled. Dirtiness was a major theme of concern. A boundary of great propriety was violated when a staff member allowed a patient to use "our" toilets and this always reflected poorly on the clinician who provided such access.
>
> Such dehumanisation was generalised to the patient toilet located in the waiting room area which for years had been available for the convenience of anyone waiting to see a clinician. Later, the installation of a buzzer system required whoever needed to use the toilet to go to the reception window and ask to be allowed in. The receptionist would press a loud buzzer announcing that the door had been open for the individual to proceed which alerted anyone in the waiting room that permission to use the toilet had been granted. These were changes justified by the argument that people were coming in off the street to use illegal drugs or were simply using the toilet "reserved" for registered patients.
>
> The issues of cleanliness, propriety, and territoriality were once again on the agenda when the old padded chairs in the waiting room were replaced with hard metal benches nailed to the floor. These were apparently installed to discourage walk-ins off the street from sitting or sleeping in the waiting room if it was cold or raining outside. They were also simpler to "clean" with a quick spray of disinfectant and a wipe down with a paper towel. Similarly, a phone that had been formerly available without request for people in the waiting room was suddenly removed. Requests to use the phone then had to be made to the receptionist who would pass the phone out through the reception window from where the call would be conducted within a few feet of the witnessing receptionist.
>
> All of these strategies ostensibly designed for safety, hygiene and fairness were at the primary expense of the most disenfranchised, neglected, censured members of society who came through our doors. These were the help seekers who struggled to maintain and manage their lives given the extremity of their needs and the paucity of resources at their disposal. These were the women and men who could not afford the luxury of a cell phone, or a bank account, or a clean toilet and a sink to wash their hands—which is particularly true for the homeless.

Nick Haslam's review of the literature reveals the presence of dehumanisation in a surprising number of fields from medicine to modern art, reminding the reader that dehumanisation is ubiquitous.[66] Curiously, it is not a question of whether we dehumanise but only *how* and *how much*. Medical dehumanisation expresses itself in various ways. *Dissimilarity*, for example, arises as a result of a clinician's perception of herself as different from the help seeker based on the fact of his illness, label and the imbalance of power between them. Dissimilarity is related to power and *objectification* where "the experience of power leads people to treat others as a means to an end rather than as ends in themselves".[67] The ranked nature of objectification is predicted by the *amount* of power held by an individual. Objectification is "an instrument of subjugation whereby the needs, interests, and experiences of those with less power are subordinated to those of the powerful".[68] Gruenfeld et al. note that philosopher Martha Nussbaum underscores the importance of "instrumentality" where "the target is a tool for one's own purpose".[69] One series of experiments, for example, showed that "high-power perceivers were more attracted to the targets' usefulness, defined in terms of the perceiver's goals, than were perceivers in low-power and baseline conditions".[70] Those with the highest power tended to objectify subordinates and peers, while people with lower power only objectified their subordinates.

There are many clinical practices contributing to objectification, including *de-individuation*, where a person's identity is lost in the anonymity of the patient group. In contrast, m*echanisation* appears to contribute to clinicians' withdrawal of empathy and to moral disengagement.[71] Such observations are relevant to community mental health settings where, despite the purported collaboration of multidisciplinary team members, there is a clear demarcation of professional ranks—likely unstated—and well-established chains of command. Here, *everyone* is at risk of being objectified by superiors or peers, except for the vulnerable help seeker who, in being the *most* subordinate of all, is objectified *by definition*.[72] Nonetheless, a clinician's ability to recognise that she is dehumanising a help seeker may well elude her, even while she is being dehumanised herself.

Prejudice: A brief accounting past to present

> *[I]t is this recognition that prejudice flows from social realities, through group identities and associated political and social ideologies, to shape the psychology of the individual, that defines the new theory of prejudice. This not only exposes our prejudices about prejudice but also shows that the key to "smashing prejudice" is not psychological readjustment but social change within which the narrative of prejudice plays an integral part.*[73]

Of considerable interest to the discussion of clinical dehumanisation and the patient/clinician divide is the emerging research on in-group/out-group biases that examines the process, function and potency of intergroup dynamics. Early investigations of prejudice first centred around "the race question" that focused on the "problematic, pathological or deviant characteristics" of people of colour that so troubled the lives of white people who oppressed them. This focus on the inadequacies of the out-group—the real victims of oppression—emerged from the interests "of colonial masters and the issues of colonial rule". It was only in the aftermath of the Second World War that the perspective shifted towards the question of what was wrong with the *oppressor*.[74] How could such incomprehensible destruction be justified in the minds and actions of those who contributed to it? Psychology examined this issue through the pioneering work of social psychologist Gordon Allport and others, whose efforts forwarded a new understanding of "racial discrimination, ideological extremism and genocide",[75] which finally challenged the perpetrators rather than the victims. The notion of "prejudice" is now fundamental to social psychology's ongoing interest in intergroup relations.[76]

The focus of this work has also developed considerably since Allport first claimed that prejudice lay in "an antipathy based upon a faulty and inflexible generalisation" that involved "thinking ill of others without sufficient warrant".[77] The problem, Allport theorised, emerged through an erroneous perception that enabled members of a dominant group to hold negative, harmful, even hateful views about members of subordinate groups. As a kind of aberration, a "fatal flaw in the human psyche", Allport's theory suggested the need for this perspective to be corrected—cognitively rectified—as it appeared to be of no benefit. But as Stephen Reicher observes, and as the autoethnographic content of our inquiry hopefully shows, prejudice is always mobilised intentionally and for gain, which calls for "collective action" not merely a shift in "individual cognition".[78]

Current research no longer construes prejudice as a flawed or useless perception, but as an integral part of the complex relational matrix between the individual and the group to whom she or he belongs. It appears to be related to "the dynamics of ongoing intergroup relations, and the way that people make sense of these relations and form a shared collective view of their social world... which serves to reflect, important social realities".[79] Reicher suggests prejudice may be understood better from the standpoint of its efficacy rather than its morality. For, those who dehumanise also value that privilege and seek to increase it. One need not look too far historically, or in this present moment, to find ample evidence for his claim. The problem, then, with those who hold a prejudiced view as a member of the dominant group "is not that they are wrong but that they are successful".[80] But neither is the picture entirely bleak on this account.

> The lesson of history is that dominant groups hardly ever just give away their power [because] [i]t is taken from them by the collective action of subordinate group members. . . . It is nonetheless true that the chances of success are much enhanced by divisions which limit the ability of dominant groups to maintain their privilege.[81]

What is described as Allport's "meta-theory" of prejudice, first focused on "(a) the pathology of the prejudiced personality, (b) the invalidity of social stereotypes, and (c) the inevitability of general psychological processes (motivational and cognitive) that produce those stereotypes (including ethnocentrism and socialisation)".[82] But current and still evolving theory now recognises the nature of individuality and personality itself as fluid and mutable, which allows us to act as individuals and group members—not only socially, but psychologically. It appears that our ability to behave as separate beings and as group members at the same time is a "highly adaptive feature of the human mind and one that makes the broad range of human social behaviour possible". This interrelationship between the self and the group is also "critical in shaping and changing people's minds, motivations and behaviours".[83] Far from being illogical, irrational or cognitively faulty, "[p]rejudices are... products of social processes of influence, communication and leadership and always have an ideological dimension".[84]

The aim of Allport's research, and that which continues to emerge in its wake, is also to resolve the problem of prejudice. Encouragingly, researchers can now create conditions demonstrating how groups can be shifted from inter- to *intragroup* ways of perceiving and acting. In learning how to move our perspective of "us versus them" to "we", the research on prejudice is confirming thrilling possibilities for greater collaboration and a reduction of prejudice. "In short, as much as groups can be used to bolster the status quo, so too can they become vehicles for resistance and *social change*".[85]

Infra-humanisation, stigma and the heartsink patient

Infra-humanisation is an emerging phenomenon in the literature we have just discussed that has special relevance for clinicians because it is so difficult to detect.[86] Its theory is concerned with the formation of in-groups and out-groups and the process by which in-group members assign themselves a greater share of "human essence".[87] Infra-humanisation does not reduce anyone to an animal or a machine but to something a little *less* human than "in-group" members. Human essence relates to what are defined as primary and secondary emotions. Primary emotions are those recognised as being shared by *both* in-group and out-group members as well as by animals. It is the *secondary* emotions that we view as most uniquely human and that we tend to assign only to members of our own in-group. Several studies have shown, for example, that a group tends to be infra-humanised if they are considered to be lacking "intelligence, language, and uniquely human emotions".[88]

Interestingly, infra-humanisation operates regardless of group status, meaning that out-group members of higher *or* lower-ranking groups may be similarly infra-humanised. In the context of a community mental health care team, this predictably occurs when clinicians infra-humanise managers, psychiatric nurses infra-humanise counsellors and social workers, administrative staff infra-humanise the clinicians and the entire team infra-humanises the patients. Infra-humanisation combines "in-group favouritism and out-group derogation", which cannot be understood as favouritism alone, because infra-humanisation is contingent on the difference between groups being *meaningful*.[89]

One group of researchers has suggested that the importance of our relationships to our significant others necessitates the creation of out-group members.[90] There is evidence that "the more a group is perceived as essential and the more that people identify with their in-group, the higher the level of infra-humanisation".[91]

> Infra-humanization, like moral exclusion, delegitimisation, and lesser-perceived humanity, probably constitute a strong defence mechanism for those who want to live in a quiet environment. It explains how one can watch apartheid, wars, and genocide on TV without being too much disturbed, or having to be sent to a psychiatric hospital.[92]

Infra-humanisation might partially explain how clinicians can be involved with institutional practices and systems they recognise as morally wrong, and devastating for the vulnerable help seeker, without being sufficiently distressed to protest or protect. Although there is sufficient research to predict the occurrence of infra-humanisation, the mechanism is still not well understood.[93] Most interestingly, this form of dehumanisation "occurs in the absence of intergroup conflict and therefore extends the scope of dehumanisation well beyond the context of cruelty and ethnic hatred", which further contributes to its invisibility.[94]

Another pernicious form of dehumanisation is stigmatisation, as we can see in the work of one group of researchers who investigated five separate factors influencing the public's interaction with those who have "mental health problems". These included (1) behaviour, (2) the reasons or causes of the behaviour, (3) perceived dangerousness of the person to others, (4) the pathologising label and (5) the person's socio-demographics—all of which appear to contribute to the avoidance and fear of the mentally ill. There is generally greater acceptance of problems related to "structural causes (e.g., stress or genetic/biological causes)" and less acceptance of problems associated with alcohol or drug misuse.[95] The ranked nature of each of these variables suggests the complexity of out-group construction. The most significant concern is the prevalence and impact of stigmatisation, given the levels of aversion expressed towards people with mental health problems. We do not like the "mentally ill" coming into our homes or marrying into our families. We do not value having them as colleagues at work or as friends, neighbours or residents in nearby group homes.[96]

Other research on stigma, stereotyping and employment has shown that public stigma tends to be *lower* if someone with mental illness reports having worked in the past three months to a year, but is otherwise higher.[97] Stigma is further complicated by the difficulty of finding and keeping employment when one is labelled with a mental illness. Not surprisingly, such attributions appear to lead to social avoidance and segregation in the workplace. It is *self-stigma*, however, which internalises the devastating and isolating effects of public stigma and, poignantly, may be why so many help seekers are identified as having "low self-esteem".

As far back as the 1950s, research indicated that a mentally ill person would likely be perceived "with fear and dislike". The strength of public aversion has been tempered in recent years with a "sophistication" of understanding and social tolerance brought about by campaigns to educate the public about mental health. These are "based on scientific research portraying mental illness as a 'disease' rather than a 'moral flaw'".[98] This strategy also supports medicalisation by legitimising symptoms as "pathology" while denying or ignoring the larger social context of the distress, and stigma persists despite ongoing campaigns to address the problem, even with the help of world-renowned celebrities. But the tenacity of stigma remains, leaving help seekers stigmatised within the institution and beyond its walls—all of which contribute to the scourge of self-stigmatisation and potential damage to every aspect of a person's private, social and work life. The case of the *heartsink* patient illustrates that stigmatisation is most grievously perpetuated by the clinician.

Another category of stigma is found in the "heartsink patient". This is an individual whose needs are perceived as all but impossible to meet within the constraints of the "mandate" for care, which causes the physician's heart to . . . sink. Such patients are legion in the halls of community mental health care.[99] Help seekers labelled with personality disorders, the most recognised being borderline personality disorder, are especially vulnerable to this form of stigma.[100] The complex needs and challenging behaviours of this cohort are largely unwelcome because they are perceived as using and abusing valuable resources and time that—so the argument goes—would be better spent on more successful outcomes.[101] Rather than being recognised as frankly discriminatory, institutional failure is laid at the feet of the "difficult" patient who "can't be helped".

The homeless person also falls into the category of the heartsink patient. Their needs are framed as so extensive that their lack of entitlement to ongoing mental health services can be justified.[102] The fragility of this cohort, their involvement with alcohol and drugs, the challenges of connecting with them and coaxing them off the street and their need for consistent and relevant care, including housing, employment and socialisation, are used to argue for the *denial* of their care. This, unlike clinical populations with "legitimate" mental illness whose greater "compliance" and socio-economic status presumably lead to outcomes worth the government's investment. But it is our aversion of homeless people—underwritten in dehumanising and discriminatory policies and protocols—that holds them in their desperate situation.[103]

The implications of "heartsink" stigmatisation are sobering. One study, for example, showed that a group of 50 mental health nurses were "the least optimistic about patients with a BPD label and. . . more negative about their experience of working with this group".[104] This diagnosis alone is so damning that it appears to contribute to the blame clinicians assign people with this diagnosis. Blame is highly correlated to the perceived control that people feel others have over their behaviours. Not surprisingly, the contempt, fear and distrust experienced by clinicians who work with this cohort contribute to impoverished levels of care. In terms of general medicine, Christopher Butler and Martyn Evans note that:

> Several authors have associated psychopathology, depression, psychosomatic illness, lower social class, being female, having thick clinical records, being older, having more acute and chronic medical problems, and making greater use of health care services with "difficult" patients.[105]

Heartsink patients can be referred to by clinicians as "black holes", "difficult", "hateful" and "health care abuser".[106] Where I worked, they were also described as "cutters", "resistant", "combative", "revolving doors", "frequent flyers", "privileged" and "non-compliant". The sense of emotional disengagement that GPs have reported when dealing with heartsink patients denies the legitimacy of the help seeker's request as well as her humanity.

> Patients' complaints were not legitimate demands on medical care, reflecting the absence of "real" illness; it was impossible to help them, or it was pointless to try because they refused what GPs thought was necessary or they were unwilling to change. Denigratory language was common and a few GPs were explicit in their dislike.[107]

In general medical practice, such aversion might reasonably relate to a bias for biomedical care, physicians' tendency to undervalue the psychological, their professional intolerance for uncertainty or even the failure of physicians to manage this population skilfully.[108] But in community mental health care, one would expect such aversion and intolerance to be overcome. Despite the nature of the work, however, the importance placed on the therapeutic relationship, and clinicians' psychiatric and psychological education, training and practice, this is not always the case.

The dark blue file

> *I don't remember her name, only that she finally stopped calling. She was a Borderline, a woman not even forty with an adult daughter who lived in town, so she had someone. She'd had repeated suicide attempts, she'd used up the system, she had a two-inch file, nothing helped, nothing worked, she expected too much and had been seen at the Centre too many times, so I was told. She was just another revolving door with a string of para-suicidal attempts behind her and another go-round would change nothing. I'd never met her, didn't even know what she looked like, but she called and called and badgered me to get her in. I was doing intake at the time—assessment and triage—and had already presented her case and been refused by the team. She didn't meet the mandate, whatever that was, but she was overdrawn.*
>
> *By the time she stopped calling, I felt skilful at blowing her off and took pride at having put out that little fire. What could I do? Her file would only*

be refused again. It was still on my desk sometime later—a month or more at least—when I heard that she'd succeeded in killing herself. I can't remember how I heard or how she did it. Pills probably, and alcohol, she abused alcohol. I vaguely remember someone asking me if I was alright. I wasn't alright. I was not alright. I think I asked if I could go to the funeral but was discouraged from doing so. Someone suggested that my presence there could be interpreted as an act of culpability. Why wouldn't it have been? Shouldn't it have been? I didn't go anyway. But I carried that blue file in my arms, along with my other work, to and from the room where staff collected their armload of active files from a cubicle in the morning and put them back at night. I carried that woman's file for six months before I could finally put it away.

The impact of dehumanising a vulnerable help seeker or colluding in such dehumanisation can leave a clinician psychologically and morally devastated by her work. There is no question that clinicians' indirect exposure to trauma in the workplace involves an inherent risk of significant emotional, cognitive and behavioural changes. The phenomenon is described in various terms, including vicarious traumatisation (VT), secondary traumatic stress (STS) and compassion fatigue (CF), which reflect the inevitable occupational hazards of clinical work. These also constitute a form of psychological trauma confirmed by a growing body of empirical research.[109]

Vicarious trauma is a fact of a community mental health clinician's life in the routine processes of assessing and working with trauma survivors but also with those dealing with the impact of all kinds of violence. Clinicians can also find themselves in the unenviable position of interrupting help seekers from going too deeply into their abuse histories to prevent them from becoming more destabilised in the absence of sufficient resources and adequate time to support them through the process. The amount of education, relational consistency and time needed to reorient and stabilise the trauma survivor are beyond the mandate or capacity of community mental health care. Group programs centred around trauma recovery models, like Dialectic Behavioural Therapy,[110] were available on an inconsistent and limited basis at my Centre. But clinicians who involved their patients in this program also shouldered the additional workload involved.

The outcome of clinicians' chronic exposure to high levels of trauma is that they "may show non-recognition of the client's experience, fragmented attention, limited empathy, intellectualisation, or dehumanisation".[111] Very high levels of secondary traumatic stress (STS), and secondary traumatic stress disorder (STSD), affect from 17% to 64% of clinicians working with trauma. Interestingly STSD, much like PTSD (post-traumatic stress disorder), is experienced by those—including clinicians—who are affected indirectly by the trauma experienced by the victim.[112] Unsurprisingly, evidence emerging from a review of 29 articles confirms that a third of them cited emotional exhaustion as the leading cause of burnout among practical psychologists. The consequences are impaired functioning, reduced competence,[113] depersonalisation and feelings of cynicism.[114] Although many clinicians do not experience compassion fatigue, these statistics are remarkably high and relevant to our discussion, given the high incidence of trauma in the complex cases routinely seen in community mental health care.[115] Indeed, the impact of trauma on clinicians working with such cohorts may reach clinical levels of severity.[116]

The insulin coma

> *I am walking late at night around the fragrant garden of the apartment complex where I live in a seaside town outside Vancouver. I am crying while I walk, raging and thinking of the man whose story I heard today that has stolen my peace and I can't sleep. He was dying of cancer and quietly distressed about what would happen to his sister when he was gone. She had been put into an insulin coma as a young woman, decades earlier. It was a barbaric, ill-informed psychiatric procedure that left her brain-injured and incapacitated the whole of her adult life. This man, and her only family member, had never married and had cared for her his whole life, at his own expense. His dignity was immense. There was no bitterness, only concern and sadness. He had no history of mental illness, was never unemployed and had no wish to hurt himself or anyone. It had simply made sense to him to contact an agency that was connected to the source of his problem, although he did not know what he was asking for when he first walked into my office.*
>
> *The needs of this man's sister fall far outside the mandate of our Centre. But he will be seen by a psychiatrist or doctor at our Centre and offered counselling if only as a humanitarian gesture, a token apology, given his story. From our standpoint, his acceptance for care is a privilege when so many service requests are denied, especially since he has no history of mental illness, medication use or previous hospitalisation. But having made it through the front gate with my help, he will be diagnosed and medicated with an anti-depressant for his anguish and maybe something else for sleep. It is a supreme irony that I am relieved to know that at least he will be seen by someone and not be left alone, even if his care requires a psychiatric diagnosis and medication to legitimise it.*

Dehumanisation in community mental health presents something of a closed loop. The clinical environment is oriented to a medicalising, reductive approach to care that pathologises the impact of social ills and inequalities which, intentionally or not, co-opts and disenfranchises the most vulnerable for its own purposes. Clinicians are also dehumanised through their ongoing exposure to a profoundly distressed and socially isolated cohort whose life circumstances they have limited means of ameliorating. The trauma stories of violence, abuse and injustice recounted by the vulnerable help seeker can, and do, vicariously traumatise the clinician who is then at an even higher risk of re-victimising the vulnerable help seeker.

The implications of medicalisation, asymmetry and dehumanisation are devastating and all encompassing. One might, therefore, wonder what justification remains for labelling *anyone* with a mental illness beyond maintaining the machine it feeds. Yet the depth and complexity of suffering related to poverty, race, gender, violence and trauma, in all its forms, together with the immense financial burden of such suffering worldwide, may not be denied. Nor is the decline of community mental health care anywhere on the immediate horizon, given the ever-increasing call for the provision of more and better mental health care. At the same time, the need to humanise and protect the vulnerable help seeker has never been greater. That said, the research on in-groups and out-groups that has evolved beyond Gordon Allport's seminal work on prejudice offers a heartening imperative. It calls us as individuals, and members of a professional collective, not only to "see" but to *work* for ways to ease and erase the dehumanising boundaries between the "vulnerable help seeker" and "mental health professional". Reynolds, Haslam and Turner articulate a rallying cry for our purpose, with resonance for any mental health clinician engaged in the project of re-humanising the vulnerable help seeker *and* themselves.

> We reject any suggestion that prejudice is rendered inevitable by the workings of human psychology—whether understood in terms of personality or general cognitive processes. Even at the very darkest moments of human history there has always been, and there will always be, the prospect of positive social and political change. It is this that offers hope for further scientific advance in understanding prejudice and its elimination.[117]

Notes

1 H.M. Evans, 'Wonder and the Clinical Encounter', *Theoretical Medicine and Bioethics*, 33 (2012), p. 128.
2 This discussion confines itself to the systems and issues related to my work environment. It would be reasonable to say that provincially funded community mental health facilities employing a case management model would share many commonalities represented and problematised in this inquiry.
3 S.J. Ziguras and G.W. Stuart, 'A Meta-Analysis of the Effectiveness of Mental Health Case Management Over 20 Years', *Psychiatric Services*, 51 (2000), p. 1410.
4 S. Ziguras, G. Stuart, and A. Jackson, 'Assessing the Evidence on Case Management', *The British Journal of Psychiatry*, 181 (2002), p. 20.
5 B. Kenny and T. Whitehead, *Insight: A Guide to Psychiatry and Psychiatric Services* (London: Crom Helm, 1973), pp. 161–67.
6 Ziguras, Stuart, and Jackson, 'Assessing the Evidence on Case Management', p. 17.
7 Concurrent disorders are those that include an addiction. A diagnosis of major depression combined with the misuse of alcohol would constitute a concurrent disorder. These diagnoses are highly prevalent in community mental health and complicate the process of diagnosis and treatment.

44 *Three opponents of wonder*

8 For a comprehensive list of services offered by a one British Columbia health authority, see: www.fraserhealth.ca/Service-Directory/Services/mental-health-and-substance-use#.X8h2QdhKjD6
9 Early and current critics have argued against psychiatry's focus on the "symptom", as do many counselling theories and other therapeutic approaches to emotional suffering. Of relevance are the socio-political dimensions of emotional distress examined, for example, by: I. Prilleltensky, 'The Role of Power in Wellness, Oppression, and Liberation: The Promise of Psychopolitical Validity', *Journal of Community Psychology*, 36 (2008). Similarly, feminist therapy seeks to educate and empower the help seeker by focusing on an analysis of power that views symptoms as evidence of *resistance* to the abuse of power, rather than pathology. Thus, "posttraumatic symptoms are explicitly framed as coping strategies and evidence of clients' attempts to manage intolerable affects and knowledge arising from the trauma". See: L.S. Brown, 'Feminist Paradigms of Trauma Treatment', *Psychotherapy: Theory, Research, Practice, Training*, 41 (2004), p. 465.
10 Psychotropic prescription drugs are deeply tied to medicalisation. Help seekers refusing medication were often denied service at my Centre, given the unstated assumption that an individual who was not sufficiently "ill" to require medication did not need our services. The work of prescribing is further complicated by: a) the high incidence of drug and alcohol addiction among the client population, b) the need to re-evaluate and re-calibrate medication initiated by other physicians less experienced with psychotropic drugs and c) the help seeker's addiction to anxiolytics or narcotics, which *can* originate during a hospital stay and requires clinical intervention.
11 P.M. Strong, 'Sociological Imperialism and the Profession of Medicine a Critical Examination of the Thesis of Medical Imperialism', *Social Science & Medicine, Part A: Medical Psychology & Medical Sociology*, 13 (1979), p. 210.
12 Ibid.
13 T. Szasz, *The Myth of Mental Illness: Foundations of a Theory of Personal Conduct* (New York: Harper & Row, 1974). Also, T. Szasz, 'The Myth of Mental Illness: 50 Years Later', *The Psychiatrist*, 35 (2011).
14 M. Cresswell, 'Szasz and His Interlocutors: Reconsidering Thomas Szasz's "Myth of Mental Illness" Thesis', *Journal for the Theory of Social Behaviour*, 38 (2008).
15 D. Rissmiller and J. Rissmiller, 'Open Forum: Evolution of the Antipsychiatry Movement into Mental Health Consumerism', *Psychiatric Services*, 57 (2006), p. 864.
16 D. Double, 'The Limits of Psychiatry', *BMJ: British Medical Journal*, 324 (2002), p. 900.
17 Rissmiller and Rissmiller, 'Open Forum: Evolution of the Antipsychiatry Movement into Mental Health Consumerism', pp. 863–64.
18 Ibid. p. 864.
19 P. Bracken and P. Thomas, 'From Szasz to Foucault: On the Role of Critical Psychiatry', *Philosophy, Psychiatry, & Psychology*, 17 (2010), pp. 219–20, 23–27.
20 Double, 'The Limits of Psychiatry', pp. 903–4.
21 Rissmiller and Rissmiller, 'Open Forum: Evolution of the Antipsychiatry Movement into Mental Health Consumerism', pp. 863–64.
22 P. Bracken and P. Thomas, 'Postpsychiatry: A New Direction for Mental Health', *BMJ: British Medical Journal*, 322 (2001), p. 724.
23 For a brief list of reputable organisations engaged in this work see: Introduction, p. xiv.
24 See J. Moncrieff's lecture: 'The Myth of the Chemical Cure: The Politics of Psychiatric Drug Treatment', University of New England, March 8, 2013, at www.youtube.com/watch?v=IV1S5zw096U

25 J. Moncrieff, 'Co-Opting Psychiatry: The Alliance Between Academic Psychiatry and the Pharmaceutical Industry', *Epidemiologia e Psichiatria Sociale*, 16 (2007), pp. 192–93.
26 An investigation of 28 studies demonstrate forest therapy to be an emerging intervention for decreasing adults' depressive symptoms. See: H. Choi, and others, 'Effects of Forest Therapy on Depressive Symptoms among Adults: A Systematic Review', *International Journal of Environmental Research and Public Health*, 14 (2017).
27 The instrumentalisation of art as therapy, mounted as an installation at the Rijksmuseum in 2014, shows how medicalisation is creating and feeding new appetites for the therapeutic. See: A. De Botton, and J. Armstrong, *Art as Therapy* (London: Phaidon Press, 2016).
28 P. Conrad, 'Medicalization and Social Control', *Annual Review of Sociology*, 18 (1992), p. 209.
29 P. Conrad, 'The Shifting Engines of Medicalization', *Journal of Health and Social Behavior*, 46 (2005), p. 3. For other allusions to medical jurisdiction, see also: pp. 4, 12.
30 For a critique of the levels of medicalisation beyond the control of physicians, see: P. Conrad and J.W. Schneider, 'Looking at Levels of Medicalisation: A Comment on Strong's Critique of the Thesis of Medical Imperialism', *Social Science & Medicine, Part A: Medical Psychology & Medical Sociology*, 14 (1980).
31 Conrad, 'The Shifting Engines of Medicalization', p. 3.
32 Ibid. p. 6. Conrad references the work of journalist Brendan Koerner, who offers a biting account on the making and selling of mental illness. See: B.I. Koerner, 'Disorders Made to Order', *Mother Jones*, 27 (2002).
33 There are two diagnostic manuals of psychiatry, the *DSM* and the *ICD*, the *International Classification of Diseases* published by the World Health Organization. The *DSM* is published by the American Psychiatric Association. Despite their similarities, the *DSM* is the most widely used in North America. See: G. Andrews, T. Slade, and L. Peters, 'Classification in Psychiatry: ICD-10 Versus DSM-IV', *British Journal of Psychiatry*, 174 (1999).
34 See: L.J. Breen and M. O'Connor, 'The Fundamental Paradox in the Grief Literature: A Critical Reflection', *OMEGA: Journal of Death & Dying*, 55 (2007).
35 M.K. Shear and others, 'Complicated Grief and Related Bereavement Issues for DSM-V', *Depression and Anxiety*, 28 (2011), 107. See also: K. Lamb, R. Pies, and S. Zisook, 'The Bereavement Exclusion for the Diagnosis of Major Depression: To Be, or Not to Be', *Psychiatry (Edgmont)*, 7 (2010), p. 20.
36 Shear and others, 'Complicated Grief and Related Bereavement Issues for DSM-V', p. 106.
37 For a balanced analysis, see: R.A. Bryant, 'Prolonged Grief in Diagnostic and Statistical Manual of Mental Disorders, 5th Edition', *Current Opinion in Psychiatry*, 27 (2014).
38 H.A. Schreier and L. Berger, 'On Medical Imperialism', *The Lancet*, 303 (1974), p. 1161.
39 These points are synthesised from Strong's work and summarised by Williams as well. See: Strong, 'Sociological Imperialism and the Profession of Medicine', pp. 199–200; S. Williams, 'Sociological Imperialism and the Profession of Medicine Revisited: Where Are We Now?', *Sociology of Health & Illness*, 23 (2001), p. 137.
40 Strong, 'Sociological Imperialism and the Profession of Medicine', p. 203.
41 Ibid. p. 212.
42 Williams, 'Sociological Imperialism and the Profession of Medicine', p. 152.
43 Racine, 'Loving in the Context of Community Mental Health', p. 114.

46 *Three opponents of wonder*

44 D.W. Maynard, 'Interaction and Asymmetry in Clinical Discourse', *American Journal of Sociology*, 97 (1991), p. 448.
45 Ibid. p. 449.
46 Ibid. p. 450.
47 D.W. Maynard, 'Perspective-Display Sequences in Conversation', *Western Journal of Communication*, 53 (1989), pp. 91–103.
48 Ibid. pp. 100–1.
49 Maynard, 'Interaction and Asymmetry in Clinical Discourse', p. 483.
50 Ibid. pp. 478–80.
51 M. Fricker, 'Powerlessness and Social Interpretation', *Episteme: A Journal of Social Epistemology*, 3 (2007), p. 100.
52 S. Brownmiller, *In Our Time: Memoir of a Revolution* (London: Dial Press, 1999), pp. 279–94.
53 Fricker, 'Powerlessness and Social Interpretation', p. 97.
54 Ibid.
55 Ibid.
56 H. Carel and I.J. Kidd, 'Epistemic Injustice in Healthcare: A Philosophical Analysis', *Medicine, Health Care and Philosophy*, 17 (2014).
57 H. Carel and I.J. Kidd, 'Epistemic Injustice and Illness-Unpublished', (2013), p. 2.
58 R. Lakeman, 'Epistemic Injustice and the Mental Health Service User', *International Journal of Mental Health Nursing*, 19 (2010), p. 151.
59 Fricker, 'Powerlessness and Social Interpretation', p. 103.
60 Carel and Kidd, 'Epistemic Injustice and Illness-Unpublished', p. 4.
61 O.S. Haque and A. Waytz, 'Dehumanization in Medicine Causes, Solutions, and Functions', *Perspectives on Psychological Science*, 7 (2012), p. 176.
62 Ibid. p. 177.
63 N. Haslam, 'Dehumanization: An Integrative Review', *Personality and Social Psychology Review*, 10 (2006), pp. 252–53.
64 K.R. Monroe, 'Cracking the Code of Genocide: The Moral Psychology of Rescuers, Bystanders, and Nazis During the Holocaust', *Political Psychology*, 29 (2008), p. 700.
65 Haslam, 'Dehumanisation: An Integrative Review', p. 253.
66 Ibid. p. 254.
67 Haque and Waytz, 'Dehumanization in Medicine Causes, Solutions, and Functions', p. 178.
68 D.H. Gruenfeld and others, 'Power and the Objectification of Social Targets', *Journal of Personality and Social Psychology*, 95 (2008), p. 111.
69 Ibid. p. 112.
70 Ibid. p. 123.
71 Haque and Waytz, 'Dehumanisation in Medicine Causes, Solutions, and Functions', pp. 177–79.
72 My italics. The authors state: "[W]e assume that subordinates are objectified almost by definition". See: Gruenfeld and others, 'Power and the Objectification of Social Targets', p. 114.
73 K.J. Reynolds, S.A. Haslam, and J.C. Turner, 'Prejudice, Social Identity and Social Change: Resolving the Allportian problematic', in *Beyond Prejudice: Extending the Social Psychology of Conflict, Inequality and Social Change*, ed. by J. Dixon and M. Levine (Cambridge: Cambridge University Press, 2012), p. 50.
74 S. Reicher, 'From Perception to Mobilisation: The Shifting Paradigm of Prejudice', in *Beyond Prejudice: Extending the Social Psychology of Conflict, Inequality and Social Change*, ed. by J. Dixon and M. Levine (Cambridge: Cambridge University Press, 2012), p. 28.

75 J. Dixon, and M. Levine, 'Introduction', in *Beyond Prejudice: Extending the Social Psychology of Conflict, Inequality and Social Change*, ed. by J. Dixon and M. Levine (Cambridge: Cambridge University Press, 2012), p. 2.
76 The emerging literature on anti-racism can arguably support the efforts of clinicians wanting to understand their own engagement in oppression vis-à-vis the problem of clinical dehumanisation. See, for example: R. Diangelo, *White Fragility: Why It's So Hard for White People to Talk About Racism* (Boston: Beacon Press, 2018).
77 Dixon and Levine, 'Introduction', p. 2.
78 Reicher, 'From Perception to Mobilisation: The Shifting Paradigm of Prejudice', p. 30.
79 Reynolds, Haslam, and Turner, 'Prejudice, Social Identity and Social Change', pp. 49–50.
80 Reicher, 'From Perception to Mobilisation: The Shifting Paradigm of Prejudice', p. 35.
81 Ibid. pp. 42–43.
82 Reynolds, Haslam, and Turner, 'Prejudice, Social Identity and Social Change', p. 54.
83 Ibid. p. 56.
84 Ibid. p. 59.
85 Ibid. p. 64.
86 J.P. Leyens and others, 'Emotional Prejudice, Essentialism, and Nationalism: The 2002 Tajfel Lecture', *European Journal of Social Psychology*, 33 (2003), p. 703.
87 S. Demoulin and others, 'The Role of In-Group Identification in Infra-Humanisation', *International Journal of Psychology*, 44 (2009), p. 4.
88 Ibid. p. 6.
89 J.P. Leyens and others, 'Emotional Prejudice, Essentialism, and Nationalism: The 2002 Tajfel Lecture', pp. 703–5.
90 Ibid. p. 704.
91 Demoulin and others, 'The Role of In-Group Identification in Infra-Humanization', p. 10.
92 Leyens and others, 'Emotional Prejudice, Essentialism, and Nationalism: The 2002 Tajfel Lecture', p. 712.
93 Demoulin and others, 'The Role of In-Group Identification in Infra-Humanization', p. 6.
94 Haslam, 'Dehumanisation: An Integrative Review', p. 255.
95 J.K. Martin, B.A. Pescosolido, and S.A. Tuch, 'Of Fear and Loathing: The Role of "Disturbing Behavior", Labels, and Causal Attributions in Shaping Public Attitudes Toward People with Mental Illness', *Journal of Health and Social Behavior*, 41 (2000), p. 208.
96 Ibid. p. 219.
97 P.W. Corrigan, K.J. Powell, and N. Rüsch, 'How Does Stigma Affect Work in People with Serious Mental Illnesses?', *Psychiatric Rehabilitation Journal*, 35 (2012), pp. 381–83.
98 Martin, Pescosolido, and Tuch, 'Of Fear and Loathing: The Role of "Disturbing Behavior", Labels, and Causal Attributions in Shaping Public Attitudes Toward People with Mental Illness', p. 209.
99 C.C. Butler and M. Evans, 'The "Heartsink" Patient Revisited', *British Journal of General Practice*, 49 (1999).
100 D. Markham, 'Attitudes Towards Patients with a Diagnosis of Borderline Personality Disorder: Social Rejection and Dangerousness', *Journal of Mental Health*, 12 (2003), 595–612. People diagnosed with BPD challenge the capacity of the system, given their tendency to self-harm, para-suicidality, the chronicity of their crises, serial hospitalisations and because they are often connected to mental health facilities for lengthy periods of time. Yet it is almost impossible to deny treatment to an individual dealing with this level of acuity during a period of crisis, on legal grounds alone.

101 Not surprisingly, the findings of one meta-analysis shows therapists' sense of personal accomplishment increases through "over-involvement" with the patient, when they spend greater amounts of time providing therapy. This is not the case when dealing with patients diagnosed with personality disorders and the challenges of hostile behaviour, self-harming, limit testing, psychosis or the threat of suicide. See: H.M. McCormack and others, 'The Prevalence and Cause (s) of Burnout Among Applied Psychologists: A Systematic Review', *Journal of Frontiers in Psychology*, 9 (2018), pp. 12–13.

102 R.E. Drake, F.C. Osher, and M.A. Wallach, 'Homelessness and Dual Diagnosis', *American Psychologist*, 46 (1991).

103 One study identifies four reasons homeless people are so negatively categorised. The first, "competitiveness", relates to businesses who "adopt unsympathetic language and attitudes" towards homeless people whose presence, they worry, will erode their competitive edge. "Worth" relates specifically to our inquiry. Thus, where "governments and their agencies. . . use language indicative of worthiness for help. . . [t]here is an attempt to ration help in a pseudo-logical way by labelling some potential clients as less deserving of help and, therefore, rightly excluded". A third reason is "appearance", given the "image of homeless people as scruffy, unkempt, dirty and repulsive", which is used to "justify street-clearing operations and improvements in a city's image" that are "wholly negative and unsympathetic". The last, "pity, charity and compassion", emerges from religious and philanthropic institutions who are more sympathetic to the plight of homeless people but whose ministrations and labels can reify the narrative of homeless people as "victims, helpless and in need charity". See: G. Tipple and S. Speak, 'Attitudes to and Interventions in Homelessness: Insights from an International Study', in *Adequate and Affordable Housing for all: Research, Policy, Practice* (Toronto, ON: University of Toronto, Centre for Urban and Community Studies, 2004), p. 2.

104 Markham, 'Attitudes Towards Patients with a Diagnosis of Borderline Personality', p. 595.

105 Butler and Evans, 'The "Heartsink" Patient Revisited', p. 230.

106 Ibid. p. 231.

107 L. Gask, C. Dowrick, and R. Morriss, 'Why Do General Practitioners Decline Training to Improve Management of Medically Unexplained Symptoms?', *Journal of General Internal Medicine*, 22 (2007), p. 567.

108 Ibid. pp. 568–69.

109 B.E. Bride, M. Radey, and C.R. Figley, 'Measuring Compassion Fatigue', *Clinical Social Work Journal*, 35 (2007), p. 155.

110 See: M. Linehan, *Cognitive-Behavioral Treatment of Borderline Personality Disorder* (London; New York: The Guilford Press, 1993).

111 R.T. Ringenbach, 'A Comparison Between Counselors Who Practice Meditation and Those Who Do Not on Compassion Fatigue, Compassion Satisfaction, Burnout and Self-Compassion' (unpublished Ph.D. dissertation, University of Akron, 2009), p. 31.

112 C.R. Figley, 'Compassion Fatigue: Psychotherapists' Chronic Lack of Self Care', *Journal of Clinical Psychology*, 58 (2002), p. 1435.

113 McCormack and others, 'The Prevalence and Cause (s) of Burnout Among Applied Psychologists: A Systematic Review', p. 3.

114 Ibid. p. 12.

115 Bride, Radey, and Figley, 'Measuring Compassion Fatigue', p. 156.

116 Figley, 'Compassion Fatigue: Psychotherapists, Chronic Lack of Self Care', pp. 1436–38.

117 Reynolds, Haslam, and Turner, 'Prejudice, Social Identity and Social Change', p. 65.

References

Andrews, G., Slade, T., and Peters, L., 'Classification in Psychiatry: ICD-10 Versus DSM-IV', *British Journal of Psychiatry*, 174 (1999), 3–5. https://doi.org/10.1192/bjp.174.1.3

Bracken, P., and Thomas, P., 'From Szasz to Foucault: On the Role of Critical Psychiatry', *Philosophy, Psychiatry, & Psychology*, 17 (2010), 219–28.

——, 'Postpsychiatry: A New Direction for Mental Health', *BMJ: British Medical Journal*, 322 (2001), 724–27. https://doi.org/10.1136/bmj.322.7288.724

Breen, L.J., and O'Connor, M., 'The Fundamental Paradox in the Grief Literature: A Critical Reflection', *OMEGA: Journal of Death & Dying*, 55 (2007), 199–218. https://doi.org/10.2190/OM.55.3.c

Bride, B.E., Radey, M., and Figley, C.R., 'Measuring Compassion Fatigue', *Clinical Social Work Journal*, 35 (2007), 155–63. https://doi.org/10.1007/s10615-007-0091-7

Brown, L.S., 'Feminist Paradigms of Trauma Treatment', *Psychotherapy: Theory, Research, Practice, Training*, 41 (2004), 464–71. https://doi.org/10.1037/0033-3204.41.4.464

Brownmiller, S., *In Our Time: Memoir of a Revolution* (London: Dial Press, 1999).

Bryant, R.A., 'Prolonged Grief in Diagnostic and Statistical Manual of Mental Disorders, 5th Edition', *Current Opinion in Psychiatry*, 27 (2014), 21–26. https://doi.org/10.1097/YCO.0000000000000031

Butler, C.C., and Evans, M., 'The "Heartsink" Patient Revisited', *British Journal of General Practice*, 49 (1999), 230–33.

Conrad, P., 'The Shifting Engines of Medicalization', *Journal of Health and Social Behavior*, 46 (2005), 3–14. https://doi.org/10.1177/002214650504600102

Conrad, P., and Schneider, J.W., 'Looking at Levels of Medicalization: A Comment on Strong's Critique of the Thesis of Medical Imperialism', *Social Science & Medicine, Part A: Medical Psychology & Medical Sociology*, 14 (1980), 75–79. https://doi.org/10.1016/S0271-7123(80)90804-4

Corrigan, P.W., Powell, K.J., and Rüsch, N., 'How Does Stigma Affect Work in People with Serious Mental Illnesses?', *Psychiatric Rehabilitation Journal*, 35 (2012), 381–84. https://doi.org/10.1037/h0094497

Cresswell, M., 'Szasz and His Interlocutors: Reconsidering Thomas Szasz's "Myth of Mental Illness" Thesis', *Journal for the Theory of Social Behaviour*, 38 (2008), 23–44. https://doi.org/10.1111/j.1468-5914.2008.00359.x

De Botton, A., and Armstrong, J., *Art as Therapy* (London: Phaidon Press, 2016).

Demoulin, S., Cortes, B.P., Viki, T.G., Rodriguez, A.P., Rodriguez, R.T., Paladino, M.P., and Leyens, J.P., 'The Role of in-Group Identification in Infra-Humanization', *International Journal of Psychology*, 44 (2009), 4–11. https://doi.org/10.1080/00207590802057654

Diangelo, R., *White Fragility: Why It's So Hard for White People to Talk About Racism* (Boston: Beacon Press, 2018).

Dixon, J., and Levine, M., 'Introduction', in *Beyond Prejudice: Extending the Social Psychology of Conflict, Inequality and Social Change*, ed. by J. Dixon and M. Levine (Cambridge: Cambridge University Press, 2012), pp. 1–23.

Double, D., 'The Limits of Psychiatry', *BMJ: British Medical Journal*, 324 (2002), 900–4. https://doi.org/10.1136/bmj.324.7342.900

Drake, R.E., Osher, F.C., and Wallach, M.A., 'Homelessness and Dual Diagnosis', *American Psychologist*, 46 (1991), 1149–58. https://doi.org/10.1037/0003-066X.46.11.1149

Evans, H.M., 'Wonder and the Clinical Encounter', *Theoretical Medicine and Bioethics*, 33 (2012), 123–36. https://doi.org/10.1007/s11017-012-9214-4

Figley, C.R., 'Compassion Fatigue: Psychotherapists' Chronic Lack of Self Care', *Journal of Clinical Psychology*, 58 (2002), 1433–41. https://doi.org/10.1002/jclp.10090

Fricker, M., 'Powerlessness and Social Interpretation', *Episteme: A Journal of Social Epistemology*, 3 (2007), 96–108. https://doi.org/10.3366/epi.2006.3.1-2.96

Gask, L., Dowrick, C., and Morriss, R., 'Why Do General Practitioners Decline Training to Improve Management of Medically Unexplained Symptoms?', *Journal of General Internal Medicine*, 22 (2007), 565–71. https://doi.org/10.1007/s11606-006-0094-z

Gruenfeld, D.H., Inesi, M.E., Magee, J.C., and Galinsky, A.D., 'Power and the Objectification of Social Targets', *Journal of Personality and Social Psychology*, 95 (2008), 111–27. https://doi.org/10.1037/0022-3514.95.1.111

Haque, O.S., and Waytz, A., 'Dehumanization in Medicine Causes, Solutions, and Functions', *Perspectives on Psychological Science*, 7 (2012), 176–86. https://doi.org/10.1177/1745691611429706

Haslam, N., 'Dehumanization: An Integrative Review', *Personality and Social Psychology Review*, 10 (2006), 252–64. https://doi.org/10.1207/s15327957pspr1003_4

Kenny, B., and Whitehead, T., *Insight: A Guide to Psychiatry and Psychiatric Services* (London: Croom Helm, 1973).

Koerner, B.I., 'Disorders Made to Order', *Mother Jones*, 27 (2002), 58–81.

Lakeman, R., 'Epistemic Injustice and the Mental Health Service User', *International Journal of Mental Health Nursing*, 19 (2010), 151–53. https://doi.org/10.1111/j.1447-0349.2010.00680.x

Lamb, K., Pies, R., and Zisook, S., 'The Bereavement Exclusion for the Diagnosis of Major Depression: To Be, or Not to Be', *Psychiatry (Edgmont)*, 7 (2010), 19–25.

Lee, I., Choi, H., Bang, K.S., Kim, S., Song, M., and Lee, B., 'Effects of Forest Therapy on Depressive Symptoms Among Adults: A Systematic Review', *International Journal of Environmental Research and Public Health*, 14 (2017). https://doi.org/10.3390/ijerph14030321

Leyens, J.P., Cortes, B., Demoulin, S., Dovidio, J.F., Fiske, S.T., Gaunt, R., Paladino, M.P., Rodriguez-Perez, A., Rodriguez-Torres, R., and Vaes, J., 'Emotional Prejudice, Essentialism, and Nationalism: The 2002 Tajfel Lecture', *European Journal of Social Psychology*, 33 (2003), 703–17. https://doi.org/10.1002/ejsp.170

Linehan, M., *Cognitive-Behavioral Treatment of Borderline Personality Disorder* (London; New York: The Guilford Press, 1993).

Markham, D., 'Attitudes Towards Patients with a Diagnosis of Borderline Personality Disorder: Social Rejection and Dangerousness', *Journal of Mental Health*, 12 (2003), 595–612. https://doi.org/10.1080/09638230310001627955

Martin, J.K., Pescosolido, B.A., and Tuch, S.A., 'Of Fear and Loathing: The Role of "Disturbing Behavior," Labels, and Causal Attributions in Shaping Public Attitudes Toward People with Mental Illness', *Journal of Health and Social Behavior*, 41 (2000), 208–23. https://doi.org/10.2307/2676306

Maynard, D.W., 'Interaction and Asymmetry in Clinical Discourse', *American Journal of Sociology*, 97 (1991), 448–95. https://doi.org/10.1086/229785

——, 'Perspective-Display Sequences in Conversation', *Western Journal of Communication*, 53 (1989), 91–113. https://doi.org/10.1080/10570318909374294

McCormack, H.M., MacIntyre, T.E., and Campbell, M.J., 'The Prevalence and Cause(s) of Burnout Among Applied Psychologists: A Systematic Review', *Journal of Frontiers in Psychology*, 9 (2018), 1–19. https://doi.org/10.3389/fpsyg.2018.01897

Moncrieff, J., 'Co-Opting Psychiatry: The Alliance Between Academic Psychiatry and the Pharmaceutical Industry', *Epidemiologia e Psichiatria Sociale*, 16 (2007), 192–96. https://doi.org/10.1017/S1121189X00002268

——, 'The Myth of the Chemical Cure: The Politics of Psychiatric Drug Treatment', University of New England, March 8, 2013. www.youtube.com/watch?v=IV1S5zw096U

Monroe, K.R., 'Cracking the Code of Genocide: The Moral Psychology of Rescuers, Bystanders, and Nazis During the Holocaust', *Political Psychology*, 29 (2008), 699–736. https://doi.org/10.1111/j.1467-9221.2008.00661.x

Prilleltensky, I., 'The Role of Power in Wellness, Oppression, and Liberation: The Promise of Psychopolitical Validity', *Journal of Community Psychology*, 36 (2008), 116–36. https://doi.org/10.1002/jcop.20225

Racine, C., 'Loving in the Context of Community Mental Health Practice: A Clinical Case Study and Reflection on Mystical Experience', *Mental Health, Religion & Culture*, 17 (2014), 109–21. https://doi.org/10.1080/13674676.2012.749849

Reicher, S., 'From Perception to Mobilisation: The Shifting Paradigm of Prejudice', in *Beyond Prejudice: Extending the Social Psychology of Conflict, Inequality and Social Change*, ed. by J. Dixon and M. Levine (Cambridge: Cambridge University Press, 2012), pp. 27–47.

Reynolds, K., Haslam, A., and Turner, J., 'Prejudice, Social Identity and Social Change: Resolving the Allportian Problematic', in *Beyond Prejudice: Extending the Social Psychology of Conflict, Inequality and Social Change*, ed. by J. Dixon and M. Levine (Cambridge: Cambridge University Press, 2012), pp. 48–69.

Ringenbach, R.T., *A Comparison Between Counselors Who Practice Meditation and Those Who Do Not on Compassion Fatigue, Compassion Satisfaction, Burnout and Self-Compassion* (unpublished Ph.D. dissertation, University of Akron, 2009).

Rissmiller, D., and Rissmiller, J., 'Open Forum: Evolution of the Antipsychiatry Movement into Mental Health Consumerism', *Psychiatric Services*, 57 (2006), 863–66. https://doi.org/10.1176/ps.2006.57.6.863

Schreier, H.A., and Berger, L., 'On Medical Imperialism', *The Lancet*, 303 (1974), 1161. https://doi.org/10.1016/S0140-6736(74)90640-0

Shear, M.K., Simon, N., Wall, M., Zisook, S., Neimeyer, R., Duan, N., Reynolds, C., Lebowitz, B., Sung, S., and Ghesquiere, A., 'Complicated Grief and Related Bereavement Issues for DSM-V', *Depression and Anxiety*, 28 (2011), 103–17. https://doi.org/10.1002/da.20780Strong, P.M., 'Sociological Imperialism and the Profession of Medicine a Critical Examination of the Thesis of Medical Imperialism', *Social Science & Medicine, Part A: Medical Psychology & Medical Sociology*, 13 (1979), 199–215. https://doi.org/10.1016/0271-7123(79)90030-0

Szasz, T., 'The Myth of Mental Illness: 50 Years Later', *The Psychiatrist*, 35 (2011), 179–82. https://doi.org/10.1192/pb.bp.110.031310

——, *The Myth of Mental Illness: Foundations of a Theory of Personal Conduct* (New York: Harper & Row, 1974).

Tipple, G., and Speak, S., 'Attitudes to and Interventions in Homelessness: Insights from an International Study', in *Adequate and Affordable Housing for All: Research, Policy, Practice* (Toronto, ON: University of Toronto, Centre for Urban and Community Studies, 2004), pp. 1–15.

Williams, S., 'Sociological Imperialism and the Profession of Medicine Revisited: Where Are We Now?', *Sociology of Health & Illness*, 23 (2001), 135–58. https://doi.org/10.1111/1467-9566.00245

Ziguras, S.J., and Stuart, G.W., 'A Meta-Analysis of the Effectiveness of Mental Health Case Management Over 20 Years', *Psychiatric Services*, 51 (2000), 1410–21. https://doi.org/10.1176/appi.ps.51.11.1410

Ziguras, S.J., Stuart, G., and Jackson, A., 'Assessing the Evidence on Case Management', *The British Journal of Psychiatry*, 181 (2002), 17–21. https://doi.org/10.1192/bjp.181.1.17

3 From behind the mask: Writing autoethnography

I have used autoethnography fluidly and intuitively in this book to "perform" and problematise moral issues rarely explored in clinical literature and to illuminate the theory under consideration. Norman Denzin observes that these "performance narratives do more than celebrate the lives and struggles of persons who have lived through violence and abuse". They refer us back "to the structures that shape and produce the violence in question".[1] These are structures autoethnography has enabled me to infiltrate, clarify and confront as a clinician who has struggled with, witnessed and perpetuated this violence within her profession. I hope to make the material in this chapter accessible and compelling enough to invite, possibly to challenge, the clinician/researcher to experiment with this form of inquiry and to discover its profoundly emergent process and thrilling potential.

> *Vulnerability doesn't mean that anything personal goes. The exposure of the self who is also a spectator has to take us somewhere we couldn't otherwise get to. It has to be essential to the argument, not a decorative flourish, not exposure for its own sake.*[2]

The chapter is organised into four parts starting with an overview of autoethnography's form that leads into a brief consideration of its major characteristics, including thick description, membership, reflexivity and narrative. An example of evocative autoethnography, "Ladies' Shoes", invites the reader behind the mask of the clinician to witness her conflicted inner moral process in the face of an ethical morass. As with all autoethnography, the reader is invited to appraise the trustworthiness and moral value of the narrative. To help with this process, several fundamental "criteria", proposed by autoethnographer Arthur Bochner, are outlined to guide and inform the reader's assessment.

Given the controversial and moral nature of autoethnography, a brief historical overview will situate autoethnography's fascinating emergence through the "paradigm wars" of the past 50 or more years. These wars describe the fight of qualitative research for parity with quantitative research and reflect the historical dominance of a reductive worldview and the defences that police its boundaries against any "illegitimate" encroachment. As we shall see, the ongoing dominance of "scientific legitimacy" is entrenched in a positivist, *quantifying, reductive* worldview despite the emergence of a good number of ideologies challenging its current authority.

We conclude with a synthesis of the most common critiques levelled at autoethnography, which typically point back to the primacy of a "generalised" worldview and the unrelenting hold of "scientific" research still dominating the world stage. Our analysis also considers the unavoidable problem of power in research, particularly narrative research, and the legitimate concerns of autoethnography's adherents and opponents.

Resisting reduction: The form and its parts

> *The genesis of autoethnography marks a milestone in the development of moral research given its focus on social justice that seeks to address and redress the problem of dehumanisation and the erosion of personal liberty.*[3]

Evocative autoethnography offers a skilful, ethically potent approach to moral research for *any* clinical researcher attempting to engage in the work of social transformation. Autoethnography is also called "auto-anthropology, autobiographical ethnography or sociology, or even personal self-narrative research and writing, and combines ethnography and autobiography". Most simply stated, this type of research aims at describing and analysing "(graphy)" the personal "(auto)" to illuminate the cultural "(ethno)".[4] A second type of autoethnography—described as "analytic"—differs significantly from evocative autoethnography in form and orientation and will be discussed a little later. But the term "autoethnography" is generally associated with its *evocative* form, as it will be here.

Autoethnography's emergence represents the fork in the road between old and new schools of ethnographers. Its performative approach focuses on the expression of emotion and a narrative style driven by the self-reflexive voice of the researcher/practitioner. Its approach is one characterised by a "postmodern scepticism" about the "generalisation of knowledge claims"[5] illustrated by a "minimalist" application of theory and criteria—for some autoethnographers more than others.[6] Above all, autoethnography embraces a transparently moral and political agenda of particular relevance to this inquiry, which is aimed at the *anti-social* and *anti-socialising* nature of the reductive worldview it opposes.

Autoethnography is taking hold in the social sciences through the leadership of an influential group of mostly American scholars[7] who are still refining and developing its form. They include, among others, Carolyn Ellis, Arthur Bochner, Norman Denzin and Laurel Richardson.[8] Autoethnography is also gaining momentum in fields related to science education,[9] medicine,[10] nursing and community mental health,[11] psychology[12] and counselling psychology.[13]

In this inquiry, autoethnography plays a significant—but not quite central—role as we have already seen in "James' Story" and elsewhere in the vignettes used throughout this inquiry. The vignette is a compelling narrative form which, like poetry, "makes another world accessible to the reader" by presenting "a lived experience" that is "emotionally and morally charged" because it is *felt*. Like poetry, the vignette presents one single "candid photo" or "epiphanic episode" through which "[p]eople organise their sense of self".[14] Michael Humphreys describes the vignette as an explicitly reflexive approach.[15]

Although the vignette's epiphanic potential lies in its reflexivity, there is always the risk the epiphany will be stillborn if it is so over-processed, over-contextualised or over-explained that there is nothing left to see or feel. One such example emerges from a scholarly article from a medical journal where even the term "autoethnography" is reduced to the acronym, "AEG".[16] Here, the narrative lies dead on the page, graphically framed within a black border to separate it from the "real research". The authors are so intent on assuring the reader they recognise the division between the "subjective" and the "objective" that their narrative translates as the kind of "decorative flourish" disparaged by autoethnographer Ruth Behar. In failing to transgress or transform the reader's perspective or—in Behar's words—to add anything to the argument, the narrative cannot qualify as autoethnography.[17] But, if mastery of execution is vital to its purpose, the question of excellence is less easily determined and the question of criteria is still being debated and established. Nonetheless, autoethnography's form comprises several fundamental aspects, including thick description, membership, narrative and reflexivity that differentiate it from other types of narrative research and that we examine next.

Thick description, membership, narrative, reflexivity

Ethnography is the theoretical field of practice aimed at deepening understanding of a given culture or group from an insider's or outsider's perspective. The ethnographer is engaged first-hand in observing, participating and closely documenting the people within a given culture or environment.[18] As a participant observer, the ethnographer uses "thick description" to develop written accounts and look for repeating patterns within that culture. These emerge in recurring themes found, for example, in songs, stories, belief systems, rituals or events.[19] Ethnography becomes *autoethnography* when this rich, detailed, evocative language focuses on the *author* within *her own* cultural context. Rather than the researcher remaining in the background, the autoethnographer is both the writer and protagonist. Her inner process, experience and response are central to the story and to an understanding of the social world she inhabits.[20]

"Thick description" is a term coined by American anthropologist Clifford Geertz that emerged in the development of ethnography.[21] It was an approach used to deepen knowledge and cultivate depth, perspective and understanding within *single* cases, as opposed to "codify[ing] abstract regularities" to generalise *across* cases.[22] Thick description, Geertz explains, was inseparable from cultural theory, given the limitations of its inner logic. Any emerging ethnographic theory must reflect back to this description and grow "out of the delicacy of its distinctions, not the sweep of its abstractions".[23] The strength of thick description lies in its *resistance* to generalisation and its ability to glean not only difference but also the refinement and subtlety of such difference. As we can already see in the autoethnographies in this inquiry, thick description helps the writer elude a generalising, reductive perspective by evoking the integrity, the *inviolability*, of the vulnerable help seeker, while asserting what is irrevocably *relational*. The "method and text"[24] of thick description also justifies a minimalist approach to the use and development of theory in autoethnography for, as Bochner reminds us, "there is nothing more theoretical than a good story".[25]

Who speaks, and on whose behalf, reflects the centrality of the element of *membership* to the interests of autoethnography. American anthropologist Davie Hayano was the first to theorise the importance of the *social* connection between the researcher and the subject in autoethnography when this form of research began to emerge.[26] Interestingly, autoethnography came to Hayano's attention in 1966 during a seminar at the London School of Economics when he heard about the story of a "shouting match" that had occurred some years before between a black and a white African: Jomo Kenyatta and L.S.B. Leakey. Their ferocious argument hinged on Kenyatta's study of his own people that brought into question the "validity of anthropological data" that did not also include a careful assessment of the "characteristics, interests, and origin of the person who did the fieldwork".[27] The notion of membership was consequently integrated into the development of autoethnography, and Hayano went on to theorise the issue.

Hayano claimed that the "membership" of the researcher to the subject(s) actually defines autoethnography, and he theorised three possible types. In each case, membership minimally required that "researchers possess the qualities of often permanent self-identification with a group, and full internal membership, as recognised both by themselves and the people of whom they are a part".[28] It was a significant step forwards in addressing the problem of research conducted within a hierarchical system that had previously placed the "subject" *below* the researcher.[29]

But even these distinctions have blurred as the field of autoethnography advances, giving way to more contemporary ideas about affiliation and "co-participant" equality.[30] Carolyn Ellis recognises even friendship as an ethical platform for moral research because it eliminates the researcher's need to "pretend". Nonetheless, such openness and sociality, no matter how sincerely expressed, can come at an unjustifiable price for the research participant. Ellis regretfully recounts, for example, how earlier in her career she and other colleagues had feigned friendship with research participants to obtain the information they required.[31] In community mental health care we find similar emotional manipulations replicated within the "therapeutic relationship" and through the use of "empathy", where the clinician conscripts the help seeker's trust in the service of clinical exigencies.[32]

It is also true that the vocabulary describing the "subject" within ethnography has evolved over time, moving her ever closer to the researcher as an "informant", a "participant", a "co-participant" and now, even a "friend". The narrowing gap between the two has changed the researcher's role from the "privileged possessor of expert knowledge" to a collaborator and community member allied with her subject.[33] This increasing intimacy has also opened the dialogue to ever more complex questions about relational possibilities that are moving autoethnography towards a form of moral practice and social activism. It is an approach with enormous salience for the clinical relationship in community mental health care and an area of research now emerging in psychological literature.[34]

Reflexivity, another fundamental element of autoethnography, plays a particularly controversial role that is becoming more widely accepted, Denzin insists, as part of a "global, reflexive, critical ethnography".[35] Reflexivity is an introspective process that mines the feeling, memory, cognition, impulse and physiological response of the researcher. Reflexivity allows her to map new knowledge about a given experience or encounter,[36] and the reflexive voice becomes the research itself, given its reflection of the researcher's experience, process and role.[37] There are also various forms—theoretical approaches—of reflexivity. Of interest to this inquiry is "confessional reflexivity" because it closely reflects my narrative interests and style.[38] Confessional reflexivity allows me to own and atone for my role in the problem being examined here. Ellis describes confessional ethnography as the story *about* the research that early ethnographers typically kept separate from their public work. The term describes an approach focused on the interaction between the researcher and the participant within the evocative writing process. Ellis prefers the term "ethnographic memoir" despite its problematic associations to memoir as a particular genre of writing, which might undermine autoethnography's legitimacy. But as a descriptor "confessional" is equally problematic, given its connotations of shame, weakness and guilt—even self-indulgence. Such connotations are already used to derogate and dismiss autoethnography's authority, which is an issue that Ellis, Behar and Bochner have addressed in their work.[39] That said, the power of reflexivity fully resides in its capacity to excavate the interior process of self and other interrogation, which in turn *transforms* the researcher's "beliefs, actions, and sense of self".[40]

In earlier conceptualisations of this term, "reflexivity" referred to one of several different practices aimed at increasing the "trustworthiness" of naturalistic research.[41] These included daily journaling, "peer debriefings" or "member checks" that helped solicit participants' response to the research. Other practices, like "triangulation", were aimed at testing one's reflexivity against various data sources, investigators, theories and methods.[42] This early formulation of reflexivity was rooted in ideas of scientific neutrality and objectivity that have given way to the transparently political and subversive aims of autoethnographers who are openly "committed to a more just social order".[43] Nonetheless, for autoethnography to claim an undisputed place in the academy, clearer criteria will likely be required, despite those autoethnographers—described as theoretically minimalist—who argue to the contrary. Patti Lather's work on validity in autoethnography has shown that the issue of criteria is very much part of the dialogue. Its development involves the ongoing work of theorising and translating quantitative criteria into their qualitative equivalent and, more specifically, their *autoethnographic* equivalent. Thus, the notion of "rigor" as a measure of quantitative merit translates into the qualitative equivalent of "trustworthiness".[44] The integrity of the writer's process within the narrative must be transparently and authentically reflected *if* she is to move—to *enlighten, to affect*—the reader. "Trustworthiness", then, becomes a cogent translation of "rigor", as it relates to the story's ethical veracity and impact. These are also early days in the development of autoethnographic criteria which, Lather cautions, will have to be fully articulated to better support "morally engaged" research.[45]

The role of reflexivity has changed significantly over time. No longer primarily or simply used to establish the legitimacy of naturalistic research as a respectably neutral player in empirical research, the self-reflexive voice is emerging in autoethnography as a radical political tool. In this inquiry, the trustworthiness of the clinician's voice lies also in its capacity to interrogate and evoke the ethical violations of clinical praxis while extending a compelling and resonant moral appeal to the reader.

Narrative presence undergirds all autoethnography and typically takes the form of a short story written in the first person with the researcher as subject.[46] But narrative can also be expressed through other creative mediums, including photography, dance, stage plays and video music, even film. The choice is contingent on the research question and the researcher's creative skill, which determine the process and outcome of the work.[47] A written narrative could be virtually anything from a poem to a comic book. In evocative autoethnography, however, the story becomes the theoretical and can be a stand-alone piece stripped of any theory or analysis, as the following autoethnographies illustrate.

In *The Academic Tourist*, for example, Robert Pelias offers a critical examination of his life as a career academic that presents a witty but poignant exposé of the pretensions of academia. As the mortified academic, Pelias mines these pretensions to uncover the hubris of the academy and the humanity of the academician trying to keep up appearances.[48] In *Girl in a Cast*, American anthropologist Ruth Behar tracks an anguishing period in her childhood to a spiritual awakening in adulthood that helps her reclaim her vulnerable and authentic voice in mainstream anthropology.[49] In *It's About Time: Narrative and the Divided Self*, Arthur Bochner connects the sudden news of his father's death to his recognition of the painful inadequacy of the academy in which he is also deeply entrenched.[50] The transformative moment occurs when Bochner sees—*as if for the first time*—what he already profoundly knows but learns anew: "I was stunned to learn how tame the academic world is in comparison to the wilderness of lived experience".[51]

These are all gripping, emotional, seamless, stand-alone pieces that qualify as autoethnography. They are revelatory, artistically crafted, convincing, evocative and speak for themselves without the need for theory or analysis. These narratives also compel an ethical response from the writer as well as the reader. In each one, a paradox emerges as a problem—an *enigma*—that points towards a moral and *relational* resolution. But this resolution is also elusive and complex because it is thwarted by the impregnable defence of the status quo that the writer is also continually negotiating.

Autoethnography offers the researcher the means to attempt a different kind of research to capture and evoke the unjust, policing mechanisms of power. Its inclusive language, unlike the obscure and specialised lexicons of the academy, makes autoethnography accessible to readers beyond *any* academic borders. The creation of a narrative presence that calls for evocation necessitates the call for the writer's abstention from professional or academic jargon that might otherwise exclude readers or, for that matter, occlude the epiphany at the centre of the story.[52] Most importantly, narrative presence enables the researcher to explore and expose protected worlds of highly personal experience—such as the hidden moral process of a clinician—that are rarely accessed in traditional research. Within these worlds, the writer can sensitise the reader to the politics of her experience and the larger truth about people different—or not so different—from herself.[53] These are the strategies that allow the writer to jump boundaries, undermine power structures and build bridges between us.

Anatomy of an autoethnography

> *[W]e need other forms of criticism, which are rigorous but not disinterested; forms of criticism which are not immune to catharsis; forms of criticism which can respond vulnerably, in ways we must begin to try to imagine.*[54]

Ladies' Shoes

> *It was my first few weeks on intake in community mental health. I had finally cinched a government job with the kind of salary and benefits package I'd waited too long to achieve. I wasn't used to dealing with doctors and psychiatrists and nurses every day it was foreign, and everything moved fast. I only had a three-month contract and no back-up. I'd left a full-time job I could no longer afford to keep, hoping that this might lead to something permanent. I could not fail. I'd lose the apartment if I couldn't keep up the mortgage payments, my beautiful apartment with the little garden, south-facing, and all mine.*
>
> *Besides the steep learning curve, the medical vibe of the place gave me an adrenaline rush with the onslaught of emergencies that came through the in-take phone lines or showed up at our door. The GP who called me that day was intense and wanted to know if he could get backing from a psychiatrist*

to force one of his patients to have dialysis who was suddenly refusing it. He needed a signature to certify his patient because this man needed dialysis right now. This man was one of "our" patients living uneventfully in a community housing situation with others who couldn't manage on their own and who were taken care of by the state. They weren't incarcerated or dangerous or locked up in a mental hospital. There was no psychiatric emergency, the resident had simply decided he'd had enough dialysis and made it clear—no thanks.

But I got the hit, the drive of this doctor who would not be refused by his patient. I could hear the quaver of fear in his voice, could hear him breathing on the other end of the phone, the insistence, the urgency, and I could see it all made sense. Or did it? What was he afraid of, what was the panic after all? The GP knew this was not standard practice, nor a clear-cut psychiatric matter; it was a physical illness and a personal choice. I had no idea how to proceed or what to say but I didn't want him to know that and went to find out. It seemed like an important task and a murky situation. One of the staff psychiatrists I approached rolled his eyes wearily when he got the gist of the story and told me to leave it with him. A signature was found before the end of the day, and the resident's wishes were over-ridden. For his own good. It felt like a small victory for me, the newbie who'd helped finesse it all.

I spoke a few days later to a staff member of this man's residence. Had she called me to tell me or had I made a follow-up call to find out how things were going? I can't remember. But I remember how it all happened in slow motion and unfolded like a film clip while we talked. Her words came slowly and deliberately, her voice was soft and tinged with sadness while she described this middle-aged man as a character who'd always endeared himself to others with his sweet ways and gentleness, his offbeat style and a penchant for wearing ladies' shoes. He'd been known, seen, valued, possibly loved, if only by this staff member and then he was—gone. He'd reached some kind of endpoint, maybe he'd known he was about to die or simply wanted to and had decided to claim this last act as his own, or tried.

Neither of us said what was really on our minds but that our hushed conversation belied. Someone had brutally imposed his will—or hers—on another human being with the same rights as anyone but with no way to claim them in his vulnerable position. His sanctity and desecration were so surprising after all, emerging like this in his death.

I didn't want to think about the details, but they arose while she kept talking in that slow, soft voice while I drifted away to wonder if they'd strapped him into a chair for this last, or almost last, dialysis. Maybe they'd restrained him in his bed or medicated him into submission beforehand. Or, had he finally acquiesced after a brow-beating from his doctor and the house staff, knowing there was no choice and doing it just to please them and get it over with? He died, anyway, a few days later.

How could it be? The rush, the excitement, the mission I'd been on just days before of talking to that doctor, of discussing it with the psychiatrist. It had all worked out only it hadn't. There I was sitting in a small, dimly lit, windowless consultation room, bowed over the desk, holding the receiver tightly to my ear and looking blankly at the wood grain of the veneer on the desk while her voice trailed on. I was stunned, nauseous with the knowledge that I had this man's *blood on my hands. But why? I hadn't done anything wrong. I'd only listened, I'd only asked, I'd only tried to help. I was only doing my job. Wasn't I only doing my job?*

How to assess the merits of an autoethnography

"Ladies' Shoes" performs some of the major themes of our inquiry and invites the reader to appraise its narrative worth.[55] But how is to be judged? Arthur Bochner provocatively suggests we should not use *any* criteria to judge an autoethnography as good or bad. He does, however, recommend six general "qualities" that help him "feel with" a story, given the centrality of feeling and emotional integrity to autoethnography's effectiveness and success.[56] In other literature related to autoethnography, these "qualities" refer to criteria.[57]

> First, I look for abundant, concrete detail. . . the commonplace, even trivial routines of everyday life. . . the flesh and blood emotions of people coping with life's contingencies. . . facts but also feelings. Second. . . complex narratives, stories told in a temporal framework that rotates between past and present reflecting. . . the curve of time. Third. . . the author's emotional credibility, vulnerability, and honesty. I expect the author to dig. . . displaying the self on the page, taking a measure of life's limitations, of the cultural scripts that resist transformation. . . . Fourth, narratives that express a tale of two selves; a believable journey from who I was to who I am, a life course reimagined or transformed by crisis. Fifth, I hold the author to a demanding standard of ethical self-consciousness. . . to show concern for how other people who are part of the teller's story are portrayed. . . and to provide a space for the listener's becoming, and for the moral commitments and convictions that underlie the story. Sixth. . . I want a story that moves me, my heart and belly as well as my head; that show[s] me what life feels like now and what it can mean.[58]

In looking at "Ladies' Shoes", Bochner's six qualities appear to coalesce in the revelatory moment of horror and moral clarity during the phone call that exposes me to my failed responsibility for this innocent man, in whose betrayal—and death—I have participated. How effectively the narrative communicates this moral imperative—and only the *reader* can say—relates to the sixth quality—*the story's ability to move us*. Without which, the *momentum*, and possibilities, or meanings, emerging from the story will fail to shift our perspective, our thinking and behaviour.[59] These six qualities, are at the heart of autoethnography's unapologetic moral project and its resistance to the ongoing imposition of a positivist—*generalising*—worldview. But in choosing this research approach to interrogate the moral ramifications of my clinical role, I also found myself at the centre of an academic and ethical maelstrom.[60]

The paradigm wars

> *I have learned that heresy is greatly maligned and, when put to good use, can begin a robust dance of agency in one's personal/political/professional life. So . . . I began writing and performing autoethnography concentrating on the body as the site from which the story is generated.*[61]

Denzin notes that social consciousness and accountability are central to the project of evocative autoethnography that has incubated through the "paradigm wars" of the past 50 years and more.[62] These are the wars between the interests of scientific-based research—quantitative research—and qualitative research that have played out between these two opposing camps, and *among* opponents within each one, in a constantly shifting ideological landscape. Denzin suggests that no fewer than seven paradigmatic shifts have taken place from the beginning of the 20th century to this present or "seventh moment". But while these shifts may cut across different historical periods and ideologies, they appear to be operating simultaneously. Far from being frozen within their historical contexts, these differing and opposing ideologies are constantly interacting, competing and informing each other in *this* present moment.[63]

Qualitative ground has been won and lost throughout these wars, although Denzin suggests that at the end of the 1990s "the key assumptions of the interpretive movement were demolished". The problem was that the "incompatibility and incommensurability" debates emerged once again to destroy the legitimacy of qualitative research as "nonscience". Of course, qualitative research does not and *cannot* employ the same criteria used to prove the validity and reliability of quantitative research.[64] But even within the qualitative camp, the criteria debate is fraught. Some argue for the need for rationalist criteria to improve the quality and standing of qualitative research. Others claim that the research community's insistence on rationalist criteria undermines the legitimacy and clout of qualitative research.[65] Still others attribute the problem of legitimacy to a setback for qualitative research caused by the growing conservatism in research practice in the past ten years.[66]

Further complicating this picture are those scholars describing quantitative and qualitative approaches as *methods* rather than paradigms, when methodology is actually secondary to the question of *paradigm*. The worldview of the researcher is, after all, informed as much methodologically as it is ontologically and epistemologically.[67]

> We can understand a paradigm as a set of fundamental beliefs (or metaphysics) that deal with ultimates or first principles. It represents *a worldview* that defines, for its holder, the nature of the "world," the individual's place in it, and the range of possible relationships to that world and its parts, as, for example, cosmologies and theologies do.[68]

To contextualise the historical emergence of this new, *third* paradigm, we consider four of these ideologies in the section ahead to show their contribution to the ever-shifting backdrop of the "paradigm wars".[69]

From positivism to postmodernism

> Some ethnographers, now, desire their work to be both "scientific" and "literary". I am one who does so desire. We recognise the historical split between scientific and literary writing that emerged in the 17th century as unstable and mutable.[70]

Quantitative research, for example, generally reflects the values and beliefs of *positivism*. This worldview claims the existence of an "apprehendable reality" apparently "driven by immutable laws and mechanisms... in the form of time and context-free generalisations, some of which take the form of cause-effect laws".[71] Positivism "has dominated... for some 400 years",[72] and describes a reductive, rationalistic, deterministic or atomistic perspective seen only by the observer. Consequently, whatever, or *whoever*, is being observed is independent of the researcher or—for our interests—*dissociated* from her. The precision made possible by such research is vital when the goal is prediction and control. But the ongoing dominance of positivism means that the "hard sciences" still command greater respect and legitimacy than "soft" sciences that do not quantify their findings.

By comparison, *post-positivism* claims the notion of an ultimate reality we can assume but never fully grasp. We can only approximate the truth by subjecting our research claims to critical examination. The research is "always subject to falsification" by being measured and compared to what is known—or agreed—and then submitted to the research community for scrutiny.[73] Its qualitative methods recognise the importance of social context and meaning-making on the part of its subjects. These include the use of case study, personal experience, introspection, life story, interview, observational, historical, interactional and visual texts that describe routine and problematic moments and meanings in individuals' lives. Denzin describes this approach as multi-method, interpretive and naturalistic.[74]

Constructivism moves beyond the notion of an ultimate truth to ideas about the fluidity of knowledge where truth is not so much established as it is informed and refined.[75] The findings are "literally created" as the research emerges through the process occurring between and among investigators and respondents. "The naturalistic paradigm asserts... that the inquirer and the respondent are interrelated with each influencing the other".[76] The outcome is consensual, co-created and evolving, as autoethnography partially demonstrates. Guba notes that it was the growing demand for this kind of research that finally resulted in the academy recognising the emergence of new values that took aim at traditional research approaches.[77]

Postmodernism shows the connection between truth and the "vocabularies and paradigms" used to describe it. Here, new relationships are forged between "authors, audiences and texts" to *resist* the methods of those who formerly used and discarded the cultures they investigated. Postmodernism recognises the significance of the story for its complexity and ability to communicate morally and ethically. It represents a move *away* from the notion of "value-free" to "value-laden" research that favours literature over the hard sciences.[78] The self-reflexive voice that emerges as the centrepiece of postmodernism reflects the many possible ways of "knowing and inquiring".[79] The researcher consequently becomes a "boundary-crosser" of a whole constellation of identities that are continually shifting and identify not only the speaker but also *the one for whom she speaks.*[80]

These four ideologies have helped trace the movement towards this emerging *third* paradigm, which is beyond the capacity or pursuits of quantitative, qualitative, or "mixed methods" research which combines the two.

> The field is on the edge of a new paradigm dialogue, a third formation existing beyond SBR[81] and mixed methods. This is the space primarily filled by non-mixed methods interpretive researchers, the empowerment discourses: critical constructionists, feminists, critical pedagogy and performance studies; oral historians. . . and interpretive interactionists. These are scholars in a different space. They seldom use terms like *validity* and *reliability*. For some, a minimalist approach to theory is endorsed. A disruptive politics of representation is the focus, as are the methods that disturb the smooth surfaces of SBR. Scholars are crafting works that move persons and communities to action.[82]

There are no tidy boundaries in autoethnography between the "ethnographic, the artistic, the epistemological, the aesthetic, and the political".[83] But despite the emergence of these new cultural perspectives and the ever-growing role of subjectivity, the orthodoxy of positivism remains intact and intractable.[84] Research failing to reflect positivist standards is still less well regarded, or rewarded, in terms of research dollars, authority, visibility or "scientific" legitimacy.[85] That said, Yvonna Lincoln, suggests the stakes are actually *much* higher.

> There is a "politics" of evidence. Beyond the questions of legitimacy, hegemony and reward structures at universities, there are larger questions, which subsume mere issues of legitimacy. Three of those questions are whether or not science has a moral aspect; who determines what counts as evidence and who is persuaded by it; and what is the nature of the "language game" which is being played out in the politics of evidence?[86]

The policing function of the dominant discourse constantly overshadows autoethnography. Bochner insists that these two ways of seeing are not so much in opposition as incommensurable and that the arguments claimed by either side are ultimately "contingent on human choices".[87] Denzin also confirms that "moral and epistemological discourses" need not be in conflict and are not antithetical to each other but can cohabit "side by side". The evidence is already found in emerging fields of study on "[r]ace, ethnicity, sexuality, class, the research rights of indigenous peoples, whiteness, and queer studies". These are fields now informing discourse that would never have occurred in the 1970s and 1980s.[88] Nonetheless, the paradigm wars rage on.

Evocative versus analytic autoethnography

Throughout this chapter we have focused on the nature and development of *evocative* autoethnography. But the contentious issue of theory-building emerges again as the central debate between analytic and evocative autoethnographers. This is a sidebar since autoethnography generally is identified with its evocative form. Nonetheless, the issue of generalisability is the main dividing line between these two types, and the argument is heated.

Denzin claims to have abandoned his analytic roots for what he believes to be higher moral ground, despite the more significant academic risks involved. He also strenuously objects to the appropriation of evocative autoethnography's creative techniques by analytic autoethnographers who, he claims, continue to oppose "poststructural,[89] antifoundational arguments" of the past quarter century.[90] Denzin chides his analytic colleagues for failing to "write messy vulnerable texts that make you cry" and for "keep[ing] politics out of their research".[91]

> Ethnography is a not an innocent practice.... Through our writing and our talk, we enact the worlds we study.... The pedagogical is always moral and political; by enacting a way of seeing and being, it challenges, contests, or endorses the official, hegemonic ways of seeing and representing the other.[92]

In contrast, analytic autoethnography calls for an approach that embraces theory-building and claims the need for broader generalisation.[93] Despite these differences, analytic autoethnography does share three characteristics of its evocative counterpart including membership, self-reflexivity and narrative.[94]

Criticism and limitations

> *Qualitative researchers are called journalists, or soft scientists. Their work is termed unscientific, or only exploratory, or entirely personal and full of bias. It is called criticism and not theory, or it is interpreted politically, as a disguised version of Marxism or humanism.*[95]

Autoethnography is subject to criticism inside and outside its academic borders, as it should be. Its most predictable "defect" appears to lie in the heresy of defying the laws of logical positivism. But this argument is specious, Lather insists, given the "increasingly definitive critique of the inadequacies of positivist assumptions in the face of the complexities of human experience".[96] Indeed, this very critique has opened a space for the recent flourishing of autoethnography, although the opposition is still attempting to tarnish its legitimacy while ignoring the gravitas of its moral project.[97]

The scientific neutrality and objectivity so cherished by a positivist worldview are also myths, Lather insists, that serve to "mystify the inherently ideological nature of research in the human sciences and legitimate privilege based on class, race, and gender".[98] But autoethnography's project is to *demystify*, which is why its methods are transgressive and performative and also why it is so fiercely opposed by those upholding the very structures autoethnography seeks to subvert. The backlash hinges on a singularly one-dimensional argument consistent with a reductive worldview. This is one that asserts that autoethnography is *not* reliable, valid, rigorous, sufficiently theorised, generalisable, scientific or legitimate *enough*, because it does not embrace the positivist project. From a positivist viewpoint, this is quite true. But as Bochner and his colleagues have asserted, and as postmodernity has shown, it *is* a myth that criteria are "beyond culture. . . ourselves and our own conventions".[99] Nonetheless, the consequences of challenging this myth are substantial, to say the least.

Power and responsibility

It is also true that autoethnography's self-reflexive voice can never be completely beyond suspicion or reproach no matter how responsibly or vulnerably it is used. The voice that tracks the researcher's moment-to-moment process and the power dynamics in which she is embedded also benefit *the researcher*. While autoethnography invites me to resist the mechanisms of power on behalf of the vulnerable help seeker, it also compromises my efforts, given my membership with the authorising institution. This authority shapes and legitimises my speech and writing as a scholar—even my clinical notes—and I hesitate to threaten it with autoethnographic candour.[100] I am well aware that my self-conscious confession and discomfort within a form that makes any evidence admissible, leaves me all too visible and vulnerable, personally, professionally *and* ethically.[101]

Despite the moral distress and sometimes-harrowing sense of culpability I have experienced as a clinician, my institutional authority is still valuable to me. This authority, William Tierney observes, continually jeopardises the integrity of my autoethnography. Postmodernity may disturb my perspective enough to help me resist slipping into the comfortable roles of "power and domination". But simply claiming membership, kinship or friendship with those I wish to authorise and dignify as an autoethnographer is *not* enough.

Especially, Tierney notes, for the researcher who does not *like* working with those with whom she is engaged in research. These are the people with whom she will never become "comrades" or "find solidarity".[102] But even if she *does* like them, her research, and integrity, will still be at risk because this solidarity can "re-instill in our relations... who is right and who is wrong". The problem is unresolvable because the researcher is the one who always holds the balance of "power, voice, and authority".[103] By refusing to essentialise the help seeker, or fall prey to the illusion that there is any real refuge from the problem of power, the danger posed by my authority is still only *partially* resolved, particularly when I wish to rescue someone—as I surely have in the context of my work.[104] Like Ruth Behar, I too have been unsettled to find myself "resisting the 'I' of the ethnographer as a privileged eye, a voyeuristic eye, an all-powerful eye".[105] There *is* no escape, because "[t]he relationship in which we involve ourselves is inherently infused with power. Our challenge is to recognise it and decide how we will function within it".[106] But if this challenge represents a razor's edge, it is also true that autoethnography places the problem of power at the forefront of its task while demanding the ethical vigilance and *exposure* of the researcher, which comes at no small cost to the researcher.[107]

Even the most successful autoethnographer remains open to the ongoing threat of eviscerating personal critique that can be emotionally wounding and academically damaging. Carolyn Ellis recounts the risk she took in sharing with her students a very personal story she had written with her husband about her decision to undergo an abortion. She had intended to open the dialogue about a sensitive issue to illustrate the potential risks of undertaking this type of research. She was less prepared for the devastating feedback from some of her students.[108]

> I am trembling by the time I finish. I want to dismiss these responses but... I push myself to face them. I know people react in these ways, but that knowledge doesn't dull the pain of seeing the condemnation in print, a pain that is part of the cost of doing autoethnography deeply and honestly.[109]

Ruth Behar suggests that the vulnerable writer also has more to lose because "boring self-revelation" is ultimately "humiliating".[110] The exposure of the writer's inner world also makes the autoethnographer something of a cultural whistle-blower and more likely to be reviled on that account.

> It is not *just* about "method or technique". Rather, qualitative research is about making the world visible in ways that implement the goals of social justice and radical progressive democracy.[111]

The issue of clinical dehumanisation at the centre of this inquiry make evocative autoethnography's demand for "radical social change" both urgent and hopeful.[112] Its proponents are courageously, if not recklessly, demonstrating how scholars can and must disclose their inner lives in their research. They are committed to the ongoing evolution of autoethnography as a form of research which recognises that "[t]he critical imagination is radically democratic, pedagogical, and interventionist".[113] Autoethnography rejects the idea of research that ignores the suffering of people at the centre. "Its ethics challenge the ethics of the marketplace, it seeks utopian transformations committed to radical democratic ideals",[114] all of which exposes and subverts the norms, beliefs and values of academic research.

Autoethnography corrects the still restricted view of what constitutes real or significant research and has enabled me to perform what *should* profoundly concern anyone seeking the help of community mental health care or working in this field.[115] The term "performance ethnography" denotes what Denzin sees as the future of autoethnography—a form of discourse and a way of being in the world that is fundamentally moral and political. Performance, he believes, will eventually blur the line between autoethnography and ethnography altogether when the self-reflexive researcher becomes the "guiding presence" in the text. At which point the critical social sciences will become "a force to be reckoned with in political and cultural arenas".[116]

But the challenge, as Tierney's reminds us, it that the self-reflective voice is never beyond the problem of the power it seeks to subvert. Even within this inquiry and the narratives I present, there are good enough reasons for caution and restraint in interrogating the professional and institutional boundaries of community mental health care. Yet, the dark side of "professional boundaries" and the epistemic injustice they hide must be clarified again and again, which is where autoethnography can shine its light most effectively.

The last word goes to Patti Lather who soberly observes that: "Only those with advanced education have a shot at piercing through the theory and the jargon and arriving at a greater understanding of social forces".[117] With this shot in view, autoethnography offers researchers in the field of community mental health care the opportunity *and* the tools to break down the barriers of this theory and jargon, and the moral obligation to try.

Notes

1 N.K. Denzin, 'Performing [Auto] Ethnography Politically', *The Review of Education, Pedagogy & Cultural Studies*, 25 (2003), p. 273.
2 R. Behar, *The Vulnerable Observer: Anthropology That Breaks Your Heart* (Boston: Beacon Press, 1996), pp. 13–14.
3 Denzin, 'Performing [Auto] Ethnography Politically', p. 258.
4 C. Ellis, T.E. Adams, and A.P. Bochner, 'Autoethnography: An Overview', *Historical Social Research/Historische Sozialforschung*, 6 (2011), p. 273.
5 L. Anderson, 'Analytic Autoethnography', *Journal of Contemporary Ethnography*, 35 (2006), p. 373.
6 A term used by Norman Denzin. See: N.K. Denzin, 'Moments, Mixed Methods, and Paradigm Dialogs', *Qualitative Inquiry*, 16 (2010), p. 424.

7 In Canada, the University of Alberta's International Institute for Qualitative Methodology is engaged in autoethnographic research and development, and their official journal is the *International Journal of Qualitative Methods*, published by SAGE.
8 Anderson, 'Analytic Autoethnography', p. 374.
9 P.C. Taylor, E.L. Taylor, and B.C. Luitel, 'Multi-Paradigmatic Transformative Research as/for Teacher Education: An Integral Perspective', in *Second International Handbook of Science Education*, ed. by K.G. Tobin, B.J. Fraser and C. McRobbie (Dordrecht, The Netherlands: Springer, 2012), pp. 373–87.
10 J. Gallé and L. Lingard, 'A Medical Student's Perspective of Participation in an Interprofessional Education Placement: An Autoethnography', *Journal of Interprofessional Care*, 24 (2010).
11 K. Foster, M. McAllister, and L. O'Brien, 'Extending the Boundaries: Autoethnography as an Emergent Method in Mental Health Nursing Research', *International Journal of Mental Health Nursing*, 15 (2006).
12 N. Devlin, 'A Critical Examination and Analysis of the Processes by Which Educational Psychologists Constructed Themselves as Ethical Professionals: To Be What I Am Not' (unpublished Ph.D. thesis, Newcastle University, 2013).
13 P. McIlveen, 'Autoethnography as a Method for Reflexive Research and Practice in Vocational Psychology', *Australian Journal of Career Development*, 17 (2008).
14 L. Richardson, 'Nine Poems Marriage and the Family', *Journal of Contemporary Ethnography*, 23 (1994), pp. 8–9.
15 M. Humphreys, 'Getting Personal: Reflexivity and Autoethnographic Vignettes', *Qualitative Inquiry*, 11 (2005).
16 Gallé and Lingard, 'A Medical Student's Perspective of Participation in an Interprofessional Education Placement: An Autoethnography'.
17 Behar, *The Vulnerable Observer: Anthropology That Breaks Your Heart*, p. 14.
18 C. Ellis, *The Ethnographic I: A Methodological Novel About Autoethnography* (Walnut Creek, CA: AltaMira Press, 2004), p. 26.
19 Ellis, Adams, and Bochner, 'Autoethnography: An Overview', p. 277.
20 Anderson, 'Analytic Autoethnography', p. 384.
21 See: C. Geertz, 'Thick Description: Toward an Interpretive Theory of Culture', in *Turning Points in Qualitative Research: Tying Knots in a Handkerchief*, ed. by Y.S. Lincoln and N.K. Denzin (Walnut Creek, CA: AltaMira Press, 2003), pp. 143–68.
22 Ibid. p. 165.
23 Ibid. pp. 164–65.
24 D.E. Reed-Danahay, *Auto/Ethnography* (New York: Berg, 1997), p. 8.
25 A. Bochner, 'It's About Time: Narrative and the Divided Self', *Qualitative Inquiry*, 3 (1997), p. 435.
26 Ellis, Adams, and Bochner, 'Autoethnography: An Overview', p. 278.
27 D.M. Hayano, 'Auto-Ethnography: Paradigms, Problems, and Prospects', *Human Organisation*, 38 (1979), pp. 99–100.
28 Ibid. p. 100.
29 Referring to a term coined by Reinharz, S. (1979), Lather observes this "rape model" of research: "career advancement of social scientists built on alienating and exploitative methods". See: P. Lather, 'Issues of Validity in Openly Ideological Research: Between a Rock and a Soft Place', *Interchange*, 17 (1986), p. 75.
30 Reed-Danahay, *Auto/Ethnography*, pp. 8–9.
31 Ellis, *The Ethnographic I: A Methodological Novel About Autoethnography*, p. 148.
32 A fine synthesis on the process of clinical manipulation is found in: M.T. Taussig, 'Reification and the Consciousness of the Patient', *Social Science & Medicine, Part B: Medical Anthropology*, 14 (1980).

33 Lather, 'Issues of Validity', p. 73.
34 The project: Psychology and the Other, now examining the moral/relational implications of Emmanuel Levinas' work within psychology and psychological praxis, has significant implications for autoethnography. See: www.psychologyandtheother.com/ Also: D.M. Goodman and M. Freeman, eds., *Psychology and the Other* (Oxford: Oxford University Press, 2015). Elsewhere, Sayers' work has examined the theories of various legendary psychoanalysts, from William James to Julia Kristeva, for their theoretical and personal perspectives on love and relationality in therapy. See: J. Sayers, *Divine Therapy: Love, Mysticism, and Psychoanalysis* (New York: Oxford University Press, 2003). See also, for example: Y. Cohen, 'Loving the Patient as the Basis for Treatment', *American Journal of Psychoanalysis*, 66 (2006).
35 Denzin, 'Performing [Auto] Ethnography Politically', p. 268.
36 C. Ellis, 'Sociological Introspection and Emotional Experience', *Symbolic Interaction*, 14 (1991), pp. 23–25.
37 S. Wall, 'An Autoethnography on Learning About Autoethnography', *International Journal of Qualitative Methods*, 5 (2008), pp. 147–48.
38 For details on all three theoretical approaches to reflexivity, see: Denzin, 'Performing [Auto] Ethnography Politically', pp. 268–70.
39 See: Ellis, *The Ethnographic I: A Methodological Novel About Autoethnography*, pp. 49–50.
40 Anderson, 'Analytic Autoethnography', pp. 382–83.
41 Guba translated quantitative criteria into applicable criteria for qualitative approaches of naturalistic research and changed the concept of *rigor* as the primary measure of quantitative excellence to *trustworthiness* as its qualitative equivalent. See: E.G. Guba, 'Criteria for Assessing the Trustworthiness of Naturalistic Inquiries', *Educational Communication and Technology*, 29 (1981), pp. 85, 87.
42 For an autoethnographic perspective of triangulation, see also: Lather, 'Issues of Validity', pp. 69, 72, 74, 77, 78.
43 Ibid. pp. 66–67.
44 J.M. Morse and others, 'Verification Strategies for Establishing Reliability and Validity in Qualitative Research', *International Journal of Qualitative Methods*, 1 (2008), p. 15.
45 See Patti Lather's excellent work in this area. Lather, 'Issues of Validity'; P. Lather, 'Fertile Obsession: Validity After Poststructuralism', *The Sociological Quarterly*, 34 (1993).
46 Ellis, *The Ethnographic I: A Methodological Novel About Autoethnography*, p. 30.
47 Ibid. p. 193.
48 R.J. Pelias, 'The Academic Tourist: An Autoethnography', *Qualitative Inquiry*, 9 (2003).
49 Behar, *The Vulnerable Observer: Anthropology That Breaks Your Heart*, pp. 104–35.
50 Bochner, 'It's About Time: Narrative and the Divided Self'.
51 Ibid. p. 421. For an emotive narrative of Bochner's involvement with his mother's death and its intersection with 9/11, see also: A. Bochner, 'Love Survives', *Qualitative Inquiry*, 8 (2002).
52 Ellis, Adams, and Bochner, 'Autoethnography: An Overview', p. 277.
53 Ibid. p. 274.
54 Behar, *The Vulnerable Observer: Anthropology That Breaks Your Heart*, p. 175.
55 Inviting the reader into the text to engage in such an evaluative process is not antithetical to the autoethnographic process but part of it, as this author illustrates. See: Humphreys, 'Getting Personal: Reflexivity and Autoethnographic Vignettes', pp. 850–51.

Writing autoethnography 71

56 A. Bochner, 'Criteria Against Ourselves', *Qualitative Inquiry*, 6 (2000), p. 270.
57 In the work of Guba or Lather, Bochner's ostensibly non-evaluative "qualities" are defined with some considerable precision, including the quality of "thick description".
58 Bochner, 'Criteria Against Ourselves', pp. 270–71.
59 Ibid. p. 271. Similar characteristics are found in: Ellis, Adams, and Bochner, 'Autoethnography: An Overview', pp. 275–77.
60 For an overview of the maelstrom, see: Denzin, 'Moments, Mixed Methods, and Paradigm Dialogs'.
61 T. Spry, 'Performing Autoethnography: An Embodied Methodological Praxis', *Qualitative inquiry,* 7 (2001), p. 709.
62 Denzin, 'Moments, Mixed Methods, and Paradigm Dialogs', pp. 420–22.
63 In 1994 Denzin noted five historical periods, and in 2001, seven historical periods. See: N.K. Denzin, 'Romancing the Text: The Qualitative Researcher-Writer-as-Bricoleur', in *Qualitative Methodologies in Music Education Research Conference*, ed. by Bulletin of the Council for Research in Music Education (Chicago: University of Illinois Press, 1994), p. 16; N.K. Denzin, 'The Reflexive Interview and a Performative Social Science', *Qualitative Research*, 1 (2001), pp. 24–25.
64 Denzin, 'Moments, Mixed Methods, and Paradigm Dialogs', p. 423.
65 L. Krefting, 'Rigor in Qualitative Research: The Assessment of Trustworthiness', *The American Journal of Occupational Therapy*, 45 (1991), p. 214.
66 S.J. Tracy, 'Qualitative Quality: Eight "Big-Tent" Criteria for Excellent Qualitative Research', *Qualitative Inquiry*, 16 (2010), p. 838.
67 E.G. Guba and Y.S. Lincoln, 'Competing Paradigms in Qualitative Research', in *Handbook of Qualitative Research*, ed. by N.K. Denzin (Thousand Oak, CA: Sage, 1994), pp. 105–17.
68 Ibid. p. 107.
69 See Table 6.2 for an overview of the differences between positivism, post-positivism and constructivism; see: Ibid. p. 112.
70 L. Richardson, 'Evaluating Ethnography', *Qualitative Inquiry*, 6 (2000), p. 253.
71 Ibid. p. 109.
72 Ibid. p. 108.
73 Ibid. p. 110.
74 Denzin, 'Romancing the Text: The Qualitative Researcher-Writer-as-Bricoleur', p. 16.
75 Guba and Lincoln, 'Competing Paradigms in Qualitative Research', pp. 110–11.
76 Guba, 'Criteria for Assessing the Trustworthiness of Naturalistic Inquiries', p. 77.
77 Ibid. pp. 75–76.
78 Ellis, Adams, and Bochner, 'Autoethnography: An Overview', p. 274.
79 Wall, 'An Autoethnography on Learning About Autoethnography', pp. 147–48.
80 Reed-Danahay, *Auto/Ethnography*, p. 3.
81 SBR is the acronym for science-based research.
82 Denzin, 'Moments, Mixed Methods, and Paradigm Dialogs', p. 424.
83 N.K. Denzin, 'Aesthetics and the Practices of Qualitative Inquiry', *Qualitative Inquiry*, 6 (2000), p. 261.
84 Lather, 'Issues of Validity', p. 63.
85 For new criteria suggested for qualitative research, see: Tracy, 'Qualitative Quality: Eight "Big-Tent" Criteria', pp. 839–40.
86 Y.S. Lincoln, 'On the Nature of Qualitative Evidence', in *Annual Meeting of the Association for the Study of Higher Education* (Sacramento, CA: November 21–24, 2002), pp. 1–23 (p. 16).
87 Bochner, 'Criteria Against Ourselves', p. 266.
88 Denzin, 'Moments, Mixed Methods, and Paradigm Dialogs', p. 424.

89 Poststructuralism is defined as the abandonment of the aims of "transcendence", characterised by a focus on "individual or particular/local resistance to the effects of power", including power legitimised as transcendental. See: M. Morris, 'The Critique of Transcendence: Poststructuralism and the Political', *Political Theory*, 32 (2004), pp. 121–122. Lather suggests that poststructuralism and autoethnography are attempts to move from "yesterday's institutions" by focusing on the "difficulties involved in representing the social rather than repressing them in pursuit of an unrealised ideal". See: Lather, 'Fertile Obsession: Validity After Poststructuralism', pp. 673, 76, 77.
90 N.K. Denzin, 'Analytic Autoethnography, or Déjà Vu All Over Again', *Journal of Contemporary Ethnography*, 35 (2006), p. 421.
91 Ibid. p. 421.
92 See: Ibid. p. 422.
93 Anderson, 'Analytic Autoethnography', p. 388.
94 Anderson proposes five main characteristics for analytic autoethnography including, membership, reflexivity, narrative visibility of the researcher, dialogue with other informants and theoretical analysis. See: Ibid. p. 378.
95 Denzin, 'Romancing the Text: The Qualitative Researcher-Writer-as-Bricoleur', p. 19.
96 Lather, 'Issues of Validity', p. 63.
97 Ibid. pp. 68–75. This critique is based on feminist research, neo-Marxist critical ethnography and Freirian "empowering" research, focused on "transformative agendas" and "research as praxis". Feminist research seeks to overcome invisibility and distortion. Marxist research attempts to show how schooling establishes social and economic inequality. Freirian research blurs "the distinctions between research, learning, and action".
98 Ibid. p. 64.
99 Bochner, 'Criteria Against Ourselves', p. 267.
100 Tierney describes the difficulty in balancing the "inner logic" of the story with the audience's need to understand and the publisher's willingness to print. See: W.G. Tierney, 'Life History's History: Subjects Foretold', *Qualitative Inquiry*, 4 (1998), p. 53.
101 Richardson, 'Evaluating Ethnography', pp. 253–54.
102 Tierney, 'Life History's History: Subjects Foretold', p. 56.
103 Ibid. pp. 56–57.
104 Ibid. p. 56.
105 Behar, *The Vulnerable Observer: Anthropology That Breaks Your Heart*, p. 17.
106 Tierney, 'Life History's History: Subjects Foretold', p. 64.
107 See: J. Taylor, 'The Intimate Insider: Negotiating the Ethics of Friendship When Doing Insider Research', *Qualitative Research*, 11 (2011).
108 Ellis, *The Ethnographic I: A Methodological Novel About Autoethnography*, pp. 75–81.
109 Ibid. p. 81.
110 Behar, *The Vulnerable Observer: Anthropology That Breaks Your Heart*, p. 13.
111 N.K. Denzin and M.D. Giardina, 'Introduction', in *Qualitative Inquiry and Human Rights,* ed. by N.K. Denzin and M.D. Giardina (Walnut Creek, CA: Left Coast Press, 2010), p. 14.
112 Denzin, 'Performing [Auto] Ethnography Politically', p. 259.
113 Ibid. p. 261.
114 Ibid.
115 Ellis, Adams, and Bochner, 'Autoethnography: An Overview', pp. 274–75.
116 Denzin, 'Performing [Auto] Ethnography Politically', p. 259.
117 Lather, 'Issues of Validity', pp. 75–76.

References

Anderson, L., 'Analytic Autoethnography', *Journal of Contemporary Ethnography*, 35 (2006), 373–95. https://doi.org/10.1177/0891241605280449

Behar, R., *The Vulnerable Observer: Anthropology That Breaks Your Heart* (Boston: Beacon Press, 1996).

Bochner, A., 'Criteria Against Ourselves', *Qualitative Inquiry*, 6 (2000), 266–72. https://doi.org/10.1177/107780040000600209

——, 'It's About Time: Narrative and the Divided Self', *Qualitative Inquiry*, 3 (1997), 418–38. https://doi.org/10.1177/107780049700300404

——, 'Love Survives', *Qualitative Inquiry*, 8 (2002), 161–69. https://doi.org/10.1177/10778004008002009

Cohen, Y., 'Loving the Patient as the Basis for Treatment', *American Journal of Psychoanalysis*, 66 (2006), 139–55. https://doi.org/10.1007/s11231-006-9012-8

Denzin, N.K., 'Aesthetics and the Practices of Qualitative Inquiry', *Qualitative Inquiry*, 6 (2000), 256–65. https://doi.org/10.1177/107780040000600208

——, 'Analytic Autoethnography, or Déjà Vu All Over Again', *Journal of Contemporary Ethnography*, 35 (2006), 419–28. https://doi.org/10.1177/0891241606286985

——, 'Moments, Mixed Methods, and Paradigm Dialogs', *Qualitative Inquiry*, 16 (2010), 419–27. https://doi.org/10.1177/1077800410364608

——, 'Performing [Auto] Ethnography Politically', *The Review of Education, Pedagogy & Cultural Studies*, 25 (2003), 257–78. https://doi.org/10.1080/10714410390225894

——, 'Romancing the Text: The Qualitative Researcher-Writer-as-Bricoleur', in *Qualitative Methodologies in Music Education Research Conference*, ed. by Bulletin of the Council for Research in Music Education (Chicago: University of Illinois Press, 1994), pp. 15–30. DOI:10.2307/40318652; www.jstor.org/stable/40318652

——, 'The Reflexive Interview and a Performative Social Science', *Qualitative Research*, 1 (2001), 23–46. https://doi.org/10.1177/146879410100100102

Denzin, N.K., and Giardina, M.D., 'Introduction', in *Qualitative Inquiry and Human Rights*, ed. by N.K. Denzin and M.D. Giardina (Walnut Creek, CA: Left Coast Press, 2010).

Devlin, N., *A Critical Examination and Analysis of the Processes by Which Educational Psychologists Constructed Themselves as Ethical Professionals: To Be What I Am Not* (unpublished Ph.D. thesis, Newcastle University, 2013).

Ellis, C., 'Sociological Introspection and Emotional Experience', *Symbolic Interaction*, 14 (1991), 23–50. https://doi.org/10.1525/si.1991.14.1.23

——, *The Ethnographic I: A Methodological Novel About Autoethnography*, Vol. 13 (Walnut Creek, CA: AltaMira Press, 2004).

Ellis, C., Adams, T.E., and Bochner, A.P., 'Autoethnography: An Overview', *Historical Social Research/Historische Sozialforschung*, 6 (2011), 273–90. https://doi.org/10.12759/hsr.36.2011.4.273-290

Foster, K., McAllister, M., and O'Brien, L., 'Extending the Boundaries: Autoethnography as an Emergent Method in Mental Health Nursing Research', *International Journal of Mental Health Nursing*, 15 (2006), 44–53. https://doi.org/10.1111/j.1447-0349.2006.00402.x

Gallé, J., and Lingard, L., 'A Medical Student's Perspective of Participation in an Interprofessional Education Placement: An Autoethnography', *Journal of Interprofessional Care*, 24 (2010), 722–33. https://doi.org/10.3109/13561820903274954

Geertz, C., 'Thick Description: Toward an Interpretive Theory of Culture', in *Turning Points in Qualitative Research: Tying Knots in a Handkerchief*, ed. by Y.S. Lincoln and N.K. Denzin (Walnut Creek, CA: AltaMira Press, 2003), pp. 143–68.

Goodman, D., and Freeman, M., eds., *Psychology and the Other* (Oxford: Oxford University Press, 2015).

Guba, E.G., 'Criteria for Assessing the Trustworthiness of Naturalistic Inquiries', *Educational Communication and Technology*, 29 (1981), 75–91.

Guba, E.G., and Lincoln, Y.S., 'Competing Paradigms in Qualitative Research', in *Handbook of Qualitative Research*, ed. by N.K. Denzin (Thousand Oaks, CA: Sage, 1994), pp. 105–17.

Hayano, D.M., 'Auto-Ethnography: Paradigms, Problems, and Prospects', *Human Organization*, 38 (1979), 99–104. https://doi.org/10.17730/humo.38.1.u761n5601t4g318v

Humphreys, M., 'Getting Personal: Reflexivity and Autoethnographic Vignettes', *Qualitative Inquiry*, 11 (2005), 840–60. https://doi.org/10.1177/1077800404269425

Krefting, L., 'Rigor in Qualitative Research: The Assessment of Trustworthiness', *The American Journal of Occupational Therapy*, 45 (1991), 214–22. https://doi.org/10.5014/ajot.45.3.214

Lather, P., 'Fertile Obsession: Validity After Poststructuralism', *The Sociological Quarterly*, 34 (1993), 673–93. https://doi.org/10.1111/j.1533-8525.1993.tb00112.x

——, 'Issues of Validity in Openly Ideological Research: Between a Rock and a Soft Place', *Interchange*, 17 (1986), 63–84. https://doi.org/10.1007/BF01807017

Lincoln, Y.S., 'On the Nature of Qualitative Evidence', in *Annual Meeting of the Association for the Study of Higher Education* (Sacramento, CA: November 21–24, 2002), pp. 1–23.

McIlveen, P., 'Autoethnography as a Method for Reflexive Research and Practice in Vocational Psychology', *Australian Journal of Career Development*, 17 (2008), 13–20. https://doi.org/10.1177/103841620801700204

Morris, M., 'The Critique of Transcendence: Poststructuralism and the Political', *Political Theory*, 32 (2004), 121–32. https://doi.org/10.1177/0090591703252835

Morse, J.M., Barrett, M., Mayan, M., Olson, K., and Spiers, J., 'Verification Strategies for Establishing Reliability and Validity in Qualitative Research', *International Journal of Qualitative Methods*, 1 (2008), 13–22. https://doi.org/10.1177/160940690200100202

Pelias, R.J., 'The Academic Tourist: An Autoethnography', *Qualitative Inquiry*, 9 (2003), 369–73. https://doi.org/10.1177/1077800403009003003

Reed-Danahay, D.E., *Auto/Ethnography: Rewriting the Self and the Social* (New York: Berg, 1997).

Richardson, L., 'Evaluating Ethnography', *Qualitative Inquiry*, 6 (2000), 253–55. https://doi.org/10.1177/107780040000600207

——, 'Nine Poems Marriage and the Family', *Journal of Contemporary Ethnography*, 23 (1994), 3–13. https://doi.org/10.1177/089124194023001001

Sayers, J., *Divine Therapy: Love, Mysticism, and Psychoanalysis* (New York: Oxford University Press, 2003). https://doi.org/10.1093/med:psych/9780198509813.001.0001

Spry, T., 'Performing Autoethnography: An Embodied Methodological Praxis', *Qualitative Inquiry*, 7 (2001), 706–32. https://doi.org/10.1177/107780040100700605

Taussig, M.T., 'Reification and the Consciousness of the Patient', *Social Science & Medicine, Part B: Medical Anthropology*, 14 (1980), 3–13. https://doi.org/10.1016/0160-7987(80)90035-6

Taylor, J., 'The Intimate Insider: Negotiating the Ethics of Friendship When Doing Insider Research', *Qualitative Research*, 11 (2011), 3–22. https://doi.org/10.1177/1468794110384447

Taylor, P.C., Taylor, E.L., and Luitel, B.C., 'Multi-Paradigmatic Transformative Research as/for Teacher Education: An Integral Perspective', in *Second International Handbook of Science Education*, ed. by K.G. Tobin, B.J. Fraser, and C.J. McRobbie (Dordrecht, The Netherlands: Springer, 2012), pp. 373–87. https://doi.org/10.1007/978-1-4020-9041-7_26

Tierney, W.G., 'Life History's History: Subjects Foretold', *Qualitative Inquiry*, 4 (1998), 49–70. https://doi.org/10.1177/107780049800400104

Tracy, S.J., 'Qualitative Quality: Eight "Big-Tent" Criteria for Excellent Qualitative Research', *Qualitative inquiry*, 16 (2010), 837–51. https://doi.org/10.1177/1077800410383121

Wall, S., 'An Autoethnography on Learning About Autoethnography', *International Journal of Qualitative Methods*, 5 (2008), 146–60. https://doi.org/10.1177/160940690600500205

4 Wonder: A turn towards the divine

It was a chance encounter in a public garden many years ago that led one afternoon to the shattering of conventional awareness and an opening to a sense of presence, perfection and awe. I have pursued this evanescence through my clinical work in community mental health care and two post-graduate degrees, trying to bring its epiphany to bear on the realities of mental health care.

The story begins in the Nitobe Memorial Garden, a formal Japanese garden on the campus of the University of British Columbia in Vancouver, where a colleague from a counselling class and I had escaped one afternoon to take turns practising "empathy skills". We sat in the open air protected from a soft summer's rain under the roof of a rustic wooden shelter surrounded by the manicured garden and a pond populated with fat, orange koi. When it was my turn to take the counselling role, my colleague began to speak quietly, thoughtfully about his life while I leaned in to listen more carefully. But as his story unfolded, I was overwhelmed by rapture.

The Nitobe Garden

> *You're talking, I see your lips move and hear the sound, but my mind is running. For what? For shelter, for validation, for a reason, for joy. I feel my mind turning over like a car with a dead battery, stalled, while an unseen driver intently turns the key, turns the key, turns the key. I am struggling to remember the name of your sister, your brother, the details of what happened. I want to hang on to the details, I'm supposed to have them in mind, but I can't. There is only You, only You and this dawning ecstasy.*
>
> *Gazing down at my arms I see my skin spiked with gooseflesh, I feel the hairs standing at attention tuned to this impossible moment. The moment endures past my fear. I dare breathe, I can trust it, can't I? This feeling is everywhere around us, but mostly here, the source is here, in this rain shelter, where he speaks while I listen. Where the rain falls in a mist around us, smudging the edges and filling all the in-betweens with something that loves me, all of me, and that I love in return with inundating gratitude that longs to express itself in great wracking sobs.*
>
> *Does he know what's happening? How can he not? He offers no clue, but the words keep coming and the story opens like a rose, petal by petal. I yearn*

towards its centre as a flower leans towards the light. With each word, each poetic pause, each gesture, he becomes more naked, more precious, the wounds and scars more clearly defined and dear. I wonder if he will undress down to his bones. The parade unreels like a film behind my eyes. I see the people he describes, meet his family members, walk through their home, stroll around his town. I endure the indignities, the penury, the loss, the unbearable loss. What can I offer him for his pain? What? Empathy? Guidance? For what? For his gift? For the joy? The sight? For his sacred story? What can I offer? Nothing. Nothing.

My body riots behind a seamless composure. I clench my teeth to keep them from chattering. A fist expands in my throat and aches with a need to cry. Finally tears break through the barrier and sit on my eyes blinding and burning me. I tip my head back to keep them from spilling down my face but there are too many waiting for release. I brush them away with the back of my hand pretending my eyes are tired and want to be rubbed. "Are you cold?" he asks me. I don't know, am I? "No, I'm fine, please go on," someone with my voice responds.

What has seeped into my pores now thunders through me like a mountain cascade. I adore him, his unbearable perfection, the golden cadence of his voice, the fine milky skin on his forehead, his heroic fear. I have to celebrate, I have to share this. I look at him and know there is even more, much more. I am you, I am you, I AM YOU! Yes, yes, I see it. I am trembling with joy, I have always loved, always been, always will be, never alone, impossible, impossible, loved always and loving this way, without knowing, but knowing, always knowing.

"Do you feel it?" My voice is hushed. My eyes probe his beautiful face for hidden evidence of an experience he is for some inexplicable reason withholding from me. A pause ensues; his eyes meet mine and then scan the rain shelter for clues to my question. He looks puzzled and returns his gaze to my face. "Feel what?" he asks, soberly. Neither of us pursues the question and seconds later he is back at the loom weaving his words. I look out at the trees beyond our enclosure and worship the spaces between the leaves, knowing what glue it is that binds these beings together, and how it is they sing.[1]

This phenomenal event crystallised the moral conundrums of praxis standing in the shadow of the authorising institution and confirmed my utter failure to respond adequately, given what I had to offer. In some ways, this event marked the end of an idealistic career as a mental health professional even before it began. But in seeing my *self* in the transfigured face of my colleague—an acquaintance from class—there was no confusion about my identity or his. Nor could this astounding recognition be interpreted as a metaphor. It was a visceral cataclysm that confirmed the pricelessness of this life—*my* life—and an immensity of love for a stranger to whom everything was owed.

This chapter shifts the emphasis on wonder as a phenomenon or "experience" for one's own exclusive gratification and wonderment towards a perspective of its moral and *relational* implications. We begin with a historical perspective that touches on wonder's origins and etymology to frame our

78 *Wonder*

preliminary understanding and demonstrate wonder's congruence to praxis. We also turn to contemporary scholarship to examine several definitions and orientations describing the current play of wonder in the literature and discussing its relevance to this inquiry. Martyn Evans' work on wonder and the clinical encounter will move the discussion towards an orientation allied to our practical and ethical interests.[2] I also diverge from Evans' construal of "clinical wonder" by orienting towards an accommodation of awe and horror that will make our definition of wonder consonant with the traumatising environment of community mental health care. I also want to ensure an understanding of wonder that reinforces the clinician's *unilateral* responsibility for the help seeker and refutes any call for mutuality or reciprocity. As we will see, the elements emerging from the notion of wonder make it less of a novelty in clinical practice than one might imagine.

A brief genealogy

> *What is the source of "wonder"? Is it something in the wonderful, or in the wonderer, in the person who experiences wonder? Or should it be located at the level of context or relationship, something that emerges in certain situations? Does it just arise, do we have to wait on it, or can it be learned or elicited? Does it really speak of something beyond? Do we have to try and indicate the level of that beyond? Does it require religious or theological language, or can it be psychologised or biologised, or would these be reductions?*[3]

A modest renaissance of interest in wonder is creating a niche in the medical humanities and inviting a more philosophical consideration and critique of the "underlying unquestioned assumptions within medical policy and practice".[4] One such question is "whether medicine is essentially a technical science or an existential practice with a centrally ethical task".[5] The interests of this inquiry chime with the latter. This evolving conversation has opened a space for the examination of wonder's moral potential in the unlikely context of community mental health care. If the overuse or misuse of "wonder" in the vernacular has diminished its value over time, wonder's ubiquity has certain virtues. Chiefly, it offers a benign, non-polarising point of departure for ethical discourse that could be more conducive to the secular environment of community mental health care than Levinas' obscure terms of reference might yet allow. I do not want the notion of *wonder* subsumed or eliminated by Levinas' ethical vision so much as integrated, developed and strengthened by it.

Several philosophers writing about wonder, including Sam Keen, Dennis Quinn, Mary-Jane Rubenstein and others, lament wonder's demise and misinterpretation claiming that the immensity of this loss is now a matter of pressing social concern. Wonder's dissolution has disconnected us from nature and eroded our sense of place in the cosmos, Keen tells us. It has robbed us of our identity, our sense of continuity and purpose and our affiliation to the sacred world we inhabit, including the universe beyond. In domesticating our world, Keen claims, we "insulate it against the intrusion of strangeness".[6] He interprets the central significance of wonder as a gift of meaning[7] that should not be simply eclipsed—or *reduced*—by an increase of knowledge.[8] Similarly, Dennis Quinn blames wonder's demise on the scientific revolution that reduced wonder to the empirical and quantifiable, making the notion of "quality" almost obsolete.[9] Wonder is now mistaken as "doubt, aesthetic delight, curiosity, the pleasure of discovery, vague religious sentiment, delight in novelty, indiscriminate approval, and sheer gush".[10] Rubenstein also bemoans the tragedy of wonder's loss and the consequences of this cultural and linguistic destitution that cheat us of those aspects of our nature that fully define our humanity.

> [W]onder's capacity to arouse and inflict terror, worship and grief is utterly decimated—or more precisely, fervently repressed—by the modern brand of wonder that connotes white bread, lunchbox superheroes and fifties sitcoms. . . . Wonder is only wonder when it remains open.[11]

Wonder emerged as the origin of Greek philosophy before following the rise of religion and reaching its apogee in the 12th and 13th centuries. But it was ultimately claimed by science's emerging project during the Renaissance and later by the interests of the Enlightenment until its subsequent demise thereafter.

Keen recounts that the Greeks "discovered"[12] the centrality of wonder to philosophy when "Plato had Socrates proclaim that it was the source and foundation of philosophy".[13] It was Theatetus, the boy whose own encounter with wonder led Socrates to claim it as the beginning of philosophy: "He who said that Iris was the child of Thaumas made a good genealogy".[14] This genealogy began with Iris, goddess of the rainbow, daughter of Thaumas, the sea god of wonders, and Electra, his wife. Iris' beauty, "divine nature" and mysterious celestial appearance were to have aroused the "passion that initiates and sustains the love of wisdom".[15] Thaumatology, Philip Fisher suggests, was the science of wonders and miracles until the Renaissance, at which time the fork in the road divided science from theology when the miraculous became superfluous to the modern notion of science.[16] Yet it was believed that the love of wisdom was initiated and sustained through Iris.[17]

Mary-Jane Rubenstein's re-interpretation of this story suggests that wonder was misappropriated to exclude the darker side of its profoundly ambivalent nature. Socrates' version of the story, she claims, left out Thaumas' other two daughters in wonder's lineage. Like Iris, her sisters, Aello and Oypetes, were winged creatures, "inter-cosmic messengers" who had the dark task of carrying humans to the underworld. Unlike Iris, the image of these harpies deteriorated over time into terrifying clawed creatures, leaving Iris and her divine beauty as wonder's only representative.[18] In silencing "the ravenous and noisome" as fundamental aspects of wonder, Rubenstein believes Socrates sanitised wonder's meaning by "declawing it" and inaccurately claiming wonder's place as the origin of philosophy. Yet it was the Socratic tradition, Rubenstein argues, that sought to keep wonder *open* before this focus was replaced by Aristotle's "remedy for wonder in the knowledge of cause and effect". Consequently, wonder's function moved from one of infinite potential for opening and expansion to one "that eliminates itself through the knowledge of causes" in the *pursuit* of answers to the mystery posed by wonder.[19] In these two perspectives, we discover the long-standing tension central to our inquiry between the *open* and *closed*. That is to say, the a-theoretical and theoretical, the anarchical and hierarchical, the affective and the rational and, as we shall discuss in the next chapter on Emmanuel Levinas, the *moral* and the *reductive*.

A brief etymology

Once we are smitten we are never healed. To be human means to be an open wound.[20]

In attempting to resuscitate wonder, these and other authors have turned to its etymology for evidence of its lost meaning. By relating wonder's meaning to Thaumas and thaumatology, for example, we discover in the Greek root *thau* a connection to something in which we also participate, although *passively*. Thus, *thaomai* "may mean to wonder or to gaze upon with wonder", while *thauma* from *thea* alludes to theatre, the place we go to be exposed to and overwhelmed by wonder. *"Thau"* also relates to the notion of theory as the focus of philosophical contemplation. In contrast, Greek words like *"thambos"* and *"tethepa"* have a stronger resonance with terror in emphasising "a condition of helplessness, bewilderment, confusion, amazement, or stupor".[21] These words apparently "derive from the idea of being struck", while the Latin *"attonius"*, for astonish, means "thunderstruck".[22]

The meaning of wonder, beginning with its German connections, may also suggest joy or delight and the pleasure often associated with it.[23] Lorraine Daston and Katharine Park suggest a connection between wonder and smiling as in the French *"merveille"*, or the Italian *"meraviglia"*, and the English *"marvel"*, dating back to the 12th century.[24] This might indicate the source of wonder and the delight it conjures as emanating from the object of wonderment itself. Daston and Park also find a strong commonality in "the vocabulary of wonder" from the 12th to the 13th century onwards that did not differentiate the sacred from the profane. It was centuries later that "the miraculous and the marvellous"[25] were differentiated as "religion" and "science". As for delight, there is also the old English *wendan*, associated with ideas of wending or turning, that Quinn suggests may describe the process of searching this way and that for an answer posed by the wonderful.[26] Such wandering might also reflect the profound and compelling pleasure—the *yearning*—that drives our pursuit of wonder's enigma.

Interestingly, wonder has lost its historical connection to "esteem-love-approval".[27] Until the 19th century, wonder and admire were used synonymously, whereas esteem is now implied in words like "wonderful" or "wonderfully". This disconnection of wonder from the binding aspects of relationship may have effectively removed it from the elevating or reverential implications of esteem and diminished its relational significance to little more than a novelty. The historical connection between admire and wonder is still found in the German *wunder*, although ambiguously. *"Verwundern"*, for example, refers to astonishment and *"bewundern"* to esteem, which might appear to connect the object of wonder with the response it elicits or even the wonder *within* it.[28]

The ideas of light, sight, reflection or mirror are also related to wonder. *"Admirare"*, for example, is the Latin root for *marvel* and *admire* as well as *miracle* and "probably derives from *mir* which refers to seeing" and may include the notion of sensing or seeing with the mind's eye. Mirror and mirage share the same root.[29] Again, this connects wonder to seeing but also *reflecting*; something akin to a mirage or a dream captured by "soft" eyes, rather than a hard, analytic gaze. In medieval mysticism, the allusion of the "inflamed/enflaming" mirror alluded to the soul's need for purification for her to "become the perfect reflective surface for the divine".[30] We also find allusions to light in the work of writers from medieval mystics to poets like Blake and Whitman and beyond who bore consistent witness to a quality of illumination that evokes an intense emotional response associated with some profound meaning.[31] The theme of light is also significant in "The Nitobe Garden" where, *"I. . . worship the spaces between the leaves, knowing what glue it is that binds these beings together"*. Evans evokes a similar quality of light in his enigmatic encounter with an ash tree, where he finds himself "fixated" by the tree's "elaborate structure" and the "precise and almost granular penetration of the air around it".[32] This light or space has a physicality or mass that is somehow magnified yet diffuse, "thick" and imbued with its own sentience. Daston and Park suggest that a departure from the root *mir* to *mira* relates to the Latin words *mirabilia* or *miracula* that refer to *objects* of wonder themselves. "Admiration" was also used synonymously with *paradox*, which Quinn defines as "contrary to or beyond *doxa*—opinion. . . as opposed to real knowledge",[33] because we find in paradox what is real and worthy of such admiration and esteem.

Another relevant historical connection is found in the old English *wundor*, related to the German *wunder* as well as *wunde*, which can mean "cut, gash" or even *wound*. Rubenstein argues that such contrasting interpretations imply wonder's ambivalent nature that connects us simultaneously to "marvel and dread, (or) amazement and terror". She also notes several biblical allusions to the word *"fear"*, which illustrate the quality of awe, dread and reverence that wonder also evokes. In describing wonder as a "kind of wound of the everyday" that must remain open or become something else, Rubenstein identifies the relevance of *openness* and *ambivalence* to our purpose.[34] It is hardly an overstatement to suggest that this *open wound* is confronted by the clinician in her every encounter with the vulnerable help seeker.

Wonder and praxis: Light, love, openness and ambivalence

The notion of wonder, as we can see, shows a fascinating congruence with the evocation of "The Nitobe Garden" and the therapeutic process, which these meanings might suggest is capable of *calling forth* the wonder-full. Mental health clinicians are exquisitely poised for this kind of apprehension, given their "listening" and witnessing practice and the historical[35] and still current connection of mental health care to the clergy and spiritual practice.[36] In her day-to-day routines, the community mental health clinician has unlimited access to a rare intimacy afforded by the raw suffering of others. *She* is continually exposed to amazement and terror within the "theatre" of the consultation room and confronted by her ambivalence. The qualities of *light, love, openness and ambivalence* found in wonder's etymology resonate with praxis and the mental health clinician's immediate experience. These are considered next, with some reference to the work of Carl Rogers, whose humanistic orientation and counselling theory are still very influential in counselling *and* medical education and practice.

Beginning with *light*, we identify the cornerstone of "talk-therapy"[37] in the practice of *reflection*. It is the therapist's task to reflect or *mirror* back observations, intuitions, feelings and aspects of the help seeker's narrative and presentation to promote insight, illumination and epiphany—to *enlighten*. The art of reflection—empathic reflection—was raised to a sophisticated level by Carl Rogers. His immense legacy now drives a clinical interest in empathy and person-centred—*patient-centred*—care that has become an industry standard. Rogers invited in a quality of connection and depth with those who came to him for help that eventually prompted him to speak of "other realities", to which he believed psychology needed to pay closer attention.[38] He also acknowledged the threat such realities posed to his profession and colleagues who were—and still are—blinkered and silenced by the dictates of the hard sciences. Daringly, he theorised that the accuracy of non-directive "reflection" was foundational to therapeutic change and claimed its impact was as transformational for the clinician as for the help seeker.[39] Remarkable and accurate as this may be, Rogers' argument and his ideas about mutuality and reciprocity[40] are nonetheless situated within a therapeutic relationship that is unequivocally *asymmetrical*.

Rogers also theorised the transformative implications of "unconditional positive regard" and "empathy", which resonate profoundly with the notions of esteem, love and approval[41] discovered in wonder's etymology. Rogers was careful to assert that these "conditions" should never seek to possess, control or satisfy the needs of the *clinician* because they represented a "caring for the client as a *separate* person".[42] But can such an assertion be justified when it cannot be ensured?

As for the issue of *love*, it is almost anathema within praxis despite the undisputed centrality of the "therapeutic relationship" and "trust" to the help seeker's process of change. It is also true that esteem, love and approval inform our ideas of affiliation, kinship, friendship,[43] community, interdependence, intimacy, tenderness and reverence, especially where positive regard for the other *elevates* the person in question.[44] Regrettably, the spectre of boundary violation pre-empts any serious examination of love in praxis[45] from an interpretation of wonder relevant to our interests.[46] As Quinn reminds us, however, the traditional view of wonder recognises the centrality of love, which must be present for the negative emotions even to arise. "In fact, this love abides and persists in all emotions as their first principle".[47] Socrates, Quinn claims, left no doubt that love is inherent in the friendship formed through the shared quest for truth. This quest is "fired by wonder" and the recognition that ultimately, "the object of wonder is not knowledge at all but love".[48]

Interestingly, the sense of *being in love* or overwhelmed by love, as I was in "The Nitobe Garden", resists qualification that might reduce my meaning to something benign—safe—or in Rubenstein's terms, "declawed".[49] This cataclysm does *not* correspond to an "appropriate" or institutional[50] "type" of love authentic enough to claim the name or "cool" enough to ensure no violation is implied. We will return to this theme in the chapters ahead.[51] For now, I will resist imposing any disclaimers on love in praxis other than to assert that love either recognises and reveres the help seeker and protects her sanctity and vulnerability or is *not* love.[52]

As for *openness*—for which Rubenstein argues—its inclusion in our definition is fundamental if the clinician is to *lean into* wonder rather than try to solve or resolve it or, for that matter, ignore or resist it. Evans' definition of wonder also suggests such openness within the clinical encounter as "an attitude of special, intense, preparatory and transfiguring attentiveness to what may be revealed as extraordinary".[53] Rogers observed that "openness to experience" was as fundamental as any other aspect of research.[54]

Such openness refers to clinicians' *and* researchers' willingness to be *disarmed*, to incline towards the unexpected or unknowable in readiness to be affected, influenced—*changed*. It is difficult to achieve in practice although psychologist, Tobin Hart claims that "deeply empathic therapists" sensitive to the feeling states of others, can "regulate" their degree of openness.[55] Without discounting an individual's proclivity or porosity for openness, it is something that can be cultivated.[56] "Openness" is prescribed, for example, for "skilled helpers" in Gerard Egan's seminal text on counselling according to the acronym "SOLER".[57] This dated model is still current in teaching clinicians how to approach another human being in distress. There is a certain poignancy about clinical professionals' need to be "taught" how to perform the open, receptive stance of the most rudimentary human response to vulnerability and pain.[58] It also takes considerable self-awareness and courage to soften one's psychological and intellectual defences to be with, contain, and *feel* extremes of emotion—from the sublime to the horrifying. Openness also chimes with spiritual practice or contemplation and has a well-established role in therapy.[59]

The final theme under consideration here—*ambivalence*—and its relevance to the "therapeutic", might arguably lie in the clinician's own emotional process, which elsewhere might be construed as counter-transference. But psychodynamic theory and the long-term therapeutic relationships typically developed by psychotherapists with their clients are not found commonly, if at all, within the framework of the community mental health environment being examined here. Of more particular relevance, then, is the clinician's ambivalence to the paradoxical and emotional extremes of wonder discovered in the face, the story, the circumstances, the countenance, the suffering and the sanctity of the vulnerable help seeker. We are ambivalent to wonder, Keen claims, because it *is* traumatic.[60]

These themes of *light, love, openness and ambivalence* are potentially uplifting as they are disturbing, mesmerising and overwhelming. In confronting the interplay of horror and awe, grief and worship, darkness and light in her work, the clinician must continually negotiate her emotional and *moral* ambivalence in a relationship where she holds the balance of power. Still, the clinician's capacity to see and reflect something *beyond*, to remain open and undefended in the face of the help seeker's anguish and vulnerability, and to love and esteem her—in opposition to every clinical sanction against such intimacy—informs not only a wonder-full perspective but a *just* one as well. This intimacy is always contingent on the clinician's ability to negotiate her own ruminating ambivalence because—at least in part—intimacy is rendered inscrutable and dangerous by the institution even though the therapeutic connection depends on it.

When wonder strikes: The mysterious hinge

How is this phenomenal encounter of seeing another as *oneself* to be decoded? Sitting with my colleague that day in the Nitobe Garden, I was shocked to find that there was no adequate *"therapeutic response"* and nothing to offer in the *"realm of possible options"*.

> *All paled in comparison to the staggering beauty and integrity I perceived in him ... which enveloped us both. Anything I could do as a counsellor would simply diminish and impose on or corrupt the perfection.... I remember scanning my mind in disbelief, finding there was nothing to be done, and coming to what seemed like more adequate, if unprofessional alternatives.... I found myself wondering if I should offer ... my*

sweater, or extend my hand to hold his, or get up from my seat to embrace him. . . . Seeing this spark of divinity before me, embraced in the sacred shelter of this relationship and knowing the depth of its meaning in my own life, I have a terrible decision to make: what can I do? What must I do for this person?[61]

What, then, is the *hinge* that accounts for this phenomenal shift that swings open and alters our perception so radically and suddenly before closing again? The help seeker's *appeal* is of particular interest in understanding what it is that insinuates itself so *wonder-fully* and problematically into the clinician's interior world as an entreaty that also announces a conflict, a contradiction, a *dilemma*. In attempting an answer, we will touch next on five philosophical "accounts of wonder" to explore how philosophers have theorised this notion.

Beginning with a *cognitive account* of wonder, Dennis Quinn, Sam Keen and Robert Fuller all refer to Piaget's theory of *accommodation* and *assimilation* for a partial answer[62] to what it means to be stricken by wonder. Jean Piaget was a Swiss developmental psychologist who focused on child development. He theorised "accommodation" as a process of cognitive disturbance that occurs when an unknown experience confronts a child. This unknown is subsequently "assimilated" through a cognitive adjustment that reconfigures the child's conceptual map to the new situation. The process is curiosity driven and enables the child to explore and understand the material world in a trajectory that is continuously moving from accommodation to assimilation.

Piaget's detractors criticised his formulation for its "theological and mythic thought" that represented a form of pre-logical thinking at odds with developmental psychology and its interest in the cognitive process.[63] Piaget's formulation might appear more sympathetic to an "open" interpretation of something preceding thought and the theoretical. Yet accommodation and assimilation seem to have less to do with an open apprehension of wonder than the drive to denature, neutralise and theorise it. For Piaget, the endpoint is cognitive mastery of the child's world, which appears to make wonder little more than a thrilling anti-chamber to *knowing*. Assimilation also reflects but one aspect of Piaget's comprehensive and controversial theoretical framework of *childhood* stages of cognitive development. Altogether, these aspects of Piaget's work seem confined to what is yet to be encountered and mastered—conquered and claimed—if only cognitively.

A more traditional view of wonder is as the seat of wisdom that moves us from the unknown to knowledge, which inheres in philosophy, poetry, the arts and "the passion that arises from the *consciousness of ignorance*".[64] Quinn explains that wonder works through our *awareness* of ignorance when it shocks us sufficiently with its mystery to jeopardise our intellectual life and challenge what we thought we knew. This view prevailed from Plato to

Descartes in upholding the "love of truth", love being the first "presupposed" of all emotions that "abides and persists" in all others and which is necessary for negative emotions to be detected. Such love is also antithetical to the sceptic unable to wonder or the pragmatist incapable of rising above the practical.[65] But this interpretation is also continually redirected towards inquiry and thinking. Hence, we may be "purged" of ignorance by writing poetry or doing philosophy, which can bring the highest pleasure.[66] Or we can transcend "mortal art" by storytelling, which the Greeks believed was a "God-like" pursuit.[67] But even these sacred practices are always in the service of knowing and knowledge, the greatest peril being ignorance or not knowing.

In contrast is Philip Fisher's *aesthetic account* of wonder as a "connection between intellectual curiosity ('I wonder if. . . '), and the pleasure of amazement".[68] His view of wonder operates through the encounter of aesthetic novelty and the hit of the first encounter accessed *only* through the faculty of sight and certain forms of art. These include architecture, painting, sculpture and some engineering projects, as opposed to "the arts of time—narration, dance, music" which, he insists, leave us immune to wonder.[69] Even conventions of syntax and grammar, Fisher claims, can trigger memory and build expectations that pre-empt wonder's possibility. He takes no account of the canon of metaphysical or mystic writers and poets whose revelatory brilliance in evoking the enigmatic and the transcendent might contest such a view. Although, Fisher does concede that on rare occasions temporal art may give way to the possibility of wonder.[70]

Fisher's perspective informs a relentless drive for "the visual, the sudden, and the unexpected", which is limited to the notion of "first sight" and the privilege of youth that declines with age.[71] Rubenstein might counter that in chasing down the new and unfamiliar for the gratification of another *now-I-get-it* moment, Fisher's perspective denies the possibility of wonder moving in another direction. He denies, that is, the movement from the ordinary to the strange or the *extraordinary*, which might challenge Fisher's definition and his keen appetite for a constant stream of novelty. Yet he insists that the "fate of the ordinary" is to remain in the shadow of whatever is rare and sudden in one's experience "like the rainbow".[72] That said, it is difficult to imagine that even a rainbow could hold more wonderment than an epiphanic encounter with another.

An *account of curiosity* offers another way to understand what underpins or opens us to wonder, although Quinn suggests curiosity should be seen as a deficiency in wonder. He also grudgingly accords curiosity "a certain commendable habit of mind in scientific inquiry"[73] but insists that its capacity to plumb unsolvable mysteries is limited.[74] Emerging from the Latin *cura*, curiosity holds an earlier association with ideas of "care, solicitude, or concern" still found in words like *pastoral care* and *curate*.[75] Related to the idea of carefulness or skilfulness, curiosity's meaning has degenerated to inquisitiveness and the vice related to the intemperance of wanting to know too much, or an excess of studiousness. With its association to the vice of lust, curiosity does not fare well in the wonder discourse. As a notion that implies a drive to be sated or a problem to be solved or pursued, curiosity fails to correspond to our search for a more "open" interpretation that might resist capture by the theoretical. Still, the quality of curiosity can help the clinician hesitate and remain—however briefly—in the destabilising openness of the unknown. Interestingly, curiosity plays a role in mindfulness and compassion practice.[76] One study suggests the importance of curiosity's role in helping psychotherapists achieve greater "attunement" with the help seeker.[77] Despite its restricted perspective, the nature of curiosity can offer something of an open space, or entryway, for wonder.

A *scientific account* of wonder is forwarded by evolutionary biologist and renowned atheist Richard Dawkins, who insists that wonder is accessible only through science. Dawkins' contempt for religion, mystery or any "benevolent overseer of our lives"[78] might undermine his claim that "the purveyors of superstition, the paranormal and astrology" are eroding science.[79] Because such purveyors presumably include the considerable population of all religious believers and spiritual seekers, scholars and scientists among them. Underscoring his derision for the Church and the mystic "happy to revel in a mystery", Dawkins insists that only the *productive* scientist can acknowledge the profundity by getting to work to find the answer.[80]

Yet, Dawkins' accounts of the natural world are mesmerising in showing how squid change colour, how insects hear, how DNA might reconstitute human beings on other planets.[81] His view of wonder also seems to deny *any* inherent value in the mystery itself or its possible connection to a *moral* or relational question. Even in attempting to "un-weave the rainbow", Dawkins argues that by understanding phenomena more deeply, their mystery can be more wonderfully known, and this may be true from the standpoint of natural phenomena.[82] He may also be justified in claiming that poets are led by "the very same spirit that moves great scientists".[83] But his perspective suggests a taste for knowledge and certainty, which seems to consign wonder to insignificance unless it can be refuted, unlocked or *proven* through science into tangible existence—like a prize.

In all these philosophical accounts of the "hinge" that opens us to wonder, we discover a focus on knowledge and resolution, solution and assimilation, and a drive that is appetitive, acquisitive and experiential. Wonder's significance as a wild card that remains untamed, unknowable and *open* is found nowhere in these formulations. They speak instead of notions more related to grasping, appropriation and mastery, which leaves unanswered the pressing question evoked by the emotionally super-charged *relational* event in "The Nitobe Garden": *"What can I do, what must I do?"* Interestingly, as we will see in the next chapter, the problem of "grasping" is at the very centre of our ethical quest. Indeed, Jantzen notes, it "should be taken literally as the founding gesture of western civilisation, whose technological economy is built on a symbolic of mastery, of grasping".[84]

Wonder and the clinician

> [T]he proper attitude of the clinician is to combine intelligence with a proper form of reverence: an attitude neither of terrified awe at responsibility, nor of immobile marvelling at the incomprehensible, but of dynamic, transfiguring wonder in the face of shared embodiment. When the doctor addresses the patient's wonderful fragility she also, thereby, reengages with her own.[85]

We move now to philosopher Martyn Evans' thoughtfully argued formulation of wonder that speaks relevantly and sensitively to the clinician and the interests of our inquiry. His analysis provides the groundwork on which to build, especially given his invitation to the research community to go further.

> No one has attempted any sustained analytic discussion on the clinical relevance of wonder, nor exploration of the ethical or aesthetic aspect of wonder in relation to medical practice from the perspective of either the clinician or the patient.[86]

Evans prioritises wonder as a *value* in medical practice[87] that calls for the replacement of the mechanised notion of medical "training" with the idea of *education* that emphasises the clinician's need for greater ethical sensitivity.[88] He argues for an easing of boundaries among competing areas of academic specialisation towards the development of a shared interdisciplinary language that might better address the needs of the patient.[89] Evans' focus on the ethical, his concern for patient welfare and his terms of reference are highly relevant to our discussion.[90]

Evans' formulation of wonder as something both "epiphanic" and "transfiguring" confirms Jantzen's observation that Western culture—and its vernacular—are embedded in its Christian roots, despite what some theologians might describe as a secular veneer.[91] Evans also concedes that wonder's ineffable significance is undeniable; "not only is metaphysics not discreditable, it is not even avoidable in thinking about our experience of the world".[92] As a consequence, his construal of wonder becomes an orientation or attitude—but *not quite* a relationship. Evans also notes that wonder is more durable than curiosity because it "survives explanation" and remains enigmatically refreshing for that reason,[93] and he confirms wonder's *openness* as something beyond reason or resolution.[94]

Evans' use of personal vignettes also reconfirms the value of autoethnography and emotional transparency in research on wonder and ethics. In one account, for example, he describes his enraptured response to a musical performance through which his life became "more nearly complete as a result of hearing and understanding... than it would have been otherwise".[95] Elsewhere, Evans describes seeing a premature infant, struggling for life in a hospital, who "emanated wonder in the invitation to see him as one of us".[96] Such evocations point to an extraordinary, life-changing apprehension that is beautiful, mysterious, *disturbing*, tacitly relational and requires metaphor and affective language to translate. Evans describes wonder as:

> [A] special kind of transfiguring encounter... a very particular attitude of special attentiveness... prompted by circumstances that may be entirely ordinary yet... yield an object in which the ordinary is transfigured by and suffused with something extraordinary as well. The attitude of wonder is thus one of altered, compellingly intensified attention to something that we immediately acknowledge as somehow important—something that might be unexpected... and towards which we will likely want to turn our faculty of understanding; something whose initial appearance to us engages our imagination before our understanding; something... larger and more significant than ourselves; something in the face of which we momentarily set aside our own concerns (and even our self-conscious awareness, in the most powerful instances).... Wonder is not the same as awe: its object need be neither sublime nor terrifying. It is closer to marvelling, yet it is not confined to static gazing but has its own dynamic leading-on to the desire to understand. It has pale echoes in curiosity, but its objects persist in our imagination, even beyond the point where we have at one level explained them.[97]

Evans' construal seeks to ignite the clinician's sense of reverence and offer moral refreshment to overcome the de-moralising drudgery of the clinical environment. But I might caution that this formulation should not exclude awe and the sublime, and for good reason. Any patient seeking general medical care is at liberty to decline treatment, in or out of hospital, even if this decision contributes to the patient's deterioration or death. Not so the vulnerable help seeker accessing mental health care, whose personal liberties can be swiftly and stunningly curtailed.

Evans is entirely persuasive in reckoning that "[w]hen the doctor addresses the patient's wonderful fragility she also, thereby, reengages with her own".[98] But, this *wonder*-full reengagement—whether tender or unsettling, astonishing or horrifying—is neither neutral nor benign in calling the clinician *to account*. To apprehend another as *oneself* is to be continually confronted by the awe-full question and its sublime implications—beyond all "therapeutic" considerations—*what can I do, what must I do for this person?*

My flower

> *My friend Mariana is howling, incoherent at the other end of a Skype call from Canada while I am here in Durham writing my thesis. Her daughter, Julia, has been committed to the psychiatric ward of the local hospital for what appears to be a psychotic breakdown. We look at each other in horror through the*

computer screen and cry while Mariana chokes out the complicated details of the past 24 hours.

We had said goodbye only weeks before after holidaying together in England, the three of us. When we met, I could see Julia was not quite herself. Her laughter was more subdued and the relaxed intimacy between us, developed from her adolescence over twenty years, had been replaced with a remoteness that eluded my efforts to connect with her. The complexity of her life and the heartache she had recently sustained helped me account for her unaccustomed gravity.

The week Mariana calls is a nightmare. I don't really know what's happening and I can't get to Julia on the other side of the world. It's maddeningly all second hand and coming from Mariana who can't stop crying. But also from one of Julia's devoted friends and two nurses I speak to during that week, as well as from Julia herself, the little ghost girl who talks to me all too briefly every day from the public phone on her ward.

Julia tries from the first day of her incarceration to frantically enlist the help of friends on the outside to find her a human rights lawyer or activist to get her out. Is she paranoid? But wouldn't she be? Her mother is denied the right to spend even the first night with her daughter who has never spent a night in any hospital let alone a locked psychiatric facility. They put her at the end of the ward and she asks to be moved closer to the nursing station because she is afraid. Because a man—a glassy-eyed inmate—had apparently appeared in the doorway of her room on a number of occasions to stare at her.

I become increasingly alarmed in the following 48 hours to hear she is taking on the staff and demanding to be released. "Julia, they will not like this. You must comply. You must. Your defiance will be interpreted as part of your illness. Tell me you understand what I am saying. You have to stop confronting them or it will not go well. Lie low for a few days, they don't have the resources to keep you in there long and there's a line up around the block waiting for your bed. This will pass; we'll get you out. I promise".

Julia is enraged with her mother the first day or two, refusing to see her when Mariana urges her daughter to relax and stay safe and quiet. She believes her mother has colluded in keeping her there. Julia tells me she feels as though the entire staff is watching her and I tell her they are. I can't help feeling a sense of guilty relief that she is at least safe until we find out what the hell is going on. I call a close friend and colleague in Canada still working in the system for a consult. "Well kiddo, you know as well as me that the hospital doesn't want her leaving if she's at risk of hopping off a bridge and she'll be let out all too soon, that's the bigger concern". Is she really at risk? She's denied being suicidal ever since she arrived, but they don't believe her.

Julia is rational and articulate on the phone and grateful to hear my voice long-distance but sounds vulnerable, young, and far away. I ask if she knows what happened. She only remembers having anxiety and a migraine and has no apparent memory or insight into her state of mind when she was sectioned, which worries me. She's vague, regressed, drugged, not herself. Julia gives me permission to speak to the night nurse, Peter. I have already told her I would happily have a conference call with the psychiatrist in her presence if she would like that. She would, she says. "Tell the nurse, tell the psychiatrist," I say.

Peter tells me they have her on two milligrams of Risperidone[99] and that she is starting to "settle" and become engaged in activities on the ward. I tell him she does not seem to be psychotic and ask for her diagnosis and why she is being held against her will. There's no diagnosis yet, Peter tells me, she's under observation. He also reminds me, not unreasonably, that it's to her benefit to be there as she'd presented with psychotic symptoms, the night she came in. He assures me of this. "But there are countless people walking the streets with psychotic symptoms who have not been sectioned," I say. Peter is silent. He does not know when she will be released. He is courteous, soft spoken. In response to my request he says he'll try to talk to one of the doctors about getting her voluntary status but can promise nothing. He's also about to go on three days leave. Mariana is upset to hear this as she and Julia greatly value Peter's kindness. The day nurse, Mariana states, is a bitch.

The following day I speak to Mariana on Skype who has been waiting for a call from the psychiatrist for three hours. I have coached her to ask him about a release date, about the diagnosis, about re-negotiating Julia's certified status to a voluntary stay in hospital to ease her distress about being locked up. But also, that she be allowed a day pass under Mariana's care, even for an hour's walk, to get her off a ward where she has been wandering for an unrelenting three days. Mariana writes down what I say and the call finally comes through.

Mariana does not want to tell the doctor too much. She's a refugee mother and she knows about imprisonment. She assures him coolly that Julia has no history of mental illness. I am uncomfortably aware of my friend's foreign accent and want this man to take her seriously. But the conversation threatens to unravel when Mariana raises her voice to inform him levelly that she is ESL[100] and that a nurse had twisted her words which resulted in Julia being assessed as less in control than she actually had been. I want her to stay calm. Mariana holds the receiver to the screen of her computer for me to hear, but the male voice on the other end is blurred. The doctor wants to know if Julia has problems with power and control, with authority. He's a moron, I think to myself.

I get off Skype and phone the hospital to reassure Julia she will likely be released in a week or less, my voice upbeat and brittle. Julia tells me she has just been given a sedative by injection after a run-in with one of the nurses. I beg her to try to listen to me, but her speech is slurred and slow and she tells me she's sorry but can't stay on the phone anymore because she needs to lie down. She is now being chemically restrained. I can't work, I can't think.

When I call Julia the following day, the transition has been successfully made. This young woman with a dancer's body and an angel's face, my friend, gifted, gutsy, funny, intelligent, politically motivated and aware, well-travelled, educated, and employed is now docile as a new born lamb. Expressing her gratitude for the kindness of the staff in a soft flat voice, she tells me it is a good place for her to be for now. She thanks me with a creepy formality for being so kind, as though we'd just been introduced. Mariana calls me later to ask what has happened. It doesn't make sense to her that her daughter has transmuted from a wild cat into this nearly inert creature seemingly overnight. "It's simple," I say. "Takes no time at all".

I try again another day, another call, another nurse. Her name is also Catherine. It takes me five or six tries to get through. It's Thursday morning. Julia has been there since Saturday night without receiving any formal psychiatric or psycho-social assessment or diagnosis. She has been held against her will without her clothes, without any counselling services, certainly without legal counsel, even without her phone that they allow her to use only five minutes a day. Despite having no history of mental illness or addiction, she has been denied even a single right to free movement while being chemically restrained for lack of compliance, and medicated with a potent anti-psychotic. It has taken a scant five days to reduce Julia to a shell.

I have a lot to say and measure my words, wanting so badly to sound professional. I introduce myself, explain my reasons for calling, my relationship to Julia, my PhD work on community mental health care, my background as a clinician and my concern that a terrible mistake has been made. The nursing notes she consults are all Catherine has in the absence of an assessment. They don't reflect that Julia has a brother, two university degrees completed with distinction, a nice apartment in a beautiful part of town, a responsible position in a respected educational institution, close friends and a significant investment in creative endeavours, as an artist in her own right. They don't mention that her parents had been jailed in their country as political dissidents. Her father, having been imprisoned for a year and tortured, had stayed behind. Mariana had fled to Canada with the children to a city whose name she'd never heard before.

"You've got a superstar on the ward, Catherine, and you don't even know it," I say. "Don't you think that Julia's response to her certification was warranted?" Catherine wants me to know that Julia is in a state-of-the-art psychiatric facility only recently opened, which provides her with the luxury of her own room and a private bath. "It's really very nice," she adds. "But how would you feel if you wound up in a situation like this, being locked up and drugged with no rights, can you imagine?" Catherine hesitatingly concedes she has thought about it and acknowledges it would be scary.

I ask if Julia has received any culturally sensitive care, or if she possibly could, while in hospital. "That comes later, in community mental health care," Catherine informs me. I don't argue there's no point. I already know all too well what kind of service will be available to Julia. I ask again about a pass for a walk outside, about having Julia's certification revoked to voluntary status, about when exactly we might expect an assessment and diagnosis. This woman has no idea how powerless I feel. Catherine is apologetic in explaining that doctors are on holiday and that they are short-staffed, which is why Julia has not been assessed yet. She says this twice, possibly to exonerate herself and I hope this means I've made a dent. Later that day, Julia is given back her clothes and allowed to go outside for a walk with her mother.

The following day she is allowed a weekend pass to be with her mother from Friday night to Monday morning. Mariana calls me on Skype the moment they get home to show me her girl, my flower, flattened by drugs and subdued by the ordeal she has survived. Her vacant eyes smile dully into the camera and she tells me softly in a child's voice that overall it was a good experience and she thinks it has helped but that it's nice to be home. She has really appreciated my help, she says again, and thanks me. I cringe to hear her speak to me like this, resisting the desire to appeal to her, "Julia, it's me! Don't say that".

She is released on Monday following the weekend and put on 2 milligrams of Risperidone that might be given as a starting dosage to someone twice her size who is suffering from hallucinations or schizophrenia. Julia has never had anything stronger than Tylenol[101] until this event. She returns to work part-time two days after discharge, despite dire warnings from the hospital psychiatrist and her family doctor about her need to take an extended leave of absence and stay on the medication. Julia sleeps with all the lights on in the bedroom of Mariana's apartment for the first week and more and is unable to return to her own apartment. At the end of the first week out of hospital, she manages to have a shower without having to ask her mother to stand outside the bathroom door because she is afraid. No wonder.

I want to believe that Julia will be able to see a psychiatrist in community mental health care well in advance of a likely waiting period of eight to twelve weeks as a result of my impassioned pleas to an intake nurse called Gloria. She works at the community mental health centre that Julia will eventually attend. Reception has put me through to her on an emergency basis and we talk. It's midnight in England, 8:00 am in Vancouver. Gloria explains that Julia's file hasn't even been received from the hospital yet and that she will be the first to know when it arrives. She's the gatekeeper. I know the job, I used to do it, I tell her so. I'm asking a huge favour. Gloria listens caringly, tenderly, while I bleed out the story over the phone to this stranger and beg her assistance. But she gently reminds me at the end of our conversation, "Catherine you know . . . that the system is . . . " "Broken, yes, I know, Gloria, I know. It's broken," I say, starting to cry. "But please, please do what you can, promise me you will do what you can. She has got to get off this medication. Please help me".[102]

The implications of "My flower" identify a possible gap in Evans' analysis of wonder that deserves close scrutiny. He is scrupulously respectful of the medical professional and at pains not to transgress. But he may overplay this card in appearing to excuse the clinician whose dehumanisation of the patient can be explained by the *clinician's* exposure to the factory-like experience described by Simone Weil.[103] The factory with its deadening routines, constraints and ethical indifference; its waste and inability to value the relational can, and *does*, degrade the clinician.[104] Yet, the privilege gap between the well-heeled, well-resourced, well-connected, well-educated and well-employed clinician and the largely disenfranchised cohort of community mental health patients makes this comparison ethically dissonant. Weil herself identifies our dehumanising propensity in claiming that "everybody despises the afflicted to some extent, although practically no one is conscious of it".[105] Evans' work specifically addresses the consequences of such contempt, but he appears to minimise the clinician's ethical responsibility by blaming the institutional "factory" for impairing the *clinician*, and the help seeker for boring her.[106] Would this not leave the most vulnerable person in the therapeutic equation in second place *after* the ennui and the dehumanisation of the clinician? Of equal interest is Evans' call for reciprocity, given its high relevance to our re-humanising project and Levinas' ethical vision—for which Carl Rogers was also criticised.

Reciprocity and mutuality

Evans' interest in "embodied human agency" suggests the benign notion of the body as the locus of wonder for the shared response of the clinician and the vulnerable help seeker.[107] Here, the collaborative possibility of "marvelling" at the body (or, even the nature of the mind), suggests a skilful way of redirecting the clinician and help seeker away from the vortex of pathology, institutional reduction and the control of the medical machine. From this perspective, Evans claims a possibility for a wonder-full clinical encounter where immediacy and reverence are palpable and possible. His observation seems both reasonable and accurate. But the problematic issue of power makes Evans' call for reciprocity tenuous, all the more so, given his perspective of asymmetry as a benefit to the help seeker. "I see no reason suddenly to drop this reciprocal requirement of acknowledgment of the Other, simply because the project of the clinical encounter is an asymmetric one (that is, primarily conceived towards the benefit of the patient)".[108]

To strengthen his point, Evans references Michelle Clifton-Soderstrom,[109] who employs a Levinasian perspective to assert the practice of medicine as "foremost an ethic", preceding even its scientific concerns.[110] Like Evans, Clifton-Soderstrom seeks an open and real dialogue between the medical professional and the patient. Unlike him, she denies the possibility of reciprocity in suggesting that "the other needs me and calls to me as a weak master to a strong slave".[111] This allusion recalls Levinas' ethical claims for the unilateral responsibility of the strong for the weak. Although interestingly, even as a weak (clinical) master, I can *never* be weaker than the strongest (*enslave*d) help seeker. Any argument to the contrary obfuscates the formidable legal power of the community mental health hierarchy in which the relationship is transacted.

The idea of reciprocity or mutuality in the clinical relationship is seductive, and its appeal may lie partially in the clinician's sincere wish to do no harm or *less* harm. It also denies or diverts scrutiny from the clinician's morally ambiguous power *over* the help seeker. That said, mental health clinicians care a great deal about their patients and routinely and earnestly attempt to subvert the reductive system in which they are also trapped, in trying to meet the help seeker as another equally fragile human being. Carl Rogers proposed exactly this in identifying *mutuality* as a central concept of his counselling theory.

This issue was also raised during a public debate with Carl Rogers in 1957 when Martin Buber famously confronted Rogers on the unavoidable inequality of power in the therapeutic relationship that Buber claimed prohibited true mutuality. This observation struck at the core of Rogers' theoretical argument as Brian Thorne has observed. Buber also insisted that the need for mutuality claimed by Rogers, while possibly capable of strengthening a person's individuality or identity, still failed to make her fully human. In the absence of true reciprocity, the individual's "awareness of others" and her "development of the responsiveness which makes for social responsibility" will be impaired.[112]

Certainly, within the context of this discussion, it is difficult to imagine how a help seeker who has been re-identified as mentally ill, "treated" or confined against her will, medicated and globally stigmatised could *easily* conjure sufficient agency to be, or become, socially responsible and engaged. Even, that is, with the help of a clinician dedicated to establishing the possibilities of wonder in her practice and to informing the help seeker's political awareness and agency beyond it.

There is no place for reciprocity in this discussion, much as the ethicist or clinician might wish, as long as the asymmetrical clinical relationship and the roles and laws governing this relationship prevail. Levinas' vision is even more unequivocal on this issue, as we will shortly see.

Final reflections

Evans' claim that "clinical" wonder need not be sublime or terrifying and is *not* the same as awe may be true in the context of the clinical space but possibly not in community mental health care, as "My flower" illustrates. If we wish to interrupt the clinician's *entrancement* with the status quo, our definition of wonder would seem incomplete without awe and ambivalence, given the terrifying violence of institutional power and the sublime appeal of the vulnerable help seeker. What is called for is a construal of wonder that harnesses the ethical potential of the clinician to recognise the help seeker as *herself*—as I recognised my colleague in "The Nitobe Garden"[113] and James in "James' Story"[114] and the unfortunate man in "Ladies' Shoes" who tried to decline his dialysis treatment.[115] It is through this perspective that the terrible question emerges: "What can I do, what must I do for this person?" and, along with it, the galvanising desire to do *something*.

In closing, we cast back to the questions asked earlier in this chapter[116] to assert that wonder appears to have many, if not infinite, sources or points of entry. Wonder emerges through what is beheld but also through the wonderer. It may announce itself gradually over time as it did in "James' Story" or cataclysmically as it did in "The Nitobe Garden". Wonder may also infiltrate the heart and mind through one's intentional turn to the disciplines of meditation, contemplation and prayer. Some would argue that wonder speaks of something *beyond* while others, as we have seen, would insist that the only mystery is the one yet to be explained, proven and claimed. I have suggested that wonder cannot be "biologised" or "psychologised", for these *are* reductions. That said, wonder does not demand the use of religious or theological language for its expression, although the language of poetry, paradox and love is central to its evocation. Of all of these questions, the most compelling is whether we "have to try to indicate the level of the beyond" in our apprehension of wonder. It is to this impenetrable "beyond", and the ethical vision of Emmanuel Levinas, that we now turn for a closer look at the face of the stranger who is no stranger at all.

Notes

1. This story was originally titled "The Third Thing". Reprinted by permission of the publisher. (Taylor & Francis Ltd, www.tandfonline.com). See: C. Racine, 'Mystical Experience of a Counsellor', *Women and Therapy*, 20 (1997), 62–64.
2. This article motivated my decision to shift the focus of this study from mysticism to wonder. See: H.M. Evans, 'Wonder and the Clinical Encounter', *Theoretical Medicine and Bioethics*, 33 (2012).
3. These questions were generously suggested by Prof. Gerard Loughlin.
4. J. Macnaughton, 'Medical Humanities' Challenge to Medicine', *Journal of Evaluation in Clinical Practice*, 17 (2011), p. 927.
5. H.M. Evans, 'Travelling Companions: Ethics and Humanities in Medicine', *Bioethica Forum*, 4 (2011), pp. 129–30.
6. S. Keen, *Apology for Wonder* (New York: Harper & Row, 1969), p. 28.
7. Ibid. p. 27.
8. Ibid. p. 26.
9. D. Quinn, *Iris Exiled: A Synoptic History of Wonder* (Lanham, MD: University Press of America, 2002), pp. 239–49.
10. Ibid. p. XII.
11. M.J. Rubenstein, *Strange Wonder: The Closure of Metaphysics and the Opening of Awe* (New York: Columbia University Press, 2008), p. 10.
12. Keen, *Apology for Wonder*, p. 62.
13. Ibid. p. 72.
14. Quinn, *Iris Exiled: A Synoptic History of Wonder*, p. IX.
15. Ibid.
16. P. Fisher, *Wonder, the Rainbow, and the Aesthetics of Rare Experiences* (Cambridge, MA: Harvard University Press, 1998), p. 11.
17. Quinn, *Iris Exiled: A Synoptic History of Wonder*, p. IX.
18. Rubenstein, *Strange Wonder: The Closure of Metaphysics and the Opening of Awe*, p. 11.
19. Ibid. p. 12.
20. J.A. Miller, *In the Throe of Wonder: Intimations of the Sacred in a Post-Modern World* (Albany, NY: State University of New York Press, 1992), p. 117.
21. Quinn, *Iris Exiled: A Synoptic History of Wonder*, pp. 6–7. See also: Keen, *Apology for Wonder*, p. 28.
22. Quinn, *Iris Exiled: A Synoptic History of Wonder*, pp. 6–7.
23. Ibid. p. 2.
24. L. Daston and K. Park, *Wonders and the Order of Nature, 1150–1750* (New York: Zone Books, 1998), p. 16.
25. Ibid.
26. Quinn, *Iris Exiled: A Synoptic History of Wonder*, p. 2.
27. Ibid. pp. 3–4.
28. Ibid.
29. Ibid.

30 This mirror was a central motif in the work of one especially controversial medieval woman, Marguerite Porete. See: M. Porete, E. Colledge, J. Grant and J.C. Marler, *The Mirror of Simple Souls* (Notre Dame, IN: University of Notre Dame Press, 1999). See: A.M. Hollywood, 'Beauvoir, Irigaray, and the Mystical', *Hypatia*, 9 (1994), p. 169.
31 E. Underhill, *Mysticism: A Study in the Nature and Development of Man's Spiritual Consciousness*, 5th edn (London: Methuen, 1914) pp. 249–56.
32 H.M. Evans, 'Transfigurings: Beauty, Wonder and the Noumenal', in *Transfigurings: The World, Wonder and Beauty* (Durham, England: June 14, 2012), p. 1.
33 Quinn, *Iris Exiled: A Synoptic History of Wonder*, pp. 8–9.
34 Rubenstein, *Strange Wonder: The Closure of Metaphysics and the Opening of Awe*, pp. 9–10.
35 Several key players advocated for the mentally ill from the late 1700s to the mid-1800s whose crusade was motivated by their religious faith. See: H.G. Koenig, M.E. McCullough, and D.B. Larson, *Handbook of Religion and Health* (New York: Oxford University Press, 2001) pp. 24–29.
36 For remarkable statistics on the involvement of clergy with the mentally ill in America, see: A.J. Weaver and others, 'What Do Psychologists Know About Working with the Clergy? An Analysis of Eight APA Journals: 1991–1994', *Professional Psychology: Research and Practice*, 28 (1997).
37 For a perspective on the loss of "talk" in contemporary psychiatry, see: G. Harris, 'Talk Doesn't Pay, So Psychiatry Turns Instead to Drug Therapy', *New York Times* (March 5, 2011).
38 C.R. Rogers, 'Some New Challenges', *American Psychologist*, 28 (1973), 385–86.
39 C.R. Rogers, 'The Nondirective Method as a Technique for Social Research', *American Journal of Sociology*, 50 (1945), p. 279.
40 See: This chapter, "Reciprocity and mutuality", pp. 94–95.
41 See: C.R. Rogers, 'The Necessary and Sufficient Conditions of Therapeutic Personality Change', *Journal of Consulting Psychology*, 21 (1957), p. 96.
42 Rogers' italics. See: ibid. p. 98.
43 This study showed that women make less distinction between friendship and kinship, which raises questions about wonder and gender in clinical care and the implications of the sense of kinship arising in the wonder-full encounter. J.M. Ackerman, D.T. Kenrick, and M. Schaller, 'Is Friendship Akin to Kinship?', *Evolution and Human Behavior*, 28 (2007).
44 See: D. Keltner and J. Haidt, 'Approaching Awe, a Moral, Spiritual, and Aesthetic Emotion', *Cognition & Emotion*, 17 (2003).
45 The authors express regret for the loss of love as a cornerstone of nursing practice relevant to this discussion. They offer reasons for its erosion and suggest the need for the cultivation of love as a practice which, as Rogers' suggests, seeks to give but not take from the patient. Yet, their analysis fails to identify the reductive paradigm in which they are also educated, indoctrinated and must collude. See: T. Stickley and D. Freshwater, 'The Art of Loving and the Therapeutic Relationship', *Nursing Inquiry*, 9 (2002).
46 During my counselling education, students were admonished *never* to touch their clients. The concern was that the help seeker could interpret such a gesture as a sexual invitation *or* violation that could cost clinicians a malpractice suit, their reputation and career.
47 Quinn, *Iris Exiled: A Synoptic History of Wonder*, p. 16.
48 Ibid. p. 87.
49 Psychotherapist Janet Sayers provocatively suggests the centrality of love to the aims of psychotherapy that "entails the oneness. . . at the heart of the mystical and the religious. . . and also the heart of falling in love, making love and being in love".

See: J. Sayers, *Divine Therapy: Love, Mysticism, and Psychoanalysis* (New York: Oxford University Press, 2003), p. 1.
50 Evans alludes to "institutional love". Also: H.M. Evans, 'Wonderful Treatment', in *Medical Humanities Companion*, ed. by P. Louhiala, I. Heath, and J. Saunders (London: Radcliffe Publishing, 2013), p. 24.
51 Ibid. pp. 30–31.
52 The prohibitions of loving are explored in: Racine, 'Loving in the Context of Community Mental Health', pp. 113–14.
53 Evans, 'Wonder and the Clinical Encounter', p. 128.
54 Rogers, 'Some New Challenges', p. 380.
55 T. Hart, 'Carl Rogers as Mystic', *The Person-Centered Journal*, 6 (1999), p. 85.
56 Lynn Underwood examines the practice of love among monks living in a monastery to compare the role of intention to the practitioner's "success". Failure to love is always the practitioner's limitation and not the responsibility of even the most difficult person he or she is attempting to love. Ownership of failure is crucial to praxis where a clinician may easily project her or his sense of failure or inadequacy onto the help seeker. See: L.G. Underwood, 'Interviews with Trappist Monks as a Contribution to Research Methodology in the Investigation of Compassionate Love', *Journal for the Theory of Social Behaviour*, 35 (2005).
57 This introductory text was part of my master's education in counselling psychology. See: G. Egan, *The Skilled Helper: A Systematic Approach to Effective Helping*, 4th edn (Belmont, CA: Thomson Brooks/Cole Publishing, 1990).
58 SOLER: **S**quarely, **O**pen, **L**ean towards the other, **E**ye contact, **R**elax. For a recent re-evaluation of this model, see: T. Stickley, 'From Soler to Surety for Effective Non-Verbal Communication', *Nurse Education in Practice*, 11 (2011).
59 For a thoughtful examination of Buddhist practice in the clinical relationship, see: A.L. Back and others, 'Compassionate Silence in the Patient-Clinician Encounter: A Contemplative Approach', *Journal of Palliative Medicine*, 12 (2009).
60 Keen, *Apology for Wonder*, p. 28.
61 Racine, 'Mystical Experience of a Counsellor', pp. 65–66. Reprinted by permission of the publisher. (Taylor & Francis Ltd, www.tandfonline.com).
62 J.H. Flavell, 'Piaget's Legacy', *Psychological Science*, 7 (1996), p. 200.
63 R. Fuller, 'Wonder and the Religious Sensibility: A Study in Religion and Emotion', *The Journal of Religion*, 86 (2006), pp. 375–76.
64 Quinn, *Iris Exiled: A Synoptic History of Wonder*, p. 5. (My italics.)
65 Ibid. p. 16.
66 Ibid. p. 45.
67 Ibid. p. 42.
68 Fisher, *Wonder, the Rainbow, and the Aesthetics of Rare Experiences*, pp. 10–11.
69 Ibid. p. 21.
70 Ibid.
71 Ibid.
72 Ibid. p. 37.
73 Ibid. p. 27.
74 Ibid. p. 26.
75 Quinn, *Iris Exiled: A Synoptic History of Wonder*, p. 26.
76 In the teaching of mindfulness practice, Daniel Siegle has developed the acronym "COAL", which stands for curiosity, openness, acceptance and love. See: D.J. Siegel, 'Mindfulness Training and Neural Integration: Differentiation of Distinct Streams of Awareness and the Cultivation of Well-Being', *Social Cognitive and Affective Neuroscience*, 2 (2007), p. 259.

77 N.G. Bruce and others, 'Psychotherapist Mindfulness and the Psychotherapy Process', *Psychotherapy: Theory, Research, Practice, Training*, 47 (2010), pp. 83–84.
78 R. Dawkins, *Unweaving the Rainbow: Science, Delusion and the Appetite for Wonder* (Boston: Houghton Mifflin, 2000), pp. 6–7.
79 Ibid. p. 118.
80 Ibid. p. 17.
81 Ibid. pp. 7–8, 75, 90, 104–5.
82 For Dawkins' scientific explanation of the rainbow, see: Ibid. pp. 42–48.
83 Ibid. p. 27.
84 G. Jantzen, *Becoming Divine: Towards a Feminist Philosophy of Religion* (Bloomington; Indianapolis: Indiana University Press, 1999), p. 233.
85 Evans, 'Wonder and the Clinical Encounter', pp. 134–35.
86 Ibid. p. 124.
87 See: H.M. Evans, 'Medical Humanities: Stranger at the Gate, or Long-Lost Friend?', *Medicine, Health Care and Philosophy*, 10 (2007), pp. 369–70.
88 Evans, 'Reflections on the Humanities in Medical Education', p. 511.
89 The differences between multidisciplinarity and interdisciplinarity are set out in: H.M. Evans and J. Macnaughton, 'Should Medical Humanities Be a Multidisciplinary or an Interdisciplinary Study?', *Medical Humanities*, 30 (2004).
90 Evans defines ethics as the "specific name" of any number of values associated with medicine from the spiritual to the political. See: Evans, 'Medical Humanities: Stranger at the Gate, or Long-Lost Friend?', p. 366.
91 "Even though Western society is largely secular. . . it is in fact the case that the western imaginary is saturated with images, values and symbols derived from the Judeo-Christian heritage". Jantzen's observation has implications for the staunchly secular environment of community mental health care, given its patriarchal underpinnings and reductive perspective. See: *Becoming Divine: Towards a Feminist Philosophy of Religion*, p. 14.
92 Evans, 'Transfigurings: Beauty, Wonder and the Noumenal', p. 6.
93 H.M. Evans, 'Wonder and the Patient', *Journal of Medical Humanities*, 36 (2015), p. 49.
94 Evans, 'Transfigurings: Beauty, Wonder and the Noumenal', p. 2.
95 Ibid. pp. 6–7.
96 Evans, 'Wonderful Treatment', p. 25.
97 Ibid. p. 27.
98 See the epigraph to this chapter section titled: Wonder and the clinician, p. 88.
99 An anti-psychotic medication.
100 ESL—English as a second language, meaning she is an immigrant.
101 Acetaminophen, found in paracetamol in the UK, is sold under the trade name of *Tylenol* in North America.
102 In five years since her hospitalisation, Julia has seen three psychiatrists and had four medication changes. She stopped the anti-psychotics with little or no psychiatrist support and has been off them for over seven months. She has fallen in love, is living with her common-law partner, they now own a home and she works full time with a fragile population in a responsible well-paid job. Julia is actively engaged in a leadership role in the community of "voice hearers" and is in demand as a public speaker. She has been relentless in working to understand her experience and to use it to help others.
103 Evans, 'Wonder and the Clinical Encounter', p. 130.
104 Ibid.
105 S. Weil, *Waiting for God* (New York: Harper, 1951), p. 40.

106 Evans suggests the doctor's humanity is "tested" and "abraded" by the boring routine of caring for unexceptional patients. "The dramatic patient encounter is exceptional. The nondramatic patient is unremarkable. The unremarkable patient becomes routine. . . uninteresting. How does one respond fully and attentively to an uninteresting patient. . . by what we might call 'patient-centered tedium'"? See: Evans, 'Wonder and the Clinical Encounter', p. 125.
107 Evans, 'Wonder and the Patient', pp. 47–49.
108 Ibid. p. 53.
109 Ibid. pp. 52–53.
110 M. Clifton-Soderstrom, 'Levinas and the Patient as Other: The Ethical Foundation of Medicine', *The Journal of Medicine and Philosophy*, 28 (2003), p. 447.
111 Ibid. p. 452.
112 B. Thorne, *Carl Rogers* (London: Sage, 1992), pp. 71–72.
113 See: This chapter, "The Nitobe Garden", pp. 76–77.
114 See: Chapter 1, "James' Story".
115 See: Chapter 3, "Ladies' Shoes", pp. 59–61.
116 See: This chapter, the epigraph at the start of the section "A Brief Genealogy", p. 78.

References

Ackerman, J.M., Kenrick, D.T., and Schaller, M., 'Is Friendship Akin to Kinship?', *Evolution and Human Behavior*, 28 (2007), 365–74. https://doi.org/10.1016/j.evolhumbehav.2007.04.004

Back, A.L., Bauer-Wu, S.M., Rushton, C.H., and Halifax, J., 'Compassionate Silence in the Patient-Clinician Encounter: A Contemplative Approach', *Journal of Palliative Medicine*, 12 (2009), 1113–17. https://doi.org/10.1089/jpm.2009.0175

Bruce, N.G., Manber, R., Shapiro, S.L., and Constantino, M.J., 'Psychotherapist Mindfulness and the Psychotherapy Process', *Psychotherapy: Theory, Research, Practice, Training*, 47 (2010), 83–97. https://doi.org/10.1037/a0018842

Clifton-Soderstrom, M., 'Levinas and the Patient as Other: The Ethical Foundation of Medicine', *Journal of Medicine and Philosophy*, 28 (2003), 447–60. https://doi.org/10.1076/jmep.28.4.447.15969

Daston, L., and Park, K., *Wonders and the Order of Nature, 1150–1750* (New York: Zone Books, 1998).

Dawkins, R., *Unweaving the Rainbow: Science, Delusion and the Appetite for Wonder* (Boston: Houghton Mifflin, 2000).

Egan, G., *The Skilled Helper: A Systematic Approach to Effective Helping*, 4th edn (Belmont, CA: Thomson Brooks/Cole Publishing, 1990).

Evans, H.M., 'Medical Humanities: Stranger at the Gate, or Long-Lost Friend?', *Medicine, Health Care and Philosophy*, 10 (2007), 363–72. https://doi.org/10.1007/s11019-007-9079-x

——, 'Reflections on the Humanities in Medical Education', *Medical Education*, 36 (2002), 508–13. https://doi.org/10.1046/j.1365-2923.2002.01225.x

——, 'Transfigurings: Beauty, Wonder and the Noumenal', in *Transfigurings: The World, Wonder and Beauty* (Durham, England: June 14, 2012), pp. 1–8. http://dro.dur.ac.uk/9726/

——, 'Travelling Companions: Ethics and Humanities in Medicine', *Bioethica Forum*, 4 (2011), 129–34.

———, 'Wonder and the Clinical Encounter', *Theoretical Medicine and Bioethics*, 33 (2012), 123–36. https://doi.org/10.1007/s11017-012-9214-4

———, 'Wonder and the Patient', *Journal of Medical Humanities*, 36 (2015), 47–58. https://doi.org/10.1007/s10912-014-9320-6

———, 'Wonderful Treatment', in *Medical Humanities Companion*, ed. by P. Louhiala, I. Heath and J. Saunders (London: Radcliffe Publishing, 2013), pp. 17–32.

Evans, H.M., and Macnaughton, J., 'Should Medical Humanities Be a Multidisciplinary or an Interdisciplinary Study?', *Medical Humanities*, 30 (2004), 1–4. https://doi.org/10.1136/jmh.2004.000143

Fisher, P., *Wonder, the Rainbow, and the Aesthetics of Rare Experiences* (Cambridge, MA: Harvard University Press, 1998).

Flavell, J.H., 'Piaget's Legacy', *Psychological Science*, 7 (1996), 200–3. https://doi.org/10.1111/j.1467-9280.1996.tb00359.x

Fuller, R., 'Wonder and the Religious Sensibility: A Study in Religion and Emotion', *Journal of Religion*, 86 (2006), 364–84. https://doi.org/10.1086/503693

Harris, G., 'Talk Doesn't Pay, So Psychiatry Turns Instead to Drug Therapy', *New York Times*, March 5, 2011.

Hart, T., 'Carl Rogers as Mystic', *The Person-Centered Journal*, 6 (1999), 81–88.

Jantzen, G., *Becoming Divine: Towards a Feminist Philosophy of Religion* (Bloomington; Indianapolis: Indiana University Press, 1999).

Keen, S., *Apology for Wonder* (New York: Harper & Row, 1969).

Keltner, D., and Haidt, J., 'Approaching Awe, a Moral, Spiritual, and Aesthetic Emotion', *Cognition & Emotion*, 17 (2003), 297–314. https://doi.org/10.1080/02699930302297

Koenig, H.G., McCullough, M.E., and Larson, D.B., *Handbook of Religion and Health* (New York: Oxford University Press, 2001). https://doi.org/10.1093/acprof:oso/9780195118667.001.0001

Macnaughton, J., 'Medical Humanities' Challenge to Medicine', *Journal of Evaluation in Clinical Practice*, 17 (2011), 927–32. https://doi.org/10.1111/j.1365-2753.2011.01728.x

Miller, J.A., *In the Throe of Wonder: Intimations of the Sacred in a Post-Modern World* (Albany, NY: State University of New York Press, 1992).

Porete, M., *The Mirror of Simple Souls*, trans. E. Colledge, J.C. Marler and J. Grant, Notre Dame Texts in Medieval Culture, Vol. 6 (Notre Dame, IN: University of Notre Dame Press, 1999).

Quinn, D., *Iris Exiled: A Synoptic History of Wonder* (Lanham, MD: University Press of America, 2002).

Racine, C., 'Loving in the Context of Community Mental Health Practice: A Clinical Case Study and Reflection on Mystical Experience', *Mental Health, Religion & Culture*, 17 (2014), 109–21. https://doi.org/10.1080/13674676.2012.749849

———, 'Mystical Experience of a Counsellor', *Women and Therapy*, 20 (1997), 61–68. https://doi.org/10.1300/J015v20n01_10

Rogers, C.R., 'Some New Challenges', *American Psychologist*, 28 (1973), 379–87. https://doi.org/10.1037/h0034621

———, 'The Necessary and Sufficient Conditions of Therapeutic Personality Change', *Journal of Consulting Psychology*, 21 (1957), 95–103. https://doi.org/10.1037/h0045357

———, 'The Nondirective Method as a Technique for Social Research', *American Journal of Sociology*, 50 (1945), 279–83. https://doi.org/10.1086/219619

Rubenstein, M.J., *Strange Wonder: The Closure of Metaphysics and the Opening of Awe* (New York: Columbia University Press, 2008).

Sayers, J., *Divine Therapy: Love, Mysticism, and Psychoanalysis, Psychologist* (New York: Oxford University Press, 2003). https://doi.org/10.1093/med:psych/9780198509813.001.0001

Siegel, D.J., 'Mindfulness Training and Neural Integration: Differentiation of Distinct Streams of Awareness and the Cultivation of Well-Being', *Social Cognitive and Affective Neuroscience*, 2 (2007), 259–63. https://doi.org/10.1093/scan/nsm034

Stickley, T., 'From Soler to Surety for Effective Non-Verbal Communication', *Nurse Education in Practice*, 11 (2011), 395–98. https://doi.org/10.1016/j.nepr.2011.03.021

Stickley, T., and Freshwater, D., 'The Art of Loving and the Therapeutic Relationship', *Nursing Inquiry*, 9 (2002), 250–56. https://doi.org/10.1046/j.1440-1800.2002.00155.x

Thorne, B., *Carl Rogers* (London: Sage, 1992).

Underhill, E., *Mysticism: A Study in the Nature and Development of Man's Spiritual Consciousness*, 5th edn (London: Methuen, 1914).

Underwood, L.G., 'Interviews with Trappist Monks as a Contribution to Research Methodology in the Investigation of Compassionate Love', *Journal for the Theory of Social Behaviour*, 35 (2005), 285–302. https://doi.org/10.1111/j.1468-5914.2005.00280.x

Weaver, A.J., Samford, J.A., Kline, A.E., Lucas, L.A., Larson, D.B., and Koenig, H.G., 'What Do Psychologists Know About Working with the Clergy? An Analysis of Eight APA Journals: 1991–1994', *Professional Psychology: Research and Practice*, 28 (1997), 471–74. https://doi.org/10.1037/0735-7028.28.5.471

Weil, S., *Waiting for God*, trans. Emma Craufurd (New York: Harper, 1951).

5 Levinas and the wholly/holy other

Introduction

Emmanuel Levinas' philosophical work focused entirely on the ethical relationship,[1] which Jacques Derrida helped bring to light by writing about him and contributing to Levinas' immense stature long before he came to prominence.[2] Derrida's popularity was responsible for bringing Levinas to the English-speaking world as was a significant interest in his work by prominent feminists who helped establish his "Anglo-American" presence. Critchley and others have claimed that Levinas' work could "hardly" be described in feminist terms.[3] But feminist Tina Chanter has argued that his construal of the feminine "Other", far from relegating women to the domestication of passive, voiceless oblivion, offers a potential space for the dialogue on women's identity.[4] Levinas is gaining currency in an ever-increasing number of clinical fields, including counselling, nursing, medical practice, psychology,[5] psychotherapy[6] and widely diverging areas of endeavour now investigating his ethical vision in growing numbers.[7]

The Face of the Other, this "fundamental event" which is both "request" and "authority",[8] is of increasing clinical interest for those calling for psychology to *mature*—at last—into a practice grounded in morality and ethics.[9] But even his most respected commentators confirm the challenge of interpreting Levinas' work. Apart from his obscure language, the sweep of Levinas' philosophical mastery is beyond the ken of most clinicians. Donna Orange cautions the unwary:

> There is no reading him well without knowing Plato, Descartes, Kant, Hegel, Husserl, and Heidegger, to whom he was responding on every page, as well as the Torah, the Talmud, and the particular forms of Judaism in which he grew up, averse to all mysticism and enthusiasm. This means that for most of us, there is no reading him well enough. In addition, we need to sense his traumatic losses, mostly unspoken.[10]

Many prominent philosophers have taken Levinas' work seriously, among them feminist philosophers Grace Jantzen, Luce Irigaray and Tina Chanter, who have critiqued his work and taken it further.[11] Jantzen, for example, turned to Levinas' ethical account in developing a "feminist imaginary" to address the problem of systemic violence.[12] She contrasted his vision to the morally indefensible discourse of religious philosophers who, before Levinas, focused primarily on the matter of one's *own* moral status. The recipients—or *victims*—of this self-centred morality were, Jantzen claimed, consequently left out of the discussion and at the mercy of a "construal of morality" that "is entirely subject centred".[13] But Levinas focused on the "other" and my ethical accountability to her—an emphasis with special relevance for the healing professions, as Jantzen accurately observes. "Those whose lives are taken up with caring for others. . . know that it is impossible to always keep one's own hands clean and that preoccupation with doing so will only make one ineffectual". By which Jantzen does "*not* mean that anything goes: it is an accountability to others, rather than a calculation of my own moral status, that is at the centre".[14]

> You know, Levinas once confided to Derrida, One often speaks of ethics to describe what I do, but what really interests me in the end is not ethics, not ethics alone, but the holy, the holiness of the holy.[15]

Levinas' focus, then, is on this holy human, wholly Other, my neighbour and dear one. She or he is "the one and only" who Levinas also calls the "*loved one*, love being the condition of the very possibility of uniqueness".[16] By which he means *irreducible*—that which cannot be thematised; broken down into components or somehow assimilated, objectified, colonised or manipulated. Levinas' phenomenal vision steps over theoretical abstraction and the ceaseless, grasping appropriative quest to know, believe or understand by making the human relationship the *starting point* of philosophy. This means we do *not* begin with a "clinical strategy" to subvert or "outgun" the atomising medical machine which has proven so resistant to our ongoing efforts to give it a human face.[17] We begin instead with the possibility of a *relationship* with the holy, *the holiness of the holy*, and the enigmatic, primordial call that comes through the human face of the other.

This chapter provides a snapshot of Levinas' life and the two most significant influences on his work—Husserl and Heidegger. We will discuss how Levinas eclipsed his teachers and challenged the entire history of Western philosophy with a revolutionary configuration of ethics that placed the *relational* prior to ontology—prior to *being*. We will also consider Levinas' argument for "disinterest" in our own self-project—a daunting task for the community mental health clinician who must serve the hierarchy and its reductive scheme. Nonetheless, disinterest makes possible another response to the help seeker's *Face* that constantly pleads for the clinician to drop her clinical façade.

Emmanuel Levinas: The man and his vision

> *To speak of Redemption in a world that remains without justice is to forget that the soul is not the demand for immortality but the impossibility of assassinating, and that consequently, the spirit is the proper concern of a just society.*[18]

Emmanuel Levinas was a Lithuanian Jew born in 1906, who received a traditional Jewish education before moving to France in 1923 to begin his studies. In 1928, he moved to Germany to study under Husserl and there discovered Heidegger whose work was to influence him profoundly. From an early age, he was influenced by the Russian classics and Shakespeare[19] and credited his exposure to Russian novels with his eventual turn to philosophy.[20] Levinas later taught at various universities in France, including the Sorbonne, and died in 1995.

Having become a French citizen and served in the military in Paris, Levinas was drafted in 1939. But by 1940 he was interned by the Germans in a Nazi prisoner of war camp and forced to hard labour for five years. Although he managed to elude the concentration camp, Levinas' family and many of his friends perished at the hands of the Nazis. One commentator has suggested that a staggering 91% of Lithuania's Jewish population died at the hands of the Nazis. Among them, 30,000 from Levinas' hometown of Kaunas were murdered over a four-month period by Nazis and Lithuanian nationalists who collaborated with the German forces.[21] The impact of the holocaust was to be foundational to his entire career. Levinas himself observed that his own biography is "dominated by the presentiment and the memory of the Nazi horror".[22]

Following the war, Levinas studied the Talmud with various renowned Jewish scholars before going on to publish some of his best known philosophical work and establishing himself as one of the most influential thinkers of the 20th century.[23] His exposure to the Nazism, his Talmudic scholarship and his lifelong critique of Heidegger's work became the crucible for his philosophical response to a century which, well into this 21st century, is still besieged by devastating violence.

Husserl and phenomenology

> *The most fundamental contribution of Husserl's phenomenology is its methodological disclosure of how meaning comes to be, how it emerges in our consciousness of the world, or more precisely, in our becoming conscious of our intentional rapport (visée) with the world. . . . The phenomenological method permits consciousness to understand its own preoccupations, to reflect upon itself and thus discover all the hidden and neglected horizons of its intentionality.*[24]

Husserl's phenomenology had a profound impact on Levinas in its aim to establish philosophy as a "science of consciousness" that might eclipse the preoccupation with empiricism and theory by focusing on the meaning of perception itself.[25] It was less a movement than a method that sought to overcome the rationalising and restricting limits of traditional philosophy. Phenomenology emphasised a direct apprehension of lived experience aimed at pure subjectivity that was more a radical approach and practice than a system of philosophy.

Its method was accomplished, Husserl claimed, by intentionally "bracketing out" or "suspending" everything but pure subjectivity so that the practitioner could return to the reduction of pure phenomenological insight.[26] Phenomenology was a "way of suspending our precognitions and prejudices in order to disclose how essential truth and meaning are generated; it was a methodological return to the beginnings, to the origins of knowledge".[27] The process was to be accomplished by resisting the influence of every construction, every social, cultural or religious assumption, assertion or imposition. Thus, could the "truth" be revealed without explaining or theorising, in advance, the phenomenon being apprehended from "within".[28]

One commentator has suggested that phenomenology became the most important strand of European thought in the 20th century although it lacked cohesion and the prominence of a real movement. But few of Husserl's students believed that what he was attempting could be achieved, nor did anyone really succeed him. Those who took his work further, including Levinas, were to challenge and change Husserl's vision in significant ways. Having written his dissertation on *The Theory of Intuition in Husserl's Phenomenology*, Levinas was also instrumental in contributing to the emergence and popularity of phenomenology in France.[29] While he re-interpreted and re-oriented phenomenology's approach towards the *ethical*, Levinas still credited Husserl for his remarkable achievement.[30]

Levinas, however, did not believe that the intentionality so fundamental to Husserl's process went far enough to ensure the possibility of the transcendent, and he judged Husserl's work as ultimately flawed. Severson notes that even in his dissertation, Levinas was unconvinced of the "*formal* or *theoretical* nature of Husserl's approach", fearing it could lead to the misunderstanding or "distortion" of the structural elements of consciousness that were of central concern to phenomenology.[31] For Levinas, phenomenology represented a return to "concrete existence" and "concrete experience" that might help overcome the limitations of philosophy's "formal logic" and "intellectualism".[32] Husserl may have wanted to oppose traditional Western philosophy, but its roots were still evident in a philosophical process that made knowledge something to be grasped or possessed.[33] Even with intentionality, Levinas insisted, the very act of thinking interfered with the emergence of pure subjectivity.[34] Levinas disagreed with Husserl's idea of consciousness as something that "discloses" an adequate representation, insisting it must instead *"overflow"* the object in a way that makes it *un*-representable and *revelatory*. "The welcoming of the face and the work of justice—which condition the birth of truth itself—are not interpretable in terms of disclosure".[35] Subjectivity could be no mere disclosure; it required the *overflowing* welcome in which "the idea of infinity is consummated".[36]

Even as late as 1983, Levinas credited Husserl's influence on his work as a phenomenologist although it did not perfectly conform to Husserl's original method.[37] However, it was for Heidegger's early work that Levinas credited the real flourishing of Husserlian phenomenology, because Heidegger recognised that "the phenomenological search for eternal truths. . . originates in *time*, in our temporal and historical existence".[38]

Heidegger and onto-theo-logy

> If Heidegger taught that the history of Western metaphysics is the history of the forgetting of Being, Levinas teaches that it is the history of the forgetting of the Other. Heidegger also forgets the Other; forgets the alterity that is beyond Being.[39]

Beyond the many ideas and thinkers with whom Levinas was engaged, Severson observes that Levinas focused his most concentrated attention on the inadequacies of Heidegger's ontology.[40] Levinas' relationship with Martin Heidegger was problematic both personally and philosophically because of Heidegger's involvement with National Socialism and Nazism but, equally, because Levinas fundamentally opposed Heidegger's thinking.[41] He believed that Heidegger's exclusive focus on the primacy of being and the problem of onto-theo-logy reduced God to the limited sphere of being and thought by placing God on equal footing with the thinker.

The onto-theo-logical nature of metaphysics in Heidegger's work placed his philosophy, Levinas argued, within the same historical "epoch" that reflects the intractable problem of onto-theology throughout "all of philosophy". In distinguishing between being as a noun and a verb, and in situating being within language itself, Heidegger's formulation of being—along with that of all Western philosophy—continued to forget the radical difference between being, beings and *beyond* being. The latter, which is at the centre of Levinas' entire project, refers to that moment or *approach* of the transcendent, which for Levinas *is* the ethical relationship. Heidegger claimed that the I of Being, of what is properly mine and what is primary, is authenticated by my death. In radical opposition, Levinas asserted the I *only* in relation to the Other, for whom I am responsible but also *for whose death* I am responsible.

This forgetfulness of the Other constitutes the remarkable blind spot in onto-theo-logy and the consequence of thinking that one can have "knowledge of God: theology".[42] Levinas argued that in substituting onto-theo-logy for thinking and logic, and mistakenly equating God with being, or being with God, our forgetfulness eventually led us to science and the suffering—the dehumanisation and de-moralisation—we are exploring in this inquiry.[43] Science, despite its profound benefits to humankind represented, Levinas argued, the totalising apparatus, "which pays attention only to beings, which subordinates them to itself, which wants to conquer and dispose of them, and which seeks power over beings. This movement thus leads to the will to power".[44] This "epoch" of onto-theology represented no less than the demise of metaphysics and the failure of the "technical world", which leads to the death of God.[45]

Another way of thinking had to be found, which Levinas discovered when he asked if God did not signify the *other of being*? By which he meant the possible subversion of being and onto-theo-logy that starts with "a certain" ethical relationship.[46] As early as 1935, Levinas was questioning the possibility of transcending ontology, which he addressed in his famous essay, "Is Ontology Fundamental?"[47] In it, he argued for a philosophy beyond ontology that pointed to a transcendence of the Good on which he was to build his primary critique of Heidegger's work. Levinas' project, to "think God as a beyond being",[48] would occupy the rest of his life.[49] His two best known works, *Totality and Infinity* and *Otherwise than Being, or Beyond Essence*, were written as major critiques of Heidegger's notion of fundamental ontology.[50]

Jeff Bloechl suggests that Levinas' departure from Husserl and Heidegger sought to overcome what seemed to be their primary conclusion that "all experience refers properly to the self", which makes *the self* both irreducible and primary.[51] Levinas' deviation from this formula refocused subjectivity as "a private and irreducible, ontological attachment" to being, which is fundamental, inescapable and constant.[52] This was "being" that engenders a chronic restlessness and exhaustion borne of all the efforts to resist "one's very self". For Levinas, the self is always constituted by what he describes as *the same*—that which is already reduced and limited through its own process—this is *not* alterity or the Other. Even "[t]he most audacious and remote knowledge does not put us into communion with the truly other; . . . it is still and always a solitude", Levinas observed.[53] The escape we seek is less from solitude than from *being*[54] which might suggest a philosopher's view of "knowledge" or a certain kind of philosopher. In the work of someone like Plato, for example, knowledge is a social process arrived at through dialogue that brings forth what in some sense *is* already known. Real freedom from ontology's rationalising appropriation that continually leads us back to *the same* is found in the relationship that originates between one particular person and me.[55] This is a relationship that awakens me with its traumatising contrast between hidebound being and the holy, between my ambitions and drive for *self*-fulfilment—my *self*-project—and my yearning for relationship. This is the event that claims me with a responsibility that "goes all the way to fission" where "I am sick with love".[56] But it is nothing like a reciprocal relationship of equals as we shall see.[57]

Levinas' radical attempt to reform this philosophical orientation to being went against the grain of philosophical thought from Plato to Heidegger.[58] But, as Severson notes, Levinas' effort to think *beyond* being still required him to work with the "philosophical tools" at hand that were ontologically loaded.

Consequently, and despite their significant differences, Heidegger and Levinas' shared aversion to intellectualism, and philosophy's long-standing neglect of time found them united in their need for another kind of language.[59]

Although Husserl and Heidegger are recognised as the two central influences on his work, Levinas was to part ways with both of them over this "contestation of the ontological by the ethical".[60] Levinas' ethical vision took aim at the whole history of European philosophy and its influence on Western civilisation that totalised and reduced "otherness" to the *same* "originary and ultimate unity".[61] This totality was all that was, and is, assimilated in the wake of Western philosophy's rationalising and reductive grasp, which is powered by "the drive for 'representation'".[62] The root problem was ontology, Levinas insisted—*ontology* is what reduces the intrinsic value of diversity and the particularity of the individual, which leads to the harrowing outcomes of totalitarianism. Within our current inquiry, these outcomes refer to the more mundane consequences of predictable institutional violence—dehumanisation, medicalisation and asymmetry—found in community mental health care in its many guises.

The Other and the Face of the Other

> *[T]aking as my point of departure the face of the other, proximity, by hearing—before all mimicry, in its facial straight forwardness, before all verbal expression, in its mortality, from the depths of the weakness—a voice that commands: an order addressed to me, not to remain indifferent to that death, not to let the other die alone; that is, an order to answer for the life of the other man (or woman), at the risk of becoming an accomplice to that death.*[63]

In simplest terms, "Otherness" refers to the "the not me" and "sameness" to "the for me".[64] The relationship between the two constitutes an ethical relationship distinguished by the "deference of the Same to the Other", which is no longer *"subordinated to ontology or to the thinking of being"*.[65] In Levinas' work there are various plays on this word. The "other" may allude to the other person for which Levinas uses the French "l'autrui", as opposed to "l'autre", which translates simply as "the other". When capitalised, the "Other" can be understood as the transcendent "trace" of the eternal, of God. Levinas also employed the face of Christ as the prototypical Face of the Other.[66]

In a riff on Hamlet's soliloquy, Levinas suggested that "[t]o be or not to be" is *not* the question, for being and its self-interest are always secondary to the evocation of the "the Face of the Other".[67] "Le Visage d'Autrui serait le commencement même de la philosophie". ("The Face of the Other person will be the actual beginning of philosophy".)[68] But who or what, exactly, is this Other? Morgan suggests this notion has been used by other philosophers over time to denote, for example, Plato's "Form of the Good", Plotinus' "the One" and Descartes' "infinite and perfect God". In Levinas' interpretation, the Other is the human being before whom I stand in a face-to-face encounter.[69] Morgan also observes the important distinction Levinas made between seeing or perceiving the face and *encountering* it. The first can be understood as "a mode of relation", but "the other is something else, something unique and originary and determinative".[70]

> This order steals into me like a thief, despite the outstretched nets of consciousness, a trauma which surprises me absolutely, always already passed in a past which was never present and remains un-representable.[71]

Levinas' inconsistent use of capitalisation in his work has challenged his interpreters and translators. One commentator goes as far as to describe Levinas' writing as "infuriatingly sloppy" for similar transgressions and other inconsistencies and contradictions.[72] But the notion of "other" as a quality of differentness or "alterity" always stands in opposition to that which is *the same*. The word play is evident throughout Levinas' work, where it is prominent even in the title of *Otherwise than Being or Beyond Essence*. Thus, otherness (alterity), the Other (the transcendent) and the other person (l'autrui) are entwined in Levinas' work, always pointing to the ethical, which is at once profoundly and practically human, relational and infinite.[73]

The "Face", or what Levinas also qualifies as the approach[74] of the Face, alludes to "[t]he dimension of the divine" that "opens forth from the human face" through the face of the stranger, the widow, the orphan.[75] These are familiar tropes in Levinas' work, which he cited from the Hebrew Bible to describe the proto-typical moral appeal of the weak to the strong.[76] Astonishingly, their inversion can also occur when the other is confronted by *my* brutality or disdain. Even those *I* oppress are capable of responding to *my* face and moral destitution,[77] which represents a remarkable act of freedom, given the seeming irrationality of such generosity.[78] Elsewhere, Levinas confirms that I *am* responsible even for the other who persecutes me.[79] Such a claim might seem indefensible, even absurd, unless we remember that Levinas is attempting to work within a phenomenological framework that is unapologetically subversive and aims to *transcend*. It may be challenging to confirm such claims, yet we can still appreciate Levinas' intention to awaken us to this felt sense. My argument does not pretend to explore or even defend all aspects of Levinas' thought. Yet, in drawing on his ethical vision I have been able to articulate and deepen what I have recognised—and embodied—in my own "clinical relationship" with the vulnerable help seeker. There are other examples confirming such claims, including Nelson Mandela's famous friendship with his own prison guards that shifted their political perspective and contributed to their enduring friendship with him.[80] In Levinas' words, *this* is the "phenomenology of sociality".[81]

Levinas' "Face" never refers to its particular features—the arrangement of the eyes, nose, mouth or ears—although it is an entirely human face. Even to notice the colour of someone's eyes is already to be outside of a social relationship with the other, for the Face cannot be reduced to mere perception.[82] We recognise the Face by its "uprightness", its defencelessness, exposure and poverty that are revealed despite any efforts to hide who we really are. Levinas' evocation of "[t]he skin of the face" being the "most naked, most destitute" conjures the impact of its raw force and the epiphany that calls to me.[83] The face is vulnerable, "nude", laid waste, devastated. It is also—paradoxically and in the same instant—exalted and *authorised* by what Levinas signifies as elevation or moral height that always points to the eternal. This is the Face that confirms my relatedness to the other—and also the "Other"—and the futility of my enormous, albeit pleasure-full, effort "to be". It is futile to turn away from the Face for my self-absorbed, narcissistic engagement in the concerns of *my* being, *my* interests, diversions, acquisitions, achievements and excesses. These can never ultimately satisfy, whereas the face inundates me with a responsibility that never ends, that "demands me, claims me, assigns me", but also grants *freedom*—not from the Other, but from the burden of my *self*.[84]

> Transcendence signifies a movement of traversing (trans) and a movement of ascending (scando). In this sense it signifies a double effort of stepping across an interval by elevation or a change of level. . . . The distance thus traversed by the gaze is transcendence. The gaze is not a climbing but a deference. In this way it is wonder and worship.[85]

Michael Morgan suggests four possible philosophical interpretations of the "normative force" of this face—that might explain its phenomenal impact upon me. The first is a "pluralist response" shaped by culture and history and having no one source. The second suggests something emerging from our psychology as a "naturalist response" or intuitive impulse. A third interpretation relates to reflexivity, free choice and our ability to engage in a rational process. Or, lastly, this normative force could be understood as a conventional response that reflects the compulsions and values of a given society.[86] But none of these "ontological" explanations adequately capture the enigma of the preconscious draw "that strips consciousness of its initiative".[87] It is this draw that announces my guilt even before my action and illuminates an ethical order manifested in, and expressed through, human relationship. Conversely, metaphysical abstractions, which Levinas called the "toys of our oratory", only achieve their meaning and purpose in the here-and-now of the face-to-face reflection of the transcendent.[88]

A case study

> This otherness and this absolute separation manifest themselves in the epiphany of the face, in the face to face. Being a grouping quite different from the synthesis, it initiates a proximity different from the one that presides over the synthesis of data, uniting them into a "world" of parts within a whole.[89]

The Face at the centre of Levinas' ethical formulation is arguably the *whole* work of community mental health care, given the clinician's constant exposure to it and the extremity of its demand. Whether the clinician responds hospitably or remains entranced in the distancing and reductive sphere of clinical biases, projections and protocols, this is *the* Face "par excellence"[90] of community mental health care. Even before taking a seat in the consultation room, this face claims me for a responsibility that my job description and clinical education have left me morally and practically unprepared, if not destitute. Nonetheless, this face cries out to me. It *howls* for understanding, for compassion, for safety, for respite, for comfort, for justice, for love, but also for its basic human rights—food, shelter, education, employment, above the hum of the factory floor, before a single word is uttered.

Sharon

> *A downcast woman walks into my counselling room. Her long hair is unkempt and unwashed and she looks exhausted and rather fearfully at me. She is so heavy she has trouble squeezing into the armed chair and has to lay back in it to make herself reasonably comfortable. Her dress hangs on her shoulders like a cotton sac and reveals the whole truth of her body. The dimpled skin on her chest and arms is blemished and discoloured where she has picked her skin. She has been ravaged by childhood sexual abuse that continued into her teen years and spends most of her days in bed too depressed to get up. She is living with crippling pain and the prognosis is bleak. She needs to work but cannot manage it physically or emotionally. Her husband earns a modest living but neither understands nor appreciates her anguish, and her children disrespect her and make her cry. She tells me she loves God but feels utterly betrayed by Him and has been poorly treated by members of her church who she loved and revered.*
>
> *Sharon is terrified to talk about wanting to kill herself for fear I will have her children taken away. I explain that social services lack the manpower and incentive to remove the teenage children from all the suicidal mothers in the land. We laugh ruefully together but she is still afraid, vigilant. I promise her that no one will take her children but I worry about their welfare and their inability to mother this suffering woman.*
>
> *One day Sharon shows me a bruise the size of a dinner plate she has made on her abdomen by pinching herself. It is a habit that mortifies her but is not easy to give up because it soothes her. She needs permission to reveal this and wants me to coax her to show me the wound. I assure her I want to see it, and with no small dignity she lifts up the hem of her dress to show me the evidence because someone has to bear witness to this much senseless suffering. I am utterly silent in the presence of this massive purple wound, the nudity laid waste, the underwear, the revelation, her solemn gaze that awaits my response, and in that moment I am overwhelmed by a dignity and anguish I find immensely personal and painful.*
>
> *From the early days of our meetings I incline myself towards this God lover and tell her, honestly, that whenever she enters the room, she brings in*

a wonderful beauty that often makes my eyes stream and for which I am profoundly grateful. Sharon looks anxiously, uncertainly, into my face to confirm my sincerity. I ask her if she can feel it in the room, the light, the spaciousness, the perfect peace. I use her language and call it "God" so she will know what I mean. She looks slowly around the room for evidence, begins to relax into her chair and finally says, quietly, "Yes, I can". Her face softens, there is nothing to be said, and we sit together in the silence for a few moments savouring the evanescence. This is the mystery that she herself evokes, recognises and loves, even while she yearns for it, even while it eludes her, and upon this we try to build a plan for her next tentative steps.

The paradox of authority and weakness

Whether she looks at me or not, she "regards me;" I must answer for her. I call face that which thus in another concerns the I—concerns me—reminding me, from behind the countenance she puts on in her portrait, of her abandonment, her defencelessness and her mortality, and her appeal to my ancient responsibility, as if she were unique in the world—beloved.[91]

Levinas' formulation of the Face shines through Sharon's actual face, her body, her wounds, her anguish and defencelessness. Her silent call echoes Levinas' frequent references to the sixth commandment, "Please do not kill me", but also, "Please help me, please be my friend". Instantly, my loyalties as a clinician are clarified and divided while what is being called for is unclear and unsettling. The "uprightness"[92] of this face, John Caruana observes, combines three aspects that constitute the sheer impact—the *shock*—of this face upon me that speaks of an integrity testifying to the "divine in the human drama".[93] Indeed, Sharon's dignity and gravitas were absolute.

The "dissymmetry" of our relationship that Levinas claims is so important between self and other is palpable in one defining moment after another as I sit with Sharon. It announces my guilt and a formidable truth clarifying that "[the] relationship between me and the other is unsurpassable". Levinas reminds us that this relationship *can* be modified by justice, which constitutes the existence of the state and citizens who are equal. But, he adds, there can be no enduring justice if "in the ethical act, in my relationship to the other. . . one forgets that I am guiltier than the others".[94]

When I confront Sharon, it appears I *have* forgotten—or possibly never knew—the extremity of my guilt although its presence and justification shine through her every pore without judgement or contempt. I observe my frustration as I attempt to impose solutions that further deny Sharon's reality and require her to exercise an agency I myself cannot, do not, exercise on her behalf. Relationship is at the centre of our every discussion, about what hurts the most in her many stories of violation and betrayal—even by her God, which is a particularly grievous loss for her. But on closer examination, even this betrayal is found to be all too human, perpetrated not by an unloving God but by certain members of her congregation and the indifference of her pastor. She feels banished, unwanted and beyond God's reach.

My relationship with this "ethical other" discloses our wonder-full rapport that casts fresh light on my practice and so-called professional judgement. The perversion of my role—of what I do and can do for, and *to*, this woman in my "care"—is fully revealed. The implications are found in the enormity of my authority over virtually every aspect of Sharon's life or, possibly, the authority of someone above me in the clinical hierarchy. This is no exaggeration, for with a single phone call, letter, clinical note or consultation with another of her care providers, I could theoretically have Sharon's fragile life besieged by the power of the law at my disposal.

Conversely, I could tell Sharon she did not "meet the mandate" and fire her from our care, nor would I be faulted. She is, after all, the prototypical "heartsink" patient whose needs are beyond the capacity—or interests—of the institution.[95] But then the Face commands me, and I am thenceforth incapable of allowing her to suffer alone. This is a call that consigns me ("[I]l y a comme un appel a moi"),[96] that "awakens" me to the violence I fear I might commit, or expose her to, despite my best intentions.[97] Here, the desire to protect this other even—or *especially*—from *myself* confirms a responsibility from which there is no release but that I am always at liberty to ignore.[98]

In what he admits is an "extreme formulation", Levinas contends that "[t]he face orders and ordains me. Its signification is an order signified",[99] even if I am powerless to do more than stand by helplessly and say, "I am here".[100] Indeed, it seemed that this was the best I could offer Sharon, so complex were her needs and so limited the resources and time I could add to those she was already receiving. Yet Levinas extends some redemption in claiming that even this woefully inadequate response—*me voici*—"is without doubt, the secret of sociality and, in its ultimate gratuity and vanity, love for the neighbour, love without concupiscence".[101]

Levinas' transcendent evocation utterly confirms the accuracy of my apprehension of Sharon's "transfigured" face, although this face shifted continually throughout our work. One moment it would evoke a wrenching tenderness and palpable sense of the divine that called out my wholehearted desire to extend myself to her. In the next, this face would relapse into the totalised perspective of a desecrated lost cause that left me earnestly wishing Sharon would just go away. Yet translating the ineffable into language is problematic, for there are *not* two different Sharons. These perceptions do *not* come at different times during our face-to-face meetings, nor are they conflated, nor are they separated—as if by a split-screen image—nor, strangely, do they actually oppose each other, despite the contrast, the *tension*, between them. This space, or *hinge*, or "node"[102] that lies between the established hierarchical order of things and that which upends it utterly and places Sharon *above* me resides in how I look at her. Nor is this "look" insignificant, Levinas confirms. "[T]he idea that the death of the other is more important than my own is an affirmation that we are not being looked at from the outside, but the essential difference between me and the other remains in my look". Such difference constitutes the immutable, irreducible—eternal "strangeness" that combines an endless obligation which "cannot be effaced".[103]

We might say that Sharon elicited a sense of wonder and reverence on which I capitalised as a clinician wishing to maintain a more humanised regard for her. Conversely, we might say that she elicited my sense of horror, despair and inadequacy that I wished to soften under the cover—or protection—of an intentionally wonder-full perspective. Yet such interpretations fail to account for the *relationship* that I am already in *up to my neck* with this woman before the question of how I am to help even emerges. That I must help her, am compelled to help her, is certain, but in no way equivalent to my ability to do so. My desire speaks for itself, as does my ambivalence and undiluted aversion. Nor are the compelling evocations of this "beloved" *imposed*. Indeed, they are *not* divorced from a certain willingness or acquiescence on my part to what Levinas so exquisitely identifies as the *welcome* of the face, which is irresistible or nearly so. Through this enigma I am confronted with an intimacy and familiarity that defy the primacy and authority of my role in this relationship and confirm *my* need of this "Other". How can this be? Sharon is obviously and very problematically subordinate to me in every conceivable way by her life circumstances and the rules of the clinical game.

The enigma is partially clarified by Levinasian scholar Richard Cohen, who observes that these two perspectives—ethics versus ontology—do *not* oppose each other along a shared continuum. They lie on different planes altogether, with the one cancelling out the other. Yet, even this assertion of the primacy of the Other—of "what ought to be"—offers Sharon scant protection. The elevated, *intimate*, view of this other who is holiness—is also fragile, tenuous, unstable and easily collapsed back to the "what is"—to the ontological reduction—that violates Sharon. This is the same reduction that underpins the mandates and protocols of my workplace. The extremity of Sharon's vulnerability discloses a responsibility for which I can also resent and blame her for my empty-handedness and despair. The step to disgust and neglect—blatant dehumanisation and abuse—lies just beyond this perimeter. Indeed, my clinical response to this face reflects Mary-Jane Rubenstein's description of wonder as something essentially ambivalent, where horror and holiness—far from opposing each other—are actually wed.[104]

Whether I act for or against Sharon, my relationship to her and responsibility for her are indisputable. These are the constituents that threaten my professional façade—and everything it represents and contributes to the project of my being—with a larger purpose whose call I am educated, socialised and *rewarded* to ignore, distrust and fear in my clinical role. But here also lies the *possibility* of the clinician's awakening to her own moral injury, and the healing invitation that awaits her in the unlikely form of the very person against whom she transgresses. All this indwells the colourless environment of a community mental health office where it's business as usual, and normalcy, respect and kindness ostensibly prevail.

Disinterest

Levinas' relational formulation is never about "thinking" or conceptualising the other. His is not a rational metaphysics that mistakes the purpose of thinking about the ultimate truth with truth itself. The problem always lies with the ontological quest for certainty and its outcome—ownership, possession, mastery, ambition, appropriation and assimilation. This quest contributes to a "sense of the malignancy of being" and the "sadness of self-interest" from which we could *release* ourselves for the "joy or accomplishment" in *"disinterest"*. "Disinterest" means turning away from the self towards the suffering other who—*like me*—is struggling with the same disappointments and inadequacies of being. Hence, disinterest can be understood as holiness.[105]

Disinterest requires that we recognise and relinquish the (im)-morality implicit in the onto-theo-logical, which Jantzen called the "symbolic of domination", because it predictably leads to violence and oppression.[106] Consequently, "we are looking for a way to get outside of ontology starting with the relationship with the other in his difference which makes objectivity impossible".[107] In this way, freedom becomes "the possibility of doing what no one can do in my place; freedom is thus the uniqueness of that responsibility",[108] but not as some joyless self-sacrifice.[109] Greater possibilities lie in imagining *beyond* what reduces our lives, the people in them and the world around us to a "series of means for further ends".[110] The need for such imagining can hardly be overstated if the mental health clinician is to actually *respond* to the wonder-full other as more than just a special experience or "privilege" for her private—if mortified—consumption.

The church

> I'd come to London on a three-and-half-hour train ride for a symposium where priests, psychiatrists and associated professionals were gathering to explore the therapeutic links between the professional and the vocational. The church was magnificent, the croissants fresh, the coffee plentiful. Gold tiles glittered from the dim recess of the apse, and the well-heeled audience took their places in the pews.
>
> The opening speaker was a young doctor who was perfectly made-up and beautifully dressed. She spoke of the torment of her medical training for half an hour with a grimace of a smile on her terrified face that never once flagged. The other presenters were middle-aged and older men, successful physicians and clerics who could extemporise with their hands in their pockets. Media savvy, self-deprecating and at the peak of their careers, they could finally say whatever they wanted and admit as much with an ironic smile. They reeked of authority, and their focus was surprisingly personal and refreshingly regretful, even wistful.
>
> Much of their talk and most of their stories were tinged with hushed reverence that borders on awe, the humble amazement and soulful gratitude for what we in this business get out of the encounter from those who come to us for help. Such sincerity should never stink of sanctimony but it almost always does.

We like talking like this—when we can—because it's true, and we feel good, we feel special for seeing and saying what is hidden. We feel free and daring because this is dangerous territory that stands in opposition to much of what we've been trained to protect and believe and not admit. But we all know that when that wonderful thing happens, everything changes. When we actually see, when we know that utter perfection sitting in front of us with his stigmatising label, his epic story and his smashed life that no one could ever fix, it's like discovering the Holy Grail, and we're confirmed and rhapsodic. "It's such a rare privilege this work, isn't it? Isn't it? Yes, it really is". This is always said as if for the first time, as though we've just noticed and we have a corner on the market that edifies us for that reason.

But the tribute never veered towards questions of power or its abuse. No one said a word about the differences in salary or status even between the doctors and priests, let alone the helpers and the helped. The only culprit ever mentioned was the "system", and we nodded our collective heads like congregants at a revival meeting each time another testimonial was given about the system that kept us from doing more, from doing enough. All the talk about the spirit-withering system added a lustre of virtue to the earnest lamentations of these powerful men, and the rest of us for that matter, who genuinely wanted to pay homage to those who'd come broken and empty-handed to our doors, with what trust and hope. But who'd somehow—marvellously, incredibly—resurrected us instead, not once but many, many, times.

There was a frisson of anarchy in the church that day that hinged on our communion with the one who is constantly revealed as more than an equal, as our teacher, as an unexpected and priceless gift, as this "great privilege". Yet, no one went further. No one talked about the injustice and our relationship with the social equivalent of "an untouchable" whom we ourselves help create but who nonetheless makes us well. This is the one on whose shoulders we stand, who rescues us from the fray of institutional chaos and holds the antidote to our own professional powerlessness, ennui and despair. No one remarked how we—the privileged—justify limiting the orbit of our effort to the homey boundaries of our professional authority and the consultation room with its many comforts. No one even hinted about who really pays for this intimate and affirming reward that allows us to be so very grateful with so little outlay. Not even me.

Responsibility

It is a passivity more passive still than any passivity that is antithetical to an act, a nudity more naked than all "academic" nudity, exposed to the point of outpouring, effusion and prayer. . . . It is a vulnerability and a paining exhausting themselves like a hemorrhage, denuding even the aspect that its nudity takes on. It is the passivity of being-for-another, which is possible only in the form of giving the very bread I eat.[111]

This question of "being" as opposed to "being-for-the-other" constantly begs the seemingly imponderable question that philosopher Philippe Nemo poses to Levinas: "But if one fears for the other and not for oneself, can one even live?" Which, Levinas agrees, is the ultimate question, but then he reframes it: "Should I be dedicated to being? By being, by persisting in being, do I not kill?"[112] We may find Levinas' repeated allusions to killing polemical or metaphoric. That we do confirms, for Jantzen, the security of academics' cocooned existence and their collusion with violence despite their efforts to act against it.[113] The same may be said of the clinician vis-à-vis the vulnerable help seeker.

In Levinas' terms, in *any* terms, should it not be argued that I have, at least on occasion, contributed to the destitution, demoralisation, degradation and *death* of the Other, no matter how peripherally, how legitimately, how "ethically" in my clinical role?[114] Which begs the question of how the morally injured clinician can be enticed to finally say as much and lay that burden down. Whatever else the clinician's role may be, her ethical responsibility is surely to reveal, interrupt and *name* what hides in the deep folds of the rational and the being that answers only to itself. Even my intention to "open to wonder" in the consultation room can be tainted by my self-consciousness and the anticipatory satisfaction arising from what I already "know" or wish to confirm.[115] Levinas' ethical formulation confirms the likelihood of my moral failure and unfulfilled responsibility, in sum, my profound unconsciousness, my blindness, my *violence*.

Curiously, this moral clarity offers the consolation of a sliver of integrity in my unacknowledged—*invisible*—survivor's guilt and grief. I may not be vindicated, but neither am I wholly dishonoured.[116] Derrida noted that Levinas himself spoke of survivor's guilt as a "guilt without fault and without debt; it is in truth an entrusted responsibility".[117] To recognise and claim what I know to be right and just in a morally compromising environment speaks of my ethical capacity to do just this. Even if such goodness is routinely sacrificed, *corrupted* and reconfigured by the institution,[118] it also "consists of taking up a position in being, such that the other counts more than myself".[119]

Nemo objects to Levinas' response by observing that even in the animal kingdom a law prevails among all species that makes it impossible to live without killing. To which Levinas asserts yet again: "In society such as it functions one cannot live without killing or at least without taking the preliminary steps for the death of someone". He then presses the point that the banality of our ability to kill does not diminish its significance. Which is why, Levinas concludes, the most important question is *not* "Why is there something instead of nothing?" but "Do I not kill by being?"[120] Is there a more fundamental question than this for the clinician to ask?

In looking more deeply into Levinas' account of responsibility, we find in his notions of passivity, dissymmetry and substitution, meanings almost indistinguishable from each other. What they describe is not a progression as much as a *suspension*, a radicalising moment of wonder that lays bare my professional identity and a spontaneous "deference" that overflows with a sense of my indebtedness to this Other. There is no reciprocity here. Any interest in reciprocity is the other person's business, Levinas insists, *not* his. "I am responsible without waiting for his reciprocity were I to die for it".[121] I am wholly responsible for the other, even for the harm this other may do—or may have done—to another or even to himself or to me. This is in addition to anything anyone else may do, be doing, or have done to harm him, or anything that might befall him. I am solely and entirely responsible, and no one can take my place in this responsibility, which makes me "un-substitutible", although *I* may be substituted for the responsibility of another. The notion of substitution is complex because it does not simply mean "I put myself in the place of someone. . . . It signifies a suffering for another in the form of expiation, which alone can permit any compassion".[122]

To clarify the point, Levinas employs a quote throughout his work taken from one of Dostoyevsky's characters: "We are all guilty for everything and everyone, and I more than all the others".[123] Such responsibility calls forth a passivity that is intense, acute, urgent, immediate, *full*, which Derrida describes as "the urgency of a destination leading to the Other and not an eternal return to self".[124] There is nothing before me in this event but a raw, unequivocal desire that is also paralysing.

In trying to understand this passivity, Michael Morgan initially suggests this passivity is *prior* to the free and active self. But ultimately, he concludes, we can only understand this passivity in the here and now, not through a temporal reading back to the time before subjectivity or action, thought, or being. It must be *now*, because I am responsible for and to the other person "before I am a person".[125] Morgan's observation speaks to the immensity of the moral impact exerted by the divinised Other on the clinician. For, in these terms, the clinician appears to be entirely dependent on the vulnerable help seeker to instruct her, show her, help her in becoming a person. Clarification and confirmation are found in Levinas' repeated allusions to my being held "hostage", "ordained", "chosen" or "*elected*" to this responsibility—which suggests the immediacy, transcendence and inviolability of this event—even if I cannot yet imagine what I am actually to *do*.

Nor is this election a privilege, Levinas cautions, but the hallmark of the morally responsible, and it *is* "hard", he confirms.[126] It is hard to be "a substitution for another, one in the place of another" and called to account for something I did not do and would rather avoid having to pay for.[127] Mental health clinicians are constantly negotiating the riptide of this imperative, this "election", in their daily encounters with the vulnerable help seeker. Moreover, the clinician is revealed to herself time and again as morally compromised if not bereft, shameful, guilty, uncertain, timid, afraid.

Derrida claims that far from being an "abdication of reason", this passivity is a sign of my receptivity.[128] It is, in sum, a welcome to *me*, the welcoming "host" who discovers to her incredulity that *she* is the one being offered hospitality *in her own home.* It is the *Other* who shows me that it is not *my* home, that *I* am the guest and the one being hosted after all. Thus, "[t]he one who welcomes is first welcomed in his own home. The one who invites is invited by the one whom she invites. The one who receives is received".[129] Such is the excessive hospitality of the Other whom the clinician confronts in the form of the vulnerable help seeker. She is the one who holds me hostage, who ordains, burdens and blesses me.

A brief critique

> *The ethical order does not prepare us for the divinity; it is the very accession to the divinity. All the rest is a dream.*[130]

Increasingly, Levinas' work is being scrutinised, critiqued and developed in fields relevant to its moral and political content, including theology, sociology, cultural theory, religion, political theory.[131] But his work has not been examined critically enough, Simon Critchley claims, and its "Achilles Heel" lies in its politics.[132] Critchley might speak for many in noting the "savage irony" of Levinas' work ultimately languishing when the overwhelming demand of his vision awaits an adequate political response.

Critchley suggests five impediments keeping Levinas' ethics from a passage to politics, three them—fraternity, monotheism, androcentrism—have particular resonance here.[133] The dialogue about clinical dehumanisation emerges, after all, from a male-based, authoritarian and legalised hierarchy, which inevitably places the help seeker at a disadvantage. Equally, the majority of clinical professionals and help seekers engaged in this clinical system are *women* who, poignantly, help hold this structure in place. But in looking towards the humanising core of Levinas' work for answers to a way *beyond*, a way *through*, Critchley reminds us that the fundamental friendship to which Levinas alludes constitutes a "fraternity" based on a classical ideal of a relationship of "brothers" who, Critchley dryly adds, "happen to male". The androcentrism explicit in Levinas' work is addressed by his critics and not easily resolved. Even the possibility of a relationship between women based on Levinas' ideal would, Critchley notes, make it "secondary" to fraternity, or simply misunderstood if not invisible. The consequence of this androcentric blind spot emerges most fascinatingly—as Critchley and Levinas' feminist critics point out—when this "essential Other" is—*herself*—essentialised. How this phenomenon plays out within our clinical exploration of the "Other" is fully articulated in the autoethnography, "The church", pp. 116–17, found earlier in this chapter.[134] Within that narrative, entranced clinicians, speaking in reverential tones, share the marvellous stories of their "transcending" experiences with the help seeker, while failing to notice that this "experience" is at the very expense of the *essentialised* Other.

The issue of fraternity and androcentrism is also part of Levinas' monotheism that connects the idea of a universal fraternity to God and community as a monotheistic whole. Within it, Critchley notes, "fraternity is ensured through the passage to God, which incidentally recalls the classical Christian, essentially Augustinian, conception of friendship".[135] But in this configuration, not only are women left behind, other nations, religious perspectives and races are as well. Like Critchley, Lin Ma disparages the inadequacy of Levinas' political thought, which, she claims, jeopardises the appeal and authority of Levinas' ethical vision given its Eurocentrism. Ma notes, for example, that in one article written in 1960, Levinas refers to people of Asian heritage as "The yellow peril" and then justifies that his comment is not racist by pleading ignorance about the culture.[136] Critchley, one of Levinas' foremost exponents, has also emphasised the problem of Levinas' "deep seated ignorance and prejudice against non-Western cultures" in an opening speech at a conference held in China in 2006.[137] Both scholars identify monotheism as a contributing factor.[138]

At least one of Levinas' interpreters has sought to separate the essential integrity of Levinas' philosophy from his personal comments about other races.[139] Other critics have been less inclined to separate the man from his work. Nor are they all in agreement that Levinas' ethical vision can be neutral, given its strong connection to a Jewish tradition in which Levinas is steeped both culturally and as a renowned Talmudic scholar.[140] Such evidence adds weight to Ma's critique about the absence of any substantial discussion of Afro-Asiatic civilisations and their connections to Western tradition in Levinas' work.[141] She informs us that Levinas at one point expressed concern that the material needs of Afro-Asiatic civilisations might ultimately "endanger the authenticity of the State of Israel and marginalize Jews and Christians".[142] Despite these unsettling, disappointing charges, it is also true that awareness of the anathema of racial discrimination and white supremacy has grown markedly in the interval between the 1960s and today. The current rash of books being published on racism for the mortified liberal white readers who are buying them attests to the ongoing failure of white people to understand their ongoing contribution to the problem.

Levinas' historical racist remarks that his critics rightly condemn are not justified on this account, but it does give them greater context. More encouragingly Critchley's and Ma's critique, while holding Levinas to account, are attempting to move his work beyond the Judaic and Greek traditions at the core of Western civilisation[143]—and the universality Levinas assigns them. The need for a just and egalitarian pluralism that is no longer dependent on—nor expected to be grateful for "European generosity"[144] is fundamental and long past due. That said, Levinas' ethical vision and the immensity of the work he dedicated to our understanding of this unsurpassable, welcoming Other and my responsibility to her or him is arguably far beyond the sum of Levinas' human failings and short-sightedness.[145]

Another insistent critique of Levinas work lies in his unequivocal condemnation of reason and logocentrism that Richard Wolin describes as a "tell-tale performative contradiction", because it is based in the very language and methods Levinas prefers to denounce as ontologically violent. The inference is always that the logical use of language is untrustworthy and ultimately dominating.[146] But if reason is always at the helm of the "will to domination" it is also true, as Wolin argues, that reason grounds and strengthens our arguments and makes truth claims and our intersubjective communications both possible and valuable.[147] There *is* more than wholesale, self-serving objectification in persuasive argumentation, and reason is more than subjugation. Indeed, reason does have "a restorative capacity and acts as balm that can heal prior wounds. . . misunderstandings and injustices.[148] Wolin also chides Levinas for his short-sightedness in reviling technology's destruction without fully acknowledging the good it can also do.[149]

In the following chapter, we will examine the ineffable language Levinas so powerfully employs to break free of the problematic egocentrism of ontology and illuminate the transcendent Otherness at the centre. But Levinas' prohibition of a lexicon of "representation" may well undermine the possibility of an accessible philosophical language.[150] Wolin argues that the binary of totality and infinity are in such strenuous opposition that it is "nearly impossible to conceptualize meaningful intersubjectivity". In withdrawing from the Face of the Other, one is immediately confronted with "totality" and a "sauve qui peut" mentality "of human self-preservation run amok".[151] Despite the irony, Wolin captures the essence of my encounter with *Sharon*,[152] whose Otherness called forth my awe and tenderness and whose burdensome totality called forth my aversion. Wolin's objection that an encounter with the Other is "so overwhelming that it entails a dissolution of the self", while "freedom is reconceptualized as being beholden to the other", is not unreasonable.[153] Such excess pushes the boundaries of credulity and impedes the translation of this phenomenon into politics. What is left, Wolin cautions, is a "dangerous" gap, between ethics and justice that is not easily resolved, given Levinas' tightly "self-enclosed conception of ethics".[154]

In addition to these critiques, feminist scholars have also contributed substantially to Levinas' work. Some have taken him to task for his male privilege, his heteronormative and prophetic language and conservatism, and for his marginalising evocations of the feminine in his construal of alterity. The latter was first identified by Simone de Beauvoir[155] and later by Luce Irigaray[156] who attempted to correct Levinas. She appealed to him to place the alterity of the feminine in a more equitable and co-creative position with the subject who transcends rather than at the expense of *she* through who he has, or *will*, transcend. We shall return to this theme in the final chapter.[157] A comprehensive analysis of critiques provoked by Levinas' construction of

Levinas and the wholly/holy other 123

eros as both the feminine and alterity is unfortunately beyond the remit of this chapter.

Elsewhere, Grace Jantzen has queried Levinas' failure to problematise his own face, the face which responds to the Other: "And it is clear that this face is indeed *his* face, the face of an adult male with sufficient ability and privilege to be able to choose its response, to make itself responsible and renounce violence". Here, Jantzen brings to our attention another example of the "privileged male" taking on the task of answering for the needs of "the ones who are helpless over against his strong self".[158] Her concern serves a useful reminder that Levinas' work offers no panacea. Indeed, such criticism is vital in balancing any potential seduction with Levinas' epiphanic vision—of what "should" be—with the actual work and sacrifice of making it real in the world.

Feminist scholar Tina Chanter argues that the limitations of Levinas' work, for which he has been pilloried, may also be misinterpretations.[159] These limitations may be insufficient to impugn the enormity of his contribution and its overall benefit to women, even if more analysis and development are justified. Still others have used Levinas to develop their own work and extend his scholarship.[160] In addition to feminist concerns, other critiques about Levinas suggest the need for more and greater analysis of his later work.[161]

Levinas' legacy is clearly still a work in progress, but these critiques offer the reader some insight into the nature, breadth and complexity of the issues being interpreted and challenged. I do not pretend to have adequate answers, but while these critiques are not insignificant, they illustrate the phenomenal imagination and complexity of Levinas' project and make him a very human figure and a man of his time, not a saint. An astute defence of Levinas' work relevant to our inquiry lies in Wolin's observation that Levinas' "ethics as first philosophy has helped to sensitize us to the instrumentalizing perils and excesses of theoretical reason. . . that, in a post-Holocaust universe should not be taken lightly".[162] Such sensitisation is far from accomplished within the context of community mental health care and our re-humanising project, which arguably makes Levinas a fine guide for the journey.

Closing reflections

The suspicions engendered by psychoanalysis, sociology and politics weigh on human identity such that we never know to whom we are speaking and what we are dealing with when we build our ideas on the basis of human facts. But we do not need this knowledge in the relationship in which the other is a neighbour, and in which before being an individuation of the genus (woman)man, a rational animal, a free will, or any essence whatever, (she)he is the persecuted one for whom I am responsible to the point of being a hostage for (her)him, and in which my responsibility, instead of disclosing me in my "essence" as a

>   *transcendental ego, divests me without stop of all that can be common to me and another (woman)man, who would thus be capable of replacing me. I am then called upon in my uniqueness as someone for whom no one else can substitute himself.*[163]

Levinas' metaphysical argument provides an astonishing ethical direction for the clinician that is always found in the relationship—in the face that has no particular attribute that might distinguish her from me but that overwhelms me with its moral height.[164] Here, in the separation between the subject and the Other—who is both the other person and *the* Other who represents God[165]—the "trace" of the infinite is discovered.[166] This trace is evident in the complexity of the help seeker's entire humanity, her speech, her face. Even the nape of her neck[167] is capable of challenging "any totalitarian or absolutist form of economy".[168] The Face is powerful enough to destroy the grip of the ego and leave the subject incapable of responding in anything less than ethical terms, although this imperative is never imposed.[169]

It is a relationship that is unchanged, Levinas tells us, even when conducted in an institution where justice is exercised and I am required to make comparisons and choices to establish fairness. If justice mediates my action within the institution, my responsibility remains undiminished even when I am confronted by competing demands. The origin of justice lies in charity and loving my neighbour, which, Chanter observes, is also a "commentary on the violence committed in the name of justice".[170] Levinas confirms the inevitability of the institution while claiming that justice is safeguarded by the "initial interpersonal relation".[171] Indeed, the system itself is mediated by my relationship with the other person through charity, and cannot exist without justice. Charity is "warped" without justice.[172]

That the plea of this Face can be ignored, feared or misconstrued by caring, committed and educated clinicians as authorisation of their professional "privilege", rather than proof of its violence, is not easily challenged. The ontological ground of a mental health clinician's caring work necessarily reduces the other and excludes—and distrusts—anything hinting of the metaphysical or requiring the suspension of belief. That said, we can find in the clinician's de-moralisation evidence of a possibility that engages her desire, perhaps her compulsion, to protect this fragile help seeker. Nonetheless, the problem lies in the clinician *herself* and the evidence of her own apparent lack of trustworthiness. Nor should we imagine the clinician is unmoved or unaffected by the help seeker. Even so, the call of the Face challenging the clinician's moral blindness does not take precedence simply or easily over her self-interest and her entrancement with the status quo.[173]

There are no simple answers for the clinician wanting to cultivate or maintain a divinised perspective of the help seeker within an institution constructed by the very reduction it perpetuates and protects. Clinicians are still professionally and institutionally bound to a medically informed, reductive "practice" that reverberates in Nemo's question: How can I live if I put the other before myself? Nonetheless, growing numbers of researchers, clinicians and therapists are turning to Levinas' ethics, to his remarkable language and to the impossible possibilities he offers those attempting to interpret and apply his wonder-full vision.

Notes

1. E. Levinas, *Ethics and Infinity: Conversations with Philippe Nemo, 1982* (Pittsburgh, PA: Duquesne University Press, 1985), p. 56.
2. For a brief overview of Levinas' current impact, see: P. Atterton and M. Calarco, 'Editors' Introduction: The Third Wave of Levinas Scholarship', in *Radicalising Levinas*, ed. by Peter Atterton and Matthew Calarco (Albany, NY: State University of New York Press, 2010).
3. S. Critchley, 'Introduction', in *The Cambridge Companion Levinas*, ed. by S. Critchley and R. Bernasconi (Cambridge: Cambridge University Press, 2002), pp. 4–5.
4. "Levinas's insistence upon otherness coincides with feminism's quest to be other than what they are". T. Chanter, 'Feminism and the Other', in *The Provocation of Levinas: Rethinking the Other*, ed. by R. Bernasconi and D. Wood (London; New York: Routledge, 1988), p. 52.
5. This special issue is devoted to Levinas. See: G. Sayre, 'Toward a Therapy for the Other', *European Journal of Psychotherapy & Counselling*, 7 (2005), p. 37.
6. See especially: D.M. Goodman and M.P. Freeman, eds., *Psychology and the Other* (Oxford: Oxford University Press, 2015).
7. Using the search term "Levinas" in the EBSCO database revealed 9,609 references ranging in subjects as diverse as corporate responsibility, literature, media and psychology, to name a few. Using the search term "Emmanuel Levinas" in Google Scholar produced 98,900 references; the search term "Levinas" produced 266,000 references.
8. See. T. Wright, P. Hughes, and A. Ainley, 'The Paradox of Morality: An interview with Emmanuel Levinas', in *The Provocation of Levinas: Rethinking the Other*, ed. by R. Bernasconi and D. Wood, trans. by A. Benjamin and T. Wright (London; New York: Routledge, 1988), pp. 168–69.
9. The author argues for the need for psychology to acquire moral relevance. See: R.N. Williams, 'Self-Betraying Emotions and the Psychology of Heteronomy', *European Journal of Psychotherapy & Counselling*, 7 (2005), p. 8.
10. D. Orange, 'Commentary on Pizer: The Refugee in the Kitchen-Variations on Hineni and Stuart Pizer's Grandfather', in *Psychology and the Other*, ed. by D. Goodman and M.P. Freeman (Oxford: Oxford University Press, 2015), p. 213.
11. S. Hand, *Emmanuel Levinas* (London; New York: Routledge, 2009), pp. 114–15.
12. G. Jantzen, *Becoming Divine: Towards a Feminist Philosophy of Religion* (Bloomington; Indianapolis: Indiana University Press, 1999), pp. 231–53.
13. Ibid. p. 229.
14. Ibid. pp. 231. See also: pp. 231–37.
15. Derrida recounts a fragment of a personal conversation with Levinas. See: J. Derrida, *Adieu to Emmanuel Levinas* (Palo Alto, CA: Stanford University Press, 1999), p. 4.
16. E. Levinas, *Entre Nous: On Thinking-of-the-Other* (New York: Cambridge University Press, 1998), p. 168.

17 J. Macnaughton, 'Medical Humanities' Challenge to Medicine', *Journal of Evaluation in Clinical Practice*, 17 (2011).
18 E. Levinas, *Difficult Freedom: Essays on Judaism* (Baltimore: Johns Hopkins University Press, 1990), p. 101.
19 Levinas, *Ethics and Infinity: Conversations with Philippe Nemo*, p. 22.
20 T. Chanter, 'Introduction', in *Feminist Interpretations of Emmanuel Levinas*, ed. by T. Chanter (University Park, PA: Pennsylvania State University Press, 2001), (p. 6).
21 Hand, *Emmanuel Levinas*, p. 170.
22 S. Malka, *Emmanuel Levinas: His Life and Legacy*, trans. by M. Kigel and S.M. Embree, (Pittsburgh, PA: Duquesne University Press, 2006), pp. XIII-XIX. See also: pp. 64–83 for a powerful description of Levinas' time in captivity.
23 E. Levinas, *Emmanuel Levinas: Basic Philosophical Writings* (Bloomington; Indianapolis: Indiana University Press, 1996), pp. 7–9.
24 E. Levinas and R. Kearney, 'Dialogue with Emmanuel Levinas', in *Face to Face with Levinas*, ed. by R. Cohen (Albany, NY: State University of New York Press, 1986), p. 14.
25 Hand, *Emmanuel Levinas*, p. 12.
26 Husserl's "phenomenological reduction" describes the purity or essence of things. This is not to be confused with the "reduction" imposed by the assimilating or objectifying impact of the rational, which Levinas describes as "the same".
27 Levinas and Kearney, 'Dialogue with Emmanuel Levinas', p. 16.
28 D. Moran, *Introduction to Phenomenology* (London; New York: Routledge, 2000), p. 4.
29 Moran notes that French phenomenology developed through Emmanuel Levinas, Maurice Merleau-Ponty, Jean-Paul Sartre, Paul Ricoeur, Julia Kristeva, Gilles Deleuze, and Jacques Derrida. See: ibid. pp. 18–19.
30 Ibid. pp. 1–18.
31 Severson describes Husserl's process of "epoché" that Levinas also employed, which recognises reality's "overlapping layers of meaning" and the relationship between them that had been unravelled to get to their underlying truth. This truth is revealed by isolating a phenomenon from "expectations and presuppositions about how an event may occur". See: E. Severson, *Levinas's Philosophy of Time: Gift, Responsibility, Diachrony, Hope* (Pittsburgh, PA: Duquesne University Press, 2013), p. 33.
32 Ibid. p. 38.
33 Moran, *Introduction to Phenomenology*, p. 328.
34 Ibid. p. 329.
35 E. Levinas, *Totality and Infinity: An Essay on Exteriority* (The Hague; Boston; London: Martinus Nijhoff, 1979), p. 28.
36 Ibid. p. 27.
37 Severson, *Levinas's Philosophy of Time: Gift, Responsibility, Diachrony, Hope*, p. 38.
38 E. Levinas, and R. Kearney, 'Dialogue with Emmanuel Levinas,' in *Face to Face with Levinas*, ed. by R.A. Cohen (Albany, NY: State University of New York Press, 1986), pp. 15–16.
39 G. Loughlin, 'Other Discourses', *New Blackfriars*, 75 (1994), p. 20.
40 Severson, *Levinas's Philosophy of Time: Gift, Responsibility, Diachrony, Hope*, p. 109.
41 The implications of Heidegger's involvement with the Nazi party are still contested. One commentator suggests that while Heidegger's involvement was far from innocent from 1933–4, there is insufficient reason to argue that the whole of his philosophy was corrupted by this episode. See: J. Young, *Heidegger, Philosophy, Nazism* (Cambridge: Cambridge University Press, 1998), pp. 1–10. Yet, the

bald facts of Heidegger's behaviour are significant. See: Hand, *Emmanuel Levinas*, p. 15. Another scholar recounts being publicly humiliated by Levinas following his presentation on Heidegger that Levinas had agreed to help jury. The author suggests this behaviour reflected Levinas' historical rage towards Heidegger's Nazi involvement and his profound philosophical antipathy to Heidegger's work. See: W.J. Richardson, 'The Irresponsible Subject', in *Ethics as First Philosophy: The Significance of Emmanuel Levinas for Philosophy, Literature and Religion*, ed. by A.T. Peperzak (New York: Routledge, 1995), pp. 123–31 (pp. 124–25).
42 E. Levinas, *God, Death, and Time* (Palo Alto, CA: Stanford University Press, 2000), pp. 121–23.
43 "Science itself, which must be considered as a reflection of being, comes from being". Ibid. p. 133.
44 Ibid. p. 124.
45 Ibid.
46 Ibid. pp. 124–25.
47 Levinas, *Emmanuel Levinas: Basic Philosophical Writings*, pp. 1–10.
48 To think God beyond being is the project of Jean-Luc Marion whose commentary is beyond the immediate focus of this book. See: J.-L. Marion, *God Without Being: Hors-Texte* (Chicago; London: University of Chicago Press, 1995).
49 Levinas, *God, Death, and Time*, p. 160.
50 P. Benson and K.L. O'Neill, 'Facing Risk: Levinas, Ethnography, and Ethics', *Anthropology of Consciousness*, 18 (2007), pp. 31–32.
51 J. Bloechl, *Liturgy of the Neighbor: Emmanuel Levinas and the Religion of Responsibility* (Pittsburgh, PA: Duquesne University Press, 1999), p. 132.
52 Ibid. p. 127.
53 Levinas, *Ethics and Infinity: Conversations with Philippe Nemo*, pp. 60–61.
54 Ibid. p. 59.
55 C. Barnett, 'Ways of Relating: Hospitality and the Acknowledgement of Otherness', *Progress in Human Geography*, 29 (2005), p. 9.
56 Levinas, *God, Death, and Time*, p. 138.
57 M.L. Morgan, *The Cambridge Introduction to Emmanuel Levinas* (Cambridge: Cambridge University Press, 2011), p. 8.
58 Derrida, *Adieu to Emmanuel Levinas*, p. 3.
59 Severson, *Levinas's Philosophy of Time: Gift, Responsibility, Diachrony, Hope*, p. 119.
60 E. Levinas, *The Levinas Reader*, ed. by S. Hand (Oxford: Basil Blackwell, 1989), p. 4.
61 Levinas, *Emmanuel Levinas: Basic Philosophical Writings*, p. X.
62 Moran, *Introduction to Phenomenology*, p. 329.
63 Levinas, *Entre Nous: On Thinking-of-the-Other*, p. 169. (My gender addition).
64 E.E. Gantt, 'Levinas, Psychotherapy, and the Ethics of Suffering', *Journal of Humanistic Psychology*, 40 (2000), p. 18.
65 My italics. Levinas, *God, Death, and Time*, p. 127.
66 Kearney to Levinas: "What do you think of when you think of the face of the other? He said, 'Christ', and I said, 'But you're a Jew', and he said, 'Yes. But Christ is the suffering Jew par excellence, for us Jews too'. He's one of us, kind of thing. And he said it in a wonderfully ecumenical way obviously". See: R. Kearney, 'The God Who May Be', in *Ideas*, with David Cayley (Toronto, Canada: Canadian Broadcasting Corporation, 2006), p. 19.
67 Levinas' play on Hamlet's words underscores his perspective that the question of being is always superseded by the *relationship* where the ethics of first philosophy rests. See: Levinas, *Ethics and Infinity: Conversations with Philippe Nemo*, p. 10.

128 *Levinas and the wholly/holy other*

68 E. Levinas, *Entre Nous: Essais Sur Le Penser-À-L'autre* (Paris: Bernard Grasset, 1991), p. 113.
69 Morgan, *The Cambridge Introduction to Emmanuel Levinas*, p. 3.
70 Ibid. p. 45.
71 E. Levinas, *Collected Philosophical Papers* (Dordrecht, The Netherlands Martinus Nijhoff, 1987), p. 171.
72 Moran, *Introduction to Phenomenology*, p. 322.
73 See: E. Levinas, *Time and the Other* (Pittsburgh, PA: Duquesne University Press, 1987), p. viii. For a lovely encapsulation of infinity and its presence as testimony, see also: Levinas, *Ethics and Infinity: Conversations with Philippe Nemo*, pp. 105–10.
74 The term "approach" is found throughout Levinas' work and denotes what is beyond volition or anticipation, or in Levinas' terms, beyond being, knowledge or the rational. The "approach" implies or evokes the neighbour, proximity, the infinite, the "saying" and, indeed, the Face whose impact upon me is unbidden and absolute. Levinas claims that "[t]o be on the ground of the signification of an approach is to be *with another* for or against a third party, with the other and the third party against oneself, in justice". See: E. Levinas, *Otherwise Than Being, or, Beyond Essence* (Pittsburgh, PA: Duquesne University Press, 1998), pp. 5, 11–12, 16, 24, 30, 36, 47–48.
75 Levinas, *Totality and Infinity: An Essay on Exteriority*, p. 78.
76 E. Levinas, *Nine Talmudic Readings* (Indianapolis: Indiana University Press, 1994), pp. 83–84.
77 Levinas, *Ethics and Infinity: Conversations with Philippe Nemo*, pp. 88–89.
78 Morgan, *The Cambridge Introduction to Emmanuel Levinas*, pp. 18–26.
79 Levinas, *Entre Nous: On Thinking-of-the-Other*, p. 106.
80 K. Weingarten, 'Immersed in America: Life after a Trip to South Africa', in *Ethical Ways of Being*, ed. by D. Kotze, et al. (Chagrin Falls, OH: Taos Publication/WorldShare Books, 2012), p. 32.
81 Levinas, *Entre Nous: On Thinking-of-the-Other*, p. 169.
82 Levinas, *Ethics and Infinity: Conversations with Philippe Nemo*, pp. 85–86.
83 Ibid. p. 86.
84 Levinas, *Entre Nous: On Thinking-of-the-Other*, p. 147.
85 Levinas, *God, Death, and Time*, pp. 163–64.
86 Morgan, *The Cambridge Introduction to Emmanuel Levinas*, p. 9.
87 Levinas, *Entre Nous: On Thinking-of-the-Other*, pp. 58–59.
88 Levinas, *Difficult Freedom: Essays on Judaism*, p. 102.
89 E. Levinas, *Entre Nous: On Thinking-of-the-Other*, pp. 185–86.
90 "Par excellence" is a verbal emphasis found repeatedly throughout Levinas' texts.
91 I have changed the gender from "him" to "her". Levinas, *Entre Nous: On Thinking-of-the-Other*, p. 227.
92 Levinas, *Entre Nous: On Thinking-of-the-Other*, pp. 130, 31, 48.
93 J. Caruana, 'Not Ethics, Not Ethics Alone, but the Holy', *Journal of Religious Ethics*, 34 (2006), p. 562.
94 Wright, Hughes, and Ainley, 'The Paradox of Morality: An Interview with Emmanuel Levinas', p. 179. See also: Levinas, *Entre Nous: On Thinking-of-the-Other*, p. 105.
95 See: Chapter 2, "Infra-humanisation, stigma and the heartsink patient", pp. 37–41. See also: C.C. Butler and M. Evans, 'The "Heartsink" Patient Revisited', *British Journal of General Practice*, 49 (1999).
96 A paraphrased translation is offered in this paragraph starting with "rapport" and ending with "Il y a comme un appel a moi" which, literally translated, means "there is like a call to me". See: Levinas, *Entre Nous: Essais Sur Le Penser-À-L'autre*, p. 114.

97 "An awakening to the other man, which is not knowledge", describes the enlightenment endowed by the face-to-face in Levinas' work. See: Levinas, *Entre Nous: On Thinking-of-the-Other*, pp. 168 and 88–89,12, 14, 18, 46, 220, 39, 40.
98 In noting the various permutations of post-metaphysical thought, which include "being-for-oneself, being- with-others or being-in-the-world, Cohen observes that Levinas placed precedence on "being-for-the-other-person" above all else including "being, essence, identity, manifestation, principle, in brief, over me". See: Levinas, *Ethics and Infinity: Conversations with Philippe Nemo*, p. 10.
99 Ibid. pp. 97–98.
100 Levinas, *Entre Nous: On Thinking-of-the-Other*, p. 149.
101 E. Levinas, 'Bad Conscience and the Inexorable', in *Face to Face with Levinas*, ed. by R.A. Cohen (Albany, NY: State University of New York Press, 1986), pp. 35–40 (pp. 38–39).
102 The "node" to which Eric Severson refers is discussed in Chapter 6: "Language, Levinas and mysticism".
103 Wright, Hughes, and Ainley, 'The Paradox of Morality: An interview with Emmanuel Levinas', p. 179.
104 Rubenstein, *Strange Wonder: The Closure of Metaphysics and the Opening of Awe*, pp. 9–11.
105 E. Levinas, 'Being in the Principle of War', in *Penser Aujourd'hui: Emmanuel Levinas,* (1991). < www.youtube.com/watch?v=-1MtMzXNGbs > See: 6.15–8.25 minutes.
106 Jantzen argues for the possibility of our divinisation by drawing on the work of Luce Irigaray and identifying the problem of systemic violence on Christianity's focus on life after death, at the expense of the living. See: Jantzen, *Becoming Divine: Towards a Feminist Philosophy of Religion*, p. 234.
107 Levinas, *God, Death, and Time*, p. 180.
108 Ibid. p. 181.
109 E. Levinas, 'Being in the Principle of War'. <www.youtube.com/watch?v=1MtMzXNGbs> [accessed 5 Dec. 2020].
110 Chanter, 'Introduction', p. 12.
111 Levinas, *Otherwise Than Being, or, Beyond Essence*, p. 72.
112 Levinas, *Ethics and Infinity: Conversations with Philippe Nemo*, p. 120.
113 Jantzen, *Becoming Divine: Towards a Feminist Philosophy of Religion*, p. 239.
114 In discussing the implications of the sixth commandment, Levinas clarifies its continuum of meaning, "which does not mean simply that you are not to go around firing a gun all the time... rather... that, in the course of your life in different ways, you kill someone. See: Wright, Hughes, and Ainley, 'The Paradox of Morality: An Interview with Emmanuel Levinas', p. 173.
115 Levinas, *Otherwise Than Being, or, Beyond Essence*, pp. 99–100.
116 "I leave the whole consoling side of this ethics to religion", Levinas claims, in acknowledging the difficulty of the responsibility ethics claims over me. See: Levinas, *Entre Nous: On Thinking-of-the-Other*, p. 108.
117 Derrida, *Adieu to Emmanuel Levinas*, p. 6.
118 Dueck notes the professional trap that necessitates the continual re-construal of the incomprehensible into the "explicable and natural". See: A. Dueck and T.D. Parsons, 'Ethics, Alterity, and Psychotherapy: A Levinasian Perspective', *Pastoral Psychology*, 55 (2007), p. 277.
119 Levinas, *Totality and Infinity: An Essay on Exteriority*, p. 247.
120 Levinas, *Ethics and Infinity: Conversations with Philippe Nemo*, p. 120.
121 Ibid. p. 98. See also: Levinas' critique of Martin Buber's concept of I and Thou as an essentially ontological event, relational though it may be in Levinas, *The Levinas Reader*, pp. 59–74.

122 Levinas, *God, Death, and Time*, p. 180.
123 Levinas, *Entre Nous: On Thinking-of-the-Other*, p. 105.
124 Derrida, *Adieu to Emmanuel Levinas*, p. 2.
125 Morgan, *Discovering Levinas*, pp. 155–60.
126 Levinas, *Entre Nous: On Thinking-of-the-Other*, p. 108.
127 Levinas, *Otherwise Than Being, or, Beyond Essence*, p. 18.
128 Ibid. p. 18.
129 Derrida, *Adieu to Emmanuel Levinas*, p. 42.
130 Levinas, *Difficult Freedom: Essays on Judaism*, p. 102.
131 S. Critchley, 'Five Problems in Levinas's View of Politics and the Sketch of a Solution to Them', *Political Theory*, 32 (2004), p. 172.
132 Ibid. p. 173.
133 These are fraternity, monotheism, androcentrism, filiality and the family, the State of Israel. See: Ibid. pp. 173–75.
134 See: "The church", pp. 116–117.
135 Ibid. p. 174.
136 L. Ma, 'All the Rest Must Be Translated: Levinas's Notion of Sense', *Journal of Chinese Philosophy*, 35 (2008), pp. 604–5.
137 Ibid. p. 600.
138 Ibid. pp. 602, 610.
139 Ibid. A reference is made here to the work of Bernasconi. p. 599.
140 Ibid. p. 599.
141 Ibid p. 604.
142 Ibid. p. 605.
143 Ibid. p. 606.
144 Ma refers to the term "European generosity" to identify its racially demeaning implications and clarify that those for whom she speaks are owed far more than a handout. See Levinas' use of this term: Ibid. p. 609.
145 One scholar, for example, has recently invoked Levinasian thought as a platform for political apology. See: B. Bahler, 'How Levinas Can (and Cannot) Help Us with Political Apology in the Context of Systemic Racism', *Religions*, 9 (2018), pp. 1–22.
146 R. Wolin, 'Levinas and Heidegger: The Anxiety of Influence', in *Heidegger's Jewish Followers: Essays on Hannah Arendt, Leo Strauss, Hans Jonas, and Emmanuel Levinas*, ed. by S. Fleischacker (Pittsburgh, PA: Duquesne University Press, 2008), p. 241.
147 Ibid. p. 238.
148 Ibid. p. 240.
149 Ibid. p. 237.
150 Ibid. p. 239.
151 Ibid. p. 241.
152 See: "Sharon", this chapter.
153 Ibid. p. 241.
154 Ibid. p. 243.
155 Chanter, 'Introduction', pp. 2–5. See also: C.E. Katz, 'Reinhabiting the House of Ruth', in *Feminist Interpretations of Emmanuel Levinas*, ed. by T. Chanter (University Park, PA: Pennsylvania State University, 2001), pp. 145–70.
156 See: L. Irigaray, 'The Fecundity of the Caress', in *Feminist Interpretations of Emmanuel Levinas*, ed. by T. Chanter (University Park, PA: Pennsylvania State University Press, 2001), pp. 119–44.
157 See: Chapter 7, "A Ride on the Mule of Wonder", pp. 184–6.
158 Jantzen, *Becoming Divine: Towards a Feminist Philosophy of Religion*, pp. 241–42.

159 Chanter, 'Introduction', pp. 32–56.
160 See, for example: M. Joy, 'Levinas: Alterity, the Feminine and Women-A Meditation', *Studies in Religion/Sciences Religieuses*, 22 (1993).
161 E.P. Ziarek, 'The Ethical Passions of Emmanuel Levinas', in *Feminist Interpretations of Emmanuel Levinas*, ed. by T. Chanter (University Park, PA: Pennsylvania State University Press, 2001), pp. 78–95.
162 Wolin, 'Levinas and Heidegger', pp. 243–244.
163 Levinas, *Otherwise Than Being, or, Beyond Essence*, p. 59 (my gender additions in brackets).
164 Levinas, *Totality and Infinity: An Essay on Exteriority*, p. 51.
165 Levinas, *Emmanuel Levinas: Basic Philosophical Writings*, pp. 7–11.
166 "I am a testimony, or a trace, or the glory of the Infinite", see: Levinas, *Collected Philosophical Papers*, p. 170.
167 Levinas apparently referred frequently in later years to Vasily Grossman's historical novel about Nazism and Stalinism. He alludes to Grossman's description of people lined up at a gate in the hopes of hearing word about their arrested friends: "each reading on the nape of the person in front of him the feelings and hopes of his misery". See: Morgan, *The Cambridge Introduction to Emmanuel Levinas*, p. 19.
168 Levinas, *Emmanuel Levinas: Basic Philosophical Writings*, pp. X-XI.
169 Ibid. p. XI.
170 Chanter, "Introduction", p. 8.
171 Levinas, *Ethics and Infinity: Conversations with Philippe Nemo*, p. 90.
172 Levinas, *Entre Nous: On Thinking-of-the-Other*, p. 121.
173 Caruana, 'Not Ethics, Not Ethics Alone, but the Holy'.

References

Atterton, P., and Calarco, M., 'Editors' Introduction: The Third Wave of Levinas Scholarship', in *Radicalizing Levinas*, ed. by P. Atterton and M. Calarco (Albany, NY: State University of New York Press, 2010).

Bahler, B., 'How Levinas Can (and Cannot) Help Us with Political Apology in the Context of Systemic Racism', *Religions*, 9 (2018), 1–22. https://doi.org/10.3390/rel9110370

Barnett, C., 'Ways of Relating: Hospitality and the Acknowledgement of Otherness', *Progress in Human Geography*, 29 (2005), 5–21. https://doi.org/10.1191/0309132505ph535oa

Benson, P., and O'Neill, K.L., 'Facing Risk: Levinas, Ethnography, and Ethics', *Anthropology of Consciousness*, 18 (2007), 29–55. https://doi.org/10.1525/ac.2007.18.2.29

Bloechl, J., *Liturgy of the Neighbor: Emmanuel Levinas and the Religion of Responsibility* (Pittsburgh, PA: Duquesne University Press, 1999).

Butler, C.C., and Evans, M., 'The "Heartsink" Patient Revisited', *British Journal of General Practice*, 49 (1999), 230–33.

Caruana, J., 'Not Ethics, Not Ethics Alone, but the Holy', *Journal of Religious Ethics*, 34 (2006), 561–83. https://doi.org/10.1111/j.1467-9795.2006.00285.x

Chanter, T., 'Feminism and the Other', in *The Provocation of Levinas: Rethinking the Other*, ed. by R. Bernasconi and D. Wood (London; New York: Routledge, 1988), pp. 32–56.

———, 'Introduction', in *Feminist Interpretations of Emmanuel Levinas* (University Park, PA: Pennsylvania State University Press, 2001), pp. 32–56.

Critchley, S., 'Five Problems in Levinas's View of Politics and the Sketch of a Solution to Them', *Political Theory*, 32 (2004), 172–85. https://doi.org/10.1177/0090591703261771

——, 'Introduction', in *The Cambridge Companion Levinas*, ed. by S. Critchley and R. Bernasconi (Cambridge: Cambridge University Press, 2002), pp. 1–32.Derrida, J., *Adieu to Emmanuel Levinas* (Palo Alto, CA: Stanford University Press, 1999).

Dueck, A., and Parsons, T.D., 'Ethics, Alterity, and Psychotherapy: A Levinasian Perspective', *Pastoral Psychology*, 55 (2007), 271–82. https://doi.org/10.1007/s11089-006-0045-y

Gantt, E.E., 'Levinas, Psychotherapy, and the Ethics of Suffering', *Journal of Humanistic Psychology*, 40 (2000), 9–28. https://doi.org/10.1177/0022167800403002

Goodman, D., and Freeman, M., eds., *Psychology and the Other* (Oxford: Oxford University Press, 2015).

Hand, S., *Emmanuel Levinas*, ed. R. Eaglestone, Routledge Critical Thinkers (London; New York: Routledge, 2009).

Irigaray, L., 'The Fecundity of the Caress', in *Feminist Interpretations of Emmanuel Levinas*, ed. by T. Chanter (University Park, PA: Pennsylvania State University Press, 2001), pp. 119–44.

Jantzen, G., *Becoming Divine: Towards a Feminist Philosophy of Religion* (Bloomington; Indianapolis: Indiana University Press, 1999).

Joy, M., 'Levinas: Alterity, the Feminine and Women: A Meditation', *Studies in Religion/Sciences Religieuses*, 22 (1993), 463–85. https://doi.org/10.1177/000842989402200405

Katz, C.E., 'Reinhabiting the House of Ruth', in *Feminist Interpretations of Emmanuel Levinas*, ed. by T. Chanter (University Park, PA: Pennsylvania State University, 2001), pp. 145–70.

Kearney, R., 'The God Who May Be', with David Cayley, *CBC Ideas* (Toronto, Canada: Canadian Broadcasting Corporation, 2006), pp. 1–22. www.cbc.ca/player/play/1473879684

Levinas, E., 'Bad Conscience and the Inexorable', in *Face to Face with Levinas*, ed. by R.A. Cohen (Albany, NY: State University of New York Press, 1986), pp. 35–40.

——, 'Being in the Principle of War in Penser Aujourd'hui: Emmanuel Levinas', 1991. www.youtube.com/watch?v=-1MtMzXNGbs

——, *Collected Philosophical Papers*, Vol. 100, trans. A. Lingis (Dordrecht, The Netherlands: Martinus Nijhoff, 1987).

——, *Difficult Freedom: Essays on Judaism*, trans. S. Hand (Baltimore: Johns Hopkins University Press, 1990).

——, *Emmanuel Levinas: Basic Philosophical Writings* (Bloomington; Indianapolis: Indiana University Press, 1996).

——, *Entre Nous: Essais Sur Le Penser-À-L'autre* (Paris: Bernard Grasset, 1991).

——, *Entre Nous: On Thinking-of-the-Other*, trans. M.B. Smith and B. Harshav (New York: Cambridge University Press, 1998).

——, *Ethics and Infinity: Conversations with Philippe Nemo*, trans. R.A. Cohen (Pittsburgh, PA: Duquesne University Press, 1985).

——, *God, Death, and Time*, trans. B. Bergo (Palo Alto, CA: Stanford University Press, 2000).

——, *Nine Talmudic Readings*, Vol. 876 (Bloomington, IN: Indiana University Press, 1994).

——, *Otherwise Than Being, or, Beyond Essence*, trans. Alphonso Lingis (Pittsburgh, PA: Duquesne University Press, 1998).
——, *The Levinas Reader*, ed. S. Hand (Oxford: Basil Blackwell, 1989).
——, *Time and the Other*, trans. R.A. Cohen (Pittsburgh, PA: Duquesne University Press, 1987).
——, *Totality and Infinity: An Essay on Exteriority*, trans. Alphonso Lingis (The Hague; Boston; London: Martinus Nijhoff, 1979).
Levinas, E., and Kearney, R., 'Dialogue with Emmanuel Levinas', in *Face to Face with Levinas*, ed. by R.A. Cohen (Albany, NY: State University of New York Press, 1986), pp. 13–33.
Loughlin, G., 'Other Discourses', *New Blackfriars*, 75 (1994), 18–31. https://doi.org/10.1111/j.1741-2005.1994.tb01463.x
Ma, L., 'All the Rest Must Be Translated: Levinas's Notion of Sense', *Journal of Chinese Philosophy*, 35 (2008), 599–612. https://doi.org /10.1111/j.1540-6253.2008.00506.x
MacNaughton, J., 'Medical Humanities' Challenge to Medicine', *Journal of Evaluation in Clinical Practice*, 17 (2011), 927–32. https://doi.org/10.1111/j.1365-2753.2011.01728.x
Malka, S., *Emmanuel Levinas: His Life and Legacy*, trans. M. Kigel and S.M. Embree, (Pittsburgh, PA: Duquesne University Press, 2006).
Marion, J.L., *God Without Being: Hors-Texte* (Chicago; London: University of Chicago Press, 1995).
Moran, D., *Introduction to Phenomenology* (London; New York: Routledge, 2000).
Morgan, M.L., *Discovering Levinas* (Cambridge: Cambridge University Press, 2007).
——, *The Cambridge Introduction to Emmanuel Levinas* (Cambridge: Cambridge University Press, 2011).
Orange, D., 'Commentary on Pizer: The Refugee in the Kitchen-Variations on Hineni and Stuart Pizer's Grandfather', in *Psychology and the Other*, ed. by D. Goodman and M. Freeman (Oxford: Oxford University Press, 2015), pp. 212–18. doi:10.1093/acprof:oso/9780199324804.003.0014
Reimer, K., 'Natural Character: Psychological Realism for the Downwardly Mobile', *Theology and Science*, 2 (2004), 89–107. https://doi.org/10.1080/1474670042000196630
Richardson, W.J., 'The Irresponsible Subject', in *Ethics as First Philosophy: The Significance of Emmanuel Levinas for Philosophy, Literature and Religion*, ed. by A.T. Peperzak (New York: Routledge, 1995), pp. 123–31.
Rubenstein, M.J., 'Dionysius, Derrida, and the Critique of "Ontotheology"', *Modern Theology*, 24 (2008), 725–41. https://doi.org/10.1111/j.1468-0025.2008.00496.x
Sayre, G., 'Toward a Therapy for the Other', *European Journal of Psychotherapy & Counselling*, 7 (2005), 37–47. https://doi.org/10.1080/13642530500087187
Severson, E., *Levinas's Philosophy of Time: Gift, Responsibility, Diachrony, Hope* (Pittsburgh, PA: Duquesne University Press, 2013).
Weingarten, K., 'Immersed in America: Life After a Trip to South Africa', in *Ethical Ways of Being*, ed. by D. Kotze, J. Myburg, J. Roux and Associates (Chagrin Falls, OH: Taos Publication/WorldShare Books, 2012), pp. 25–36.
Williams, R.N., 'Self-Betraying Emotions and the Psychology of Heteronomy', *European Journal of Psychotherapy & Counselling*, 7 (2005), 7–16. https://doi.org/10.1080/13642530500087351
Wolin, R., 'Levinas and Heidegger: The Anxiety of Influence', in *Heidegger's Jewish Followers: Essays on Hannah Arendt, Leo Strauss, Hans Jonas, and Emmanuel

Levinas, ed. by S. Fleischacker (Pittsburgh, PA: Duquesne University Press, 2008), pp. 219–244.

Wright, T., Hughes, P., and Ainley, A., 'The Paradox of Morality: An Interview with Emmanuel Levinas', in *The Provocation of Levinas: Rethinking the Other*, ed. by R. Bernasconi and D. Wood, trans. by A. Benjamin and T. Wright (London; New York: Routledge, 1988), pp. 168–80.

Young, J., *Heidegger, Philosophy, Nazism* (Cambridge: Cambridge University Press, 1998). https://doi.org/10.1017/CBO9780511583322

Ziarek, E.P., 'The Ethical Passions of Emmanuel Levinas', in *Feminist Interpretations of Emmanuel Levinas*, ed. by T. Chanter (University Park, PA: Pennsylvania State University Press, 2001), pp. 78–95.

6 Clinical application and beyond: The function of the holy

It is to the function of the holy, the language Levinas used to conjure it, and examples of research currently attempting to "apply" his epiphanic ethics that we now turn. Levinas' ethical vision illustrates how our orientation to mental health and therapy is creating more harm than good, is inadequate to the task or no longer relevant. It shows that our construal of mental illness is operating out of an outmoded paradigm that fails to address the real issues and injustices in people's lives.[1] But translating Levinas into praxis remains problematic, although emerging scholarship is helping us imagine Levinas' ethics into practice.

The first half of this chapter reviews the role of the holy in the context of community mental health and the "dazzling" responsibility to which the clinician finds herself "ordained" and "held hostage". We will consider the influence of early mysticism on the linguistic strategies Levinas employed to overcome the vortex of ontology and claim the primacy of the relational. We will also examine the intersection of mysticism in psychiatry and clinical practice to explore its connections and disjunctions with Levinas' vision. The last half of the chapter examines the "possible/impossible" of clinical application, beginning with disgraced Canadian humanitarian Jean Vanier, whose work had offered such promise in reflecting the "possible" of Levinas' vision. The chapter concludes with examples of the work of theorists and therapists engaging with Levinas in theory and practice. Their efforts confront institutional dehumanisation and challenge the theoretical mainstays of psychology towards *re*-moralising the field as a whole.

The function of the holy revisited

Simon Critchley neatly summarises the "one big thing" that drove Levinas' entire philosophy, which, across the evolution of his work and the subjects, arguments, and language he used to evoke it, comes to this: "[E]thics is first philosophy, where ethics is understood as a relation of infinite responsibility to the other person".[2] The sum of Levinas' project was this, and he developed it in the shadow of the "useless suffering"[3] wreaked by the Holocaust. Through it, he animated the unassailability and pre-eminence of this infinite responsibility to identify the roots of totalising violence and its subversion, in the possibility of a particular relationship.

As we saw in Chapter 5, Sharon's story lays bare the ultimate nature of this relationship by clarifying the oversight of institutional violence found in the de-moralised clinician's "wonder blindness"—*and* guilt. This "particular" relationship is the *entire* argument for the holy—*and* its meaning—in secular clinical praxis, from which all other possible "functions" or "applications" flow as tributaries from a source. Severson notes that "[f]or Levinas, philosophy begins in the midst of violence and disappointment, but points towards a primordial peace, the echo of which still reverberates in the face of the other, that face that cries out, Do not kill me".[4] This is Sharon's face "par excellence".

When I confess to Sharon that her presence in my office moves me to tears, I acknowledge my own abjection in the face of the holy that floods our space and my awareness with a revelation of kinship and tenderness I crave and fear. "I myself lose self-certainty and self-assured mastery, confronted with the Other which calls my categories into question by not fitting tidily into them".[5] More devastatingly, *I* am called into question, very personally, as precisely and enigmatically as Levinas claims. In the light of this holiness, my clinical role is transmuted from a label, a function, a job, to an ultimate bond. The help seeker's height and proximity tell me so.

Height and proximity were important signifiers in Levinas' lexicon that give language to his ethical vision. "[T]he ascendency of the other is exercised upon the same to the point of interrupting it, leaving it speechless".[6] What Levinas calls "the same" alludes to ontology and the reductive violation I *myself* enact unknowingly—unconsciously as a sleepwalker—on the help seeker who always exceeds me. Even while I cling to my authority and the delusion of my neutrality and innocence as a "clinician", it is the ontological reduction hidden in plain sight that renders me speechless when the contrast with the help seeker's *height* rectifies my perspective. "Height stands as the dimension of perfection, largely because of the asymmetry and the general sense of the escape of the other from my horizon".[7] As his work evolved, Levinas shifted his emphasis on height to *proximity* to avoid limiting the notion of the transcendent. Height does not evoke ethical transcendence, Levinas cautions, as much as the idea of closeness. Hence, the *approach* of the face or the nearness of the Other—and the responsibility this implies.[8]

> The relationship of proximity cannot be reduced to any modality of distance or geometrical contiguity, nor to the simple 'representation' of a neighbour; it is already an assignation, an extremely urgent assignation—an obligation, anachronously prior to any commitment.[9]

Importantly, proximity *never* implies "mutuality" or "reciprocity.[10] Nor does it reflect the I and Thou relation for which Levinas chided Buber, because the ethical relationship "is more than an empty contact which may always be renewed and of which spiritual friendship is the apogee".[11] There is no mutuality or equivalency to be found in Levinas' relational transaction as an imaginary meeting point of "equals" discovered somewhere between the downward trajectory of the awed clinician and the upward trajectory of the ascending—*transcending*—vulnerable Other. But regardless how "elevated" the help seeker may *seem* before the "speechless" clinician, or the degree of hallowed proximity involved, it remains within the clinicians' capacity, if not her jurisdiction and mandate, to violate and assume.[12] Nonetheless, my responsibility *is* unilateral and unequivocal—trumped by any question of reciprocity.[13]

In Levinasian terms, the holy infers anarchy. "[P]roximity is *anarchically* a relationship with a singularity without the mediation of any principle, any ideality", that "concretely corresponds to my relationship with my neighbour".[14] This singularity represents what is both beyond me and unutterably intimate—an assignation!—as that which Levinas signifies as Other, God, the transcendent, the trace, the *holy*. Levinas captures the nature of the insurrection through his language. Thus, anarchy "troubles being"; it is "persecution" and "obsession", the latter leading to what Levinas calls a "defection" of the ego from consciousness, which constitutes the very "inversion" of consciousness.[15] Interestingly, this anarchy upends everything—but not as disorder, for "[d]isorder is but another order and what is diffuse is thematisable".[16] Hence, anarchy "brings to a halt the ontological play which. . . is consciousness".[17] For Levinas, "ontology" always refers to "any relation to otherness that is reducible to comprehension or understanding".[18] The work of overcoming this ontological bind is accomplished, Levinas cautions, by the "refusal to allow oneself to be tamed or domesticated by a theme".[19]

By heeding this anarchical Face and resisting—or attempting to resist—the domesticating influence of the status quo, we might presume or hope that the holy will infiltrate the chinks in the ontological armour of clinical implacability. Even a momentary illumination in an environment where violence is normalised and hidden by the very language of *care* and *empathy* it employs, can open the clinician to another, better, way. But it is always a choice, and the demands are significant because they call for the clinician's unilateral *disarmament* and the redirection of her agency "for" the other.

Language and the holy

Is Levinas' language too obscure for our purposes? Donna Orange wonders if his vision is too extreme for clinical practice, suggesting it might point to one's masochism or messianic grandiosity to wish to carry, if only briefly, the anguish of the help seeker. But as Orange also observes, if we were fundamentally *for* ourselves, which Levinas identified as the crucial error and basis of Sartre's "teleological project", along with "all of Western ontology",[20] then the one-for-the-other at the centre of Levinasian ethics would not even be possible.[21] "For" is the operative word, Levinas insists. "My responsibility for the other is the *for* of the relationship".[22]

> In the expression "the one-for-the-other," the "for-" cannot be reduced to the reference of one thing said [un dit] to another said [un autre dit], or of one theme to another. To make that claim would be to remain with the idea of signification as a Said. But we are going to look for what signification might mean as Saying.
> The "for-" is the way in which *woman*/man approaches *her*/his neighbour, the way in which a relationship with the other is set up that is no longer proportionate to the one. It is a relationship of nearness where the responsibility of the one for the other is played out.[23]

In his riff on the simple word "for", we discover the obscurity and play of Levinas' language and its imperative drive towards the other, which is as enigmatic and non-linear as it is absolute. This "for" is imbued with all the gravitas of Levinas' transcendent vision that he translates as a phenomenologist. He does not develop his work through argumentation, but through "semi-poetic, rhapsodic and grammatically elusive meditations around certain central intuitions or metaphors" to evoke the paradox—the *epiphany*—to which his ethics always point.[24] Paul Davies observes that Levinas' "ethical language" actually prohibits an exit from "the scene of an enigma" by indefinitely extending the paradox, which points back to philosophy's failure but never toward the answers we seek from his moral edict.[25] This enigma also stymies the efforts of researchers attempting to develop clinical "applications" based on Levinas' vision. The problem is that even the *idea* of "legitimate scientific research" or theory, essentially totalises Levinas' project, which is to *subvert* any such reductive endeavours.[26] Given the magnitude of this enigma, Levinasian scholars are of two minds as to whether it can be even calibrated as a human response worthy of the call. Levinas himself suggests that the answer lies in "maturity and patience for insoluble problems", while conceding that to say as much is a "pathetic formula".[27]

> I do not know how to draw the solution to insoluble problems. It is still sleeping in the bottom of a box; but a box over which persons who have drawn close to each other keep watch. I have no idea other than the idea of the idea that one should have. . . . I have the idea of a possibility in which the impossible may be sleeping.[28]

While the impossible sleeps, clinical researchers attempting to apply Levinas' work all risk re-inscribing the violence his vision seeks to disrupt. Interestingly, current efforts to address clinical reduction through an engagement with spirituality and theology in psychiatry, confront similar challenges. Given mysticism's enduring appeal to the collective imagination and its subversive implications, the following digression on the intersection of mystical experience and psychopathology offers additional context to Levinas' ethical project and his use of language.

Mystical experience and mysticism

A thread on "mystical experience" in psychological literature examines the connection of spiritual and religious experience with psychosis and forms part of the emerging field on spirituality, theology and health.[29] It is an unlikely discourse, given science's historical distrust and ambivalence towards the theological, although the debate rages on and, as Jantzen reminds us:

> Whether we like it or not the biblical texts and religion built upon them have shaped the consciousness of Western civilisation; and we cannot, without violence to ourselves, cut ourselves off from our own formation. We can only struggle with it and against it: we ignore it at our peril.[30]

The interface between spirituality, religion and psychosis reflects the ongoing and profound neglect of spirituality in clinical practice. Jackson and Fulford suggest that medicating or pathologising spiritual or mystical experience is as unethical as withholding treatment from someone with legitimate mental illness.[31] But the legitimacy—or accuracy—of such "experience" is still in question and not easily resolved. Concepts like spirituality, psychopathology and even "psychosis" also vary in meaning, leaving the problem of definition unresolved. Adding further confusion, the research falls roughly into three camps representing pro and anti-psychiatry orientations. Thus, some clinicians fail to recognise any overlap between the pathological and the spiritual. Others pathologise any spiritual experience, and still others tend to see all pathology as spiritually based, including proponents like R. D. Laing and others like him who are anti-psychiatry.[32] Equally important, Christopher Cook notes, "the relevance... of mysticism to psychiatry extends beyond issues of diagnosis and treatment", because the community itself is impoverished "where psychiatry colludes in pathologising such experiences".[33]

Not unlike Levinas' work, research on spirituality, theology and mental health challenges the boundaries of the dominant discourse by interrogating clinical power and what constitutes pathology—and "treatment". It does so at considerable cost to the ineffable notions under examination, for these are necessarily *reduced* by the scientific models to which they must conform by being "operationalised" to fit within a reductive framework.[34] This exploding field of research is also innovative, professionally risky and controversial in drawing on scholars like William James, Evelyn Underhill and Walter Stace, among others, whose work has significantly influenced modern psychology's understanding of "mystical experience".[35] Thus, we discover Ralph Hood's innovative mysticism scale[36] informed by the work of Walter Stace.[37] More recent scales have been developed to identify and measure similar "exceptional" experience.[38] Other clinical literature cites William James' four main characteristics of mystical experience[39] to help legitimise bona fide mystical "experience". Elsewhere, Cook, employs Evelyn Underhill's concept of mysticism to appeal to psychiatry to broaden its perspective beyond pathology.[40] It is also true that Williams, Underhill and Stace offer but a fragment of the mystical canon they explore, although the contribution of these scholars is largely undisputed. Interestingly, the pioneering work on "mystical experience with psychotic features"[41] was among the first in challenging the *DSM IV*[42] to recognise and preserve the legitimacy of such experience in 1985.[43] Since then, the robust emergence of research on spirituality, religion and mental health worldwide has become as diverse as it is fascinating and heatedly political.[44]

Our fascination with mystical "experience", however, does not closely reflect the accounts of the early mystics where this kind of apprehension was understated—or not even mentioned. The origins of mysticism emerge from the work of an unknown writer named Dionysius the Areopagite, who produced a body of texts composed in the fifth or sixth century that continues to inform our interest in mysticism today. Mark McIntosh claims that Dionysius is unfairly blamed for shifting the early practice of mystical theology to what has become the modernised interpretation of an individual ecstatic experience we call "mystical". But this should not be mistaken for the original meaning of ekstasis (ecstasy), which was "a standing outside oneself to be all the more available to the beloved".[45] The rapturous beauty of Dionysius' language, expressed in one of his most famous passages, is evidence of the timeless appeal of a phenomenon now being explored by psychiatry and the project of mental health:

> The divine longing (theios erōs) is Good seeking good for the sake of good. That yearning (erōs) which creates all the goodness of the world preexisted superabundantly within the Good and did not allow it to remain without issue. . . . This divine yearning brings ecstasy so that the lover belongs not to the self but to the beloved.[46]

It is also true that early mysticism had a more integrated, communal and coherent context that focused on a lifelong commitment to spiritual practice and asceticism. The path to the knowledge of God was through the arduous journey of purgation, illumination and contemplation, or union, with God. A more accurate description of "mysticism" might be understood as "contemplation", which "in earlier eras referred to the most intimate and transforming encounter with God", while the term "mysticism" might be considered an "academic invention".[47] Other accounts describe mysticism as "a part or element of religion. . . as a process or way of life. . . an attempt to express a direct consciousness of the presence of God".[48] Mysticism describes a quality of consciousness that "allows us to see the mystical element of religion as a process, a form of life, and not merely as a matter of raw experience, even of some special kind".[49] Affective mysticism also represents "a particular form of discourse... a source for doing theology... a certain type of knowing... a kind of intersubjectivity, and a set of texts from a variety of traditions requiring a complex hermeneutics".[50] As we can see, the contemporary reinterpretation of mysticism as an "experience" has annihilated its religious and historical significance and uprooted its social, cultural and communal origins and function.

The evolving field of spirituality, theology and health and the discourse on mystical experience have, nonetheless, opened up a remarkable space where clinical reduction and our perspective of the help seeker are being challenged. This space invites a re-consideration of the professional prohibitions of "loving", where the clinical implications of the "holy" might be clarified and the psycho-spiritual needs, values and "lived experience" of clinical populations properly dignified. That said, the discourse on "mystical experience" in mental health care is not engaged in the ethical relationship that Levinas' vision informs. Nor does it explore the nature of the *wonder-full* phenomena that clinicians encounter in their relational work with those labelled "mentally ill". Regrettably, the personal perspective of the clinician remains virtually unreported in this literature. Research on spirituality, theology and mental health is also primarily quantitative, focused on definition, pathology and the perspective of the help seeker. This does not diminish the significance of this field of inquiry or the value of its remarkable and growing contribution. Introducing a wild card like "mystical experience" into clinical research represents a bold and humanising project—not unlike Levinas' ethical vision. But here the similarity ends.[51]

Language, Levinas and mysticism

> *It is a dazzling, where the eye takes more than it can hold, an igniting of the skin, which touches and does not touch what is beyond the graspable, and burns. It is a passivity or a passion in which desire can be recognised, in which the "more in the less" awakens by its most ardent, noblest and most ancient flame a thought given over to thinking more than it thinks.*[52]

Levinas' ethical vision is highly allergic to *any* construal of the mystical or its "experience". Despite his own use of paradox, hyperbole and exaggeration,[53] which often reads like mystical poetry, Levinas mistrusted poetry, associating it with "mystification, pagan magic, and sorcery".[54] He insisted that transcendence related exclusively to the *holy* but not the *sacred*, to which he ascribed a kind of ecstatic affective experience that he believed seduces the self away from its real purpose. Caruana's analysis examines the connection between ethics and the holy in Levinas' work, relating it to the primary teaching of Judaism that links the human other and "the saintliness of God" to the maintenance of our human bond.[55] Holiness is corrupted, Levinas insisted, when the transporting ecstasy of the sacred and its solitary drive towards the divine derails us from our path towards the other, becoming, once again, a "form of violence".[56] Levinas' concern about the dangers of affectivity echoes those Christian theologians who decry the contemporary definition of the mystical as "an experience" that is reduced by the self for its own gratification. Whereas, transcendence is that which is fulfilled by the ethical terms of my obligation to my neighbour.

Nonetheless, the *language* of early mysticism was of considerable interest to Levinas, as it was to those postmodern philosophers who have turned to the linguistic strategies of negative—apophatic—theology to look pointedly for an apprehension capable of *transcending* the subject-object distinction.[57] This distinction concerns the seemingly intractable issue of *how* to extricate the "object" from the reductions of the "subject" and is highly relevant here. The object in this discussion is the vulnerable help seeker, and the subject the clinician who observes, distances, labels, objectifies and in some real ways *owns* the object of her scrutiny. Levinas sought to interrogate and subvert this distinction through language that has been criticised for its obscurity[58] and sometimes delirious excess aimed at protecting the uncontainable Other.[59] Derrida described Levinas' words as being "carried away" in a "discourse that opens each signification to its other".[60] Michael Morgan has suggested that Levinas used this form of language to illustrate the inadequacy of earlier arguments made by philosophers from Descartes to Heidegger, and to shock his reader into another way of seeing.[61] Amy Hollywood might suggest this kind of language is purposeful because it *preaches*.[62] It also *prays* as Critchley reminds us, because "the face-to-face relation with the other is not a relation of perception or vision, but is always linguistic... not something I see, but something I speak to". Levinas described it as "'expression', 'invocation' and 'prayer'".[63]

We find in Levinas' language, linguistic strategies that "provoke the collapse of binary language"[64] by creating a space for the writer—and *reader*—to apprehend and testify to an event *beyond being*. This, "despite the constraints of social, political and ecclesial structures"[65] against which some early so-called mystics famously resisted—including two of the greatest apophatic theologians from the late 13th and early 14th centuries, Meister Eckhart and Marguerite Porete.[66] One such strategy is found in the themes of "unsaying" and "the saying and the said", which, as Levinas' work matured, emerged through his increasingly paradoxical language and explicit attempts at "unsaying the said".[67] In "the said", the Other is already reduced, assimilated, thematised and waiting to be reborn in the "saying" through the immediacy of the human encounter where one person can address another in such terms as: "After you, sir". Sociality as simple as this testifies to the condition of being held hostage to the other. In Levinasian terms, "the saying", which is fundamentally and always goodness, friendship and hospitality, *recuperates* the "said".[68] These are the deterrents of ontology. The act of "saying" describes a "primordial passivity" that shows my beginnings start with the other who precedes me and to whom I am bound "in obligation to a responsibility that did not begin with me".[69] How and where the saying and the said connect is more elusive, Severson admits.

> [T]here is no *how* that explains this node of contact between the saying and the said; it is beyond the reach of philosophical investigation.... This node makes the impossible possible. Despite its predisposition to violence and economy, fleshed bodies can nevertheless be sites for the irruption of the holy.[70]

Bernard McGinn's work on the language of love in mysticism offers another perspective on Levinas' evocations of desire, need and tenderness.[71] The connection between ineffability and the erotic language of love in some mystical literature describes the wonder-full encounter with the divine as akin to falling in love, or being in love.[72] Here also is where the language of paradox is employed "in the delicate game of creating strategies" to allow us to express what "lies outside of the normal canons of speech".[73] Paradox, with its complicated stylistic devices, is used to subvert and disrupt the limitations of language, and the reader's psychological defences, enabling the writer to *evoke* the very states of consciousness in the reader she is attempting to translate.[74]

The connection between the erotic and the evocation of the divine in mystical literature is still under scrutiny, although in Christianity and Judaism this connection reflected a view of God as both lover and love. Thus, the early influence of the *Song of Songs* was—among other interpretations—understood to describe the relationship of God to the individual.[75] Far from representing some distant abstraction of goodness, or sexual sublimation, these evocations translate something transcendent and deeply personal. The embodiment of such desire is not necessarily more important than other forms of love, McGinn observes, but possibly more powerful in its evocation and more valuable for that reason.[76] Some mystical writers are infamous for the language of erotic love they used to capture the ineffable—a quality beyond "the usual categories of knowing and loving".[77]

Levinas' writing bears the hallmark of the apophatic—negative theology—in its epiphanies and paradoxes that strain towards the ineffable, the cerebral, the wordless, the transcendent. Yet, his visceral, super-charged evocations also conjure the "sensory impressions" of affective—kataphatic—mysticism[78] which is emotional, effusive, *embodied* and immanent.[79] Levinas fully understood the implications of the language he employed to point to worlds *beyond*. One of his best known interpreters, Richard Cohen, has observed that Levinas

144 *Clinical application and beyond*

acknowledged that *only* language had the power to "break the continuity of being or of history".[80]

Clinical application or impossibility
Jean Vanier: A cautionary tale of a failed saint

Having examined the function and language of the holy, we now turn to possible exemplars and examples of Levinasian ethics in praxis, beginning with Jean Vanier. His work and life were to have comprised the entire first half of this chapter until the stunning news of his sexual abuses came to light following his death. I have substantially abbreviated Vanier's story but include it here as a cautionary tale. It serves as a sober reminder that the most transcendent language, devout adherence to spiritual practice and charity, and the warmth and charm that can enlist a global army to its cause may still hide a great darkness. This is the darkness that rests in ontology's totalising violence to which Levinas' work fully attests.

Vanier was known as a Canadian humanitarian, theologian and philosopher[81] and was the son of one of Canada's former governor generals, Georges Vanier, and mother, Pauline.[82] He dedicated his life to the cause of intellectually disabled adults and to extending, he claimed, an experiment of peacemaking into the world made possible by sharing one's life with the weak.[83] He was well connected to the global community, and his contribution to the dialogue on peacemaking was considerable.[84] Admittedly, his conservative Catholicism influenced his stand on abortion[85] as well as his reported evasion of issues related to advancing women's role in the Catholic Church,[86] and his psychological interpretation of homosexuality as deviance.[87] But this conservatism was mitigated by his refreshing counter-cultural vision that appeared to resist institutional dehumanisation. He was a hero who stood on the margins with those he championed. Seemingly without blemish, his public profile was irreproachable, and even before his death, it was expected he would be canonised.

Raised a devout Catholic,[88] Vanier was deeply influenced by his mother's spiritual director and Dominican priest, Thomas Philippe, who was accused in 2014, well after his death, of sexually abusing a significant number of women in his role as spiritual director over almost three decades.[89] Vanier was shocked. How could this be? This put into question the well-rehearsed story of L'Arche and how Philippe had prompted Vanier towards his vocation during a summer sabbatical in France when Vanier was away from his work as a young philosophy professor at the University of Toronto. Philippe had introduced Vanier to the plight of the intellectually disabled in a local psychiatric hospital and, horrified by the dehumanisation he found there, Vanier felt "called" to address the injustice. He and Philippe subsequently established a home with two men from this hospital to live with them in a run-down house they called L'Arche (The

Arc) in the hopes of re-humanising their lives. But soon, the story goes, Vanier's relationship with these men revealed his need *for them* as he began, in their company, to grapple with his own "human weakness" and "longings".[90] This is the weakness, he said, that "carries within it a secret power. The cry and the trust that flow from weakness can open up hearts. The one who is weaker can call forth powers of love in the one who is stronger".[91] It was an idealised story that fulfilled the need of the many who were touched by it.

Vanier's person and project seemed to reflect the highest ideals of Levinasian thought, philosophically, theologically, politically and practically. Both Levinas and Vanier appeared to share an incontestable rationality arguing for the abandonment of the self for the other as the only way through the problem of violence and dehumanisation. Both embraced a view of the transcendent irreducible other, albeit from differing perspectives, to inform arguments that seemed to reach similar and passionate conclusions. Like Levinas, Vanier consistently attested to the ineffable in calling his adherents to abandon the culture of competition and become "downwardly mobile".[92] He drew liberally and compellingly on biblical allusions, the notion of Jesus's presence in the other and on the stories of intellectually disabled individuals who had forged his awareness and life. Vanier's writing was nothing like Levinas' prophetic and obscure language. But the paradox they both pursued acknowledged the primacy and holiness of the other who does and *should* precede all else.

Also, like Levinas, Vanier's formulation of the relational went far beyond typical notions of "service" to others. Consequently, the role of non-disabled "assistants" who live in L'Arche with its "members" is not to help so much as to enter into friendship, a "covenant of love", as brothers and sisters, so they can share their lives.[93] Because the assistants who come to L'Arche tend not to stay for long, Vanier described his as a "pilgrim community".[94] The L'Arche brand has been long associated with the wholesome, joyful, *relational* possibilities of genuine community and communion for adults living with intellectual disabilities and their "assistants"—paid and volunteer—with whom they supposedly live as equals in loving homes.[95]

Levinas, however, made no pretence of ever knowing how his vision could be applied in the real world. But Vanier spent a lifetime showing the world how it *could* be done as a quintessentially "downwardly mobile" spiritual superstar who enthralled his many followers and supporters. Even Levinas admitted the irresistible draw of saintliness.

> [W]e cannot not admire saintliness. Not the sacred, but saintliness: that is, the person who in his (*or her*) being is more attached to the being of the other than to his (or her) own. . . . [It] is in saintliness that the human begins; not in the accomplishment of saintliness, in the value.[96]

Vanier died on May 7, 2019, and his obituary in the *New York Times* features an undated photograph of him walking in a demonstration in support of people with disabilities holding the hands of the two people flanking him in wheelchairs. Vanier towers above them, the white hair on his bowed head attests to a lifetime of responsibility and love. Here, the article claims, was "a teacher and moral leader who converted his desire to help people into a worldwide movement" and whose work was lauded by the pope.[97]

Nine months after his death, Vanier was revealed as a serial sexual abuser whose fall from grace left his supporters and admirers gasping. The story emerged in the Canadian press through the *Globe and Mail* on February 21, 2020, announcing that Vanier had been accused of sexually abusing at least six adult women from within his own community over a period of 35 years (1970–2005). More women may come forward over time; others may have already died. These were not disabled residents of L'Arche homes, but women from his community, including assistants and nuns. The abuses were apparently initiated by Vanier under the guise of spiritual direction with women incapable of resisting his authority. The details describe Vanier's behaviour as "inappropriate", "coercive" and "non-consensual". One of his victims has reported that Vanier would tell her: " 'This is not us, this is Mary and Jesus. You are chosen, you are special, this is secret'".[98]

Equally disturbing, Vanier's actions closely mirrored the style of abuse perpetrated by the man he described as his spiritual father, Thomas Philippe, who had played such a central role in Vanier's life from even before the genesis of L'Arche. A mesmerising chronology of collusion and predation can be pieced together from the summary of the external inquiry conducted by GCPS and commissioned by the L'Arche Foundation following allegations against Philippe, and later, Vanier himself.[99] Equally stunning was the revelation that a "small clandestine group... subscribed to and participated in some of the deviant sexual practices of disgraced priest Thomas Philippe", to which Vanier also belonged, although he "publicly denied knowledge of the practices".[100] This is corroborated by an archive of extensive correspondence Vanier maintained with Philippe over many years.

L'Arche Foundation has been dealt a blow that some have speculated could bring an end to this global community. Others have argued if not pled that the good done by this foundation should not perish because of Vanier's actions— none more loudly than from within the foundation itself. It is also a given that the evidence about Vanier's behaviour will never be tested in a court of law. Nor will the full number of sexually assaulted women ever be known. Which leaves us to ask: What is the real value of Vanier's legacy given his protracted abuse of vulnerable women and trusting acolytes and the moral betrayal of all who contributed wholeheartedly to L'Arche's ultimate success? It is a question beyond this discussion that surely deserves more consideration. Vanier's actions have a systemic context embedded in the substrate of "being" and the violence his project leaves unchallenged, which surely warrants a more focused feminist analysis. This is the context to which Levinas repeatedly speaks and that has made possible the desecration of those women who Vanier wilfully violated.

> To accept being, in other words, is to fall prey to a philosophy of success, the worship of the real, a fatalism without moral resources, for it boils down to saying that what is, by virtue of its appearance as being, is what must be.[101]

Whatever similarities might possibly remain between Levinas and Vanier's vision are obliterated by this spectacular turn of events. But Vanier's story provides confirming and sobering evidence of our ongoing and misguided love of saints that even Levinas corroborates. Equally, it speaks to the ubiquity and banality of systemic, self-serving violence that goes to the heart of this inquiry. Such violence not only can but does occur even within the most benign humanitarian contexts—which Levinas' oeuvre is wholly dedicated to elucidating and challenging.

Bringing the other into community mental health care

> [H]erein lies possibly the main challenge when using Levinas' ethics in science and research: How to maintain the radicalism of his critique of the symbolic order when this is to be communicated in a scientific context that expects clarification of statements and ideas?[102]

Philosopher Richard Kearney has suggested that Levinas' view of the transcendent, while accurate, is too austere for his taste in its namelessness and awe. "We all need creature comfort, and we need a name to pray to and a story to tell and to fit into when we talk about our relationship to the divine".[103] Kearney's observation addresses the profound vulnerability of the help seeker and the responsibility of the clinician who is so well placed to *respond* in personal, practical and hospitable ways to these creaturely needs—no matter how symbolically or ritually. Yet, I am inclined to speak for the austerity of Levinas' uncompromising vision and its "infinite and relentless burden", whose responsibility cannot be "resisted" or diluted simply because of its "extremity or inconvenience". To oppose this austerity is to oppose "otherness and its demand" and to risk "promoting one or another form of disrespect".[104]

With this delicate balance in mind, the remainder of this chapter illustrates the breadth of the discourse and the possibilities and pitfalls of "applying" Levinas' a-theoretical approach.

Translating Levinas for health professionals

In her timely call for a Levinasian perspective to humanise clinical care, Débora Vieira Almeida understands that the difficulty of standing up for the other stems from the absence of a theoretical framework that could allow us to discuss the issue at a scientific level.[105] If her reference to the scientific and theoretical seems to overlook Levinas' central project of seeing through and overwhelming the categorical, Almeida is well aware of the problem.

> [H]ealth professionals deal with distinct dimensions in their practice: that of ontology, a dimension which knows and takes possession of the other (to know a pathology, the treatment, for example), and that of the alterity, which will never be understood due to being beyond the limits of comprehension of an I health professional.[106]

Almeida proposes a theory for humanisation based on a Levinasian model that translates the "I-other relationship in and through the act of caring" to that of the "I-health professional".[107] She aims to show how Levinasian ethics could shift the clinician's sense of *role* to one of *relationship* and the notion of illness and treatment to *Other* and to *caring*. Similarly, she translates Levinas' idea of "being held hostage" as the "I-health professional" becoming "hostage of the guarantee not to treat it as an object".[108] Of course, such a guarantee cannot be made or apprehended in the absence of the holy that infuses the call of the Other. Nor, for that matter, is it forced or imposed in the presence of the holy. Almeida also explores the idea of the infinite as a type of knowledge "different from that which the *I* can grasp in the sense of dominating", which she seems to translate as "knowledge that teaches humanity to the I".[109] Levinas might argue that any such knowledge could only give way to its totalising implications. If so, this could leave the clinician to continue refreshing herself at the fountain of this wonder-full Other without feeling or fulfilling any responsibility at all.

Almeida's project is nonetheless courageous, and her practical translations are relevant to clinical care and true to Levinas' formulation. *How* Levinas' ethics are to be taught, practised and applied within Almeida's theory is less clear. Levinas' greatest allure for our re-humanising project seems to lie in the confirmation of the clinician's *desire* for the "holy", which is so conspicuously absent in clinical literature, nor should we be surprised. The holy poses a daring and urgent challenge to clinical reduction and the power structure that upholds it. But if so, then what? Almeida concludes:

> To conceive of the other towards the "I health professional" . . . demands that the technical and scientific knowledges of the professional be submitted to the demands of the other; demands that the public policies always have the purpose of serving Other justly, attributing a character of singularity to the concept.[110]

Almeida's sentiments are in perfect accord with our inquiry and might be readily endorsed by the ethics committee of any community mental health centre.

Clinical application and beyond 149

But her proposition leaves the reader wishing she had plumbed the boggy depths of the reduction she is trying to subvert more deeply or shown more clearly how her theory could work. Nonetheless, this nurse educator continues to engage in the worthy task of humanising clinical care and teaching humanisation to nurses.[111]

The razor's edge

The call for caution in attempting to bridge the gap between the clinician and vulnerable help seeker may not offer much consolation or assistance—but does it provide *any* protection worth mentioning? It *is* challenging to plead for friendship, inclusivity and an orientation that might make a humanising difference without also hovering one's finger nervously over the alarm bell. John Swinton, psychiatric nurse, priest and scholar in the field of disability and mental health, was also influenced by Vanier's emphasis "on friendship and mutuality-in-community".[112] He argues for a quality of "belonging" beyond the simple idea of "inclusivity" and identifies the "evil" of dehumanisation that harms the help seeker as well as the clinician.[113] But in forwarding friendship and love as the "solution", he appears to recant in the same moment by also cautioning against the dangers of blurred boundaries, misunderstanding and misconduct that could potentially harm the help seeker.[114] Swinton is right to say as much, although such friendship and love are not in the order of a perspective that would *elevate* or humanise the other. From this perspective, the help seeker seems to be at risk either way, whether from clinical reduction, distance and objectivity or through the kind of potentially dangerous friendship Swinton prescribes.

My need, *my desire*, for the vulnerable other is possibly the most difficult, radical aspect of Levinas' vision, given the legitimate concerns about the gross abuses perpetrated by Jean Vanier. There is also the worry of abusing the vulnerable help seeker in subtler ways. For example, in claiming that the strong may *not progress*, overcome their darkness, violence and loneliness *without* the weak and destitute, we risk diminishing the horror in the lives of the "other". We risk essentialising her or him for our own purposes.[115] But in returning to the social and transcendent spirit of Levinas' ethical vision, Catherine Chalier reminds us that Levinas does not mean we are necessarily happy to be burdened by the responsibility he describes and that we "will most likely try to forget it".[116] And yet, regardless of our ambivalence, Adriaan Peperzak insists that within such responsibility also lies our heart's *desire*.

> Desire transcends economy by desiring the other—not for satisfaction or consolation, not as a partner in love, but as the one whose face orients my life and thereby grants it significance. In desire, I discover that I am not enclosed within myself, because I am "always already" to and for the Other, responsible, hostage, substitute.[117]

150 *Clinical application and beyond*

Desire and love are also anathema to the therapeutic relationship, operating as they do through the paradigm of "the same" where any hint of desire is reducible to the bogeyman—and the potential *fact*—of abuse.[118] Yet desire and love are implicit in the daunting enormity of responsibility commanded by the Face. Consequently, the clinician *must ensure* the magnetic claim of this Face never seriously challenges her position and authority over the vulnerable help seeker. She must execute this manoeuvre at almost any cost, even of her *own* moral convictions, despite the undeniable evidence of the violence before her. This is precisely how a clinician can continue to violate the other even when she looks into her eyes.

Daisy May

> *May, who lived alone and was about 65, tiny, grey-haired, unremarkable, and complaining, was telling us about the insignificant details of her past week in a defeated voice while we listened. My colleague and I were running a CBT*[119] *group in the windowless meeting room and checking in with each member of the dozen people sitting around the table to see how well everyone had managed their goals for the week, before getting the session underway.*
>
> *I began to take an interest in what May was saying as she started to recount actually getting herself out of bed several mornings in a row, having a shower, getting dressed, forcing herself to make and eat breakfast and not allowing herself to go back to bed and to sleep. The people around the table were becoming equally interested in what was a significant deviation from her habit of staying in bed until lunch and in her pyjamas until dinnertime. Yet, there was no sense of victory in her report, no pride or elation about this accomplishment or its possibility. At the end of the brief monologue, she stopped for a moment before looking around the room to include everyone in the unanswered question she had posed herself that week. After doing everything the manual had said to do, and making a commitment to the group knowing something had to change, May was left with an unanswered question.*
>
> *"But then what?" She asked in a plaintive voice, clearly needing an answer, deserving an answer. "So I do all of this, I make all this effort. I'm finished reading the paper by 7:30 in the morning and I don't allow myself to turn on the TV. But then what?" She searched the faces of her peers. "Do you know what I mean? What's the point? I don't know what the point is". The room was silent. I met my colleague's eyes and we shared a small bitter-sweet smile before looking away from each other and back to May who was waiting. Smooth as silk my colleague congratulated May for her significant revolution, expressing regret that we couldn't explore that issue here and glossing over her important question, the only question really, by asking the next person for his report.*
>
> *May looked puzzled or possibly chastened by my colleague's kindly but dismissive response, and I watched her gaze soberly down at the table in front of her looking still and small. When her neighbour started to speak, I heard my own inner voice leap to May's defence with no small vehemence and conviction. "You got that right sister. You got that dead right," I thought, looking at her, reading her humiliation and wanting so badly to take it away. When she*

finally looked into my face I smiled lovingly, I hoped, wanting her to catch my warmth, my allegiance. But she looked away quickly, possibly imagining that I was patronising her which, I suppose, I was.

Cultural competence under a Levinasian microscope

To determine the ethical integrity of any clinical "application" we arguably need only look through a Levinasian lens to verify it as the real thing or another reduction in disguise. Social work educators Adital Ben-Ari and Roni Strier discuss this ethical trompe l'oeil in examining the increasing interest in "cultural competence". As a notion now emerging in clinical care and community mental health care, cultural competence emphasises the institution's awareness of its need to deal more sensitively, knowledgeably and justly with differences. These refer to socio-economic and life circumstances, race, culture, age, sexual orientation, gender, religious or spiritual practices and beliefs. The supposed virtue of cultural competence lies in its capacity to recognise and address the embeddedness of such difference in the varying quality of care an individual is likely to receive.[120] Levinas, however, speaks to concerns more significant and subtler than these by recognising the other's irreducible alterity. This alterity—this *otherness*— Jeffrey Bloechl observes, represents no particular cultural or religious framework, despite Levinas' Jewish heritage and scholarship. The *moral* issue always takes precedence over the cultural or epistemological.[121]

Levinas' view identifies the fallacy of cultural competence as a "necessary and sufficient condition for working effectively with differences". Nor can it be "taught, learned, trained and attained",[122] Ben-Ari and Strier conclude. Cultural competence has nothing to do with my encounter with the other who opens me to my moral identity and ethical yearning in an event "announcing my having already been found".[123] It is just another reductive exercise that *generalises* the help seeker while it presumes to specify and honour difference for her benefit. Certainly, the clinician is always responsible for recognising and addressing social, cultural or religious difference and the many concerning implications of diversity and discrimination in the context of her work. But to assume the *ethical* priority of cultural competence is to miss the point that even the most refined understanding of cultural or social differences still reduces the help seeker to another category. Cultural competence shares nothing in common with the transcendent "trace of the *who knows where*"[124] that inheres in each of us and has no generalisable parts.[125]

Levinas in collaboration with other ethical orientations

Levinas' work is also emerging in potentially fascinating collaborations. Martyn Kovan, for example, calls for a collaboration of Levinasian and Buddhist ethics that could allow two compatible ethical orientations to address their separate weaknesses and build on their respective strengths.[126] Buddhism's rise in North America already describes an impressive and growing influence in psychology and medicine.[127] As an ethical practice, Buddhism arguably supports Levinas' project of uncovering and addressing the ontological roots of violence by identifying our inextricable connection with each other.[128] The Mahayana Buddhist practice of "taking all blames into one"[129] or the Theravadan practice of the Brahma Viharas[130] are but two practices sympathetic to Levinas' perspective of an un-substitutable responsibility for the other. Such practices are gaining interest in clinical literature and being developed as applications in widely differing medical contexts, from psychiatry to oncology.[131] Kovan argues that such a collaboration could address the ambiguities of situations with differing yet equally defensible ethical positions that he believes Levinas' work lacks the capacity to clarify fully. That said, Levinas' stand on violence and personal responsibility is unequivocal.[132]

> [V]iolence is not... the storm that destroys a harvest, or the master who mistreats his slave, or a totalitarian state that vilifies its citizens, or the conquest and subjection of men in war. Violence is to be found in any action in which one acts as if one were alone to act: as if the rest of the universe were there only to receive the action. Violence is consequently also any action which we endure without at every point collaborating in it.[133]

Kovan also seeks a more nuanced answer concerning who or what may be more or less ethical. To clarify his point, he offers a riveting analysis of a life-and-death situation between an American Buddhist peace activist and two Burmese Buddhists on opposing sides of the Burmese revolution.[134] Each has a defensible ethical position, but how from a Levinasian perspective do we judge the merits of each one? Kovan claims the answer lies in a closer collaboration of Levinas and Buddhism. The value of such a hybrid could be imagined for the clinician juggling competing ethical demands, while supporting the help seeker to assess and navigate the moral complexities of her own life, distress and care within the mental health system.[135]

The lonely self

> *The possibility of sacrifice as a meaning of the human adventure! Possibility of the meaningful, despite death, though it be without resurrection! The ultimate meaning of love without concupiscence, and of an I no longer hateful.*[136]

Levinas' vision illuminates the naivety and irresponsibility of a "therapeutic" perspective that makes the vulnerable help seeker the lonely centre of her universe. The need to redirect this focus could hardly be more apparent when cherished notions of what constitutes the "therapeutic" or "best practice" are revealed in ways large and small to be anti-social if not ludicrous.

What do you do?

> *A colleague from down the hall, a psych nurse, comes into my office and looks around the room before addressing me. "Do you have handouts for your patients?" She gives me a brief smile but seems in a bit of a rush and doesn't sit down to tell me what the matter is. "Uh, handouts?" I say, uncertainly, standing up from my chair and looking around the room to see if she'd seen something I'd somehow missed in my own office. "Yeah, you know, just a one-pager. I need something on self-esteem". "Self-esteem?" I say, echoing her question as though I am deaf or unfamiliar with her language. "Yeah, I've got a patient in with me right now with low self-esteem who could really do with a handout, just a one-pager, that's all I need. Don't you have one?" "Ah, no, actually," I say. She is looking at me quizzically, waiting for a reasonable answer that might account for such an unprofessional oversight. Perhaps she thinks I'm simply out of handouts and need to print some more. It is inconceivable to her that I, a therapist, would not have a tool as basic as this to give people with low self-esteem, given that virtually everyone who comes into this place supposedly suffers from it. It's a term I never use, it's meaningless, it's demeaning, I hate it.*
>
> *I feel slightly flustered as I watch her walk towards the door. "Would you like me to see your patient?" I ask, following behind her, trying to be helpful, but realising with a sinking heart that my offer may have just offended or alarmed her. "No, no, no, no". She says quickly, confirming my fear, and raising her palm to stop me from continuing. "I just thought you might have something . . . " There's another pause. "Yes, well, uh, I don't," I say, stating the obvious. The situation is not getting any better and I don't know why I feel so sheepish. She looks at me appraisingly from the doorway and asks, "What do you do?" "What do I do? For self-esteem issues you mean?" "Yeah, what do you do for your patients?" Not having a reasonable answer on the tip of my tongue, and seeing just how far apart we are on this issue, I say the only thing that comes to mind. "I talk to them". I might also have added, "I sit with them". But I didn't want to sound like a complete idiot.*

In moving towards an argument for the other, Cohen observes that Levinas flatly contradicted the psychological perspective of his day that interpreted "need as lack".[137] This view still prevails in theorising our drive to control or fulfil ourselves socially, materially or even spiritually. But for Levinas, this drive does *not* represent our need for satisfaction and gratification as much as our desire to escape ourselves through the transcendent—"the desire for the truly other—escape from self-enclosure".[138]

Cohen also suggests that Levinas' account of responsibility could be relevant to those at risk of suicide who fail to recognise the hell of their own self-absorption and despair as an expression of their unfulfilled desire *for* the other. Cohen's suggestion is relevant, if not fundamental, but he may not appreciate the efficiency of the institution—or the well-intended clinician—to mediate against such a view. There is nothing substantial enough in institutional diagnostics, psychotropic medication or treatment plans to confirm the help seeker's sense of relatedness, responsibility or *place*. Beyond that is the violence of the isolating system that reifies the help seeker's identity as the sole architect of her abysmal fate. Her clinical file, pathology and circumstances appear to prove as much—to say nothing of the stigma that will, almost inevitably, burden her. The picture is further complicated by the absence of any clear consensus on what even constitutes "recovery" or "mental illness".[139] Echoing Levinas, Cohen accurately observes that mental health is "not simple conformity to social conventions. . . but responsible participation in the moral dimensions of social life, which may mean standing on one's own against certain social conventions".[140] His observation speaks as much, or more, for the clinician as for the help seeker. But, the delicacy and difficulty—the *risk*—of resistance cannot be underestimated when the clinician stands against institutional conventions—and the power of the law—in confronting the most naive and *human* expectations of the vulnerable help seeker.

Safe as in church

> *Please don't talk yet. . . . I understand . . . you're beside yourself . . . would you like to take your coat off? Please sit down . . . that's it. Do you want to put your purse on the floor? Would you like a drink of water? Let's take a minute shall we? Please don't apologise. . . . This is the place to let these tears go. . . . Would you like some Kleenex? Yes, I do hear you, your husband, the children, the job, the attempt, the whole thing. . . . I hate to stop you from talking but I don't want you say too much until you know who you are talking to. It seems like an interruption and you've waited weeks to get in here and it's our first meeting and you're spilling over. . . but I work by some rules you need to understand. There will be time to talk. . . . Take some nice big breaths . . . that's it. You've been crying like this for a week? But look what you've been through. You almost died. I am so sorry for your pain. . . . We'll wait until you're ready . . . but don't talk yet. . . . I'm trying . . . to protect you.*
>
> She stops suddenly to look at me, her hand on the Kleenex she is still holding to her nose, the question clear in her startled eyes.
>
> *No, no, I'm safe, of course I'm safe. Don't I look safe? Check me out, look at me. Hi there! Of course I am. But . . . there are things we have to talk about first, so you can decide what you want to tell me, but also, what you might . . . not want to say. Do you understand what I'm telling you? This is really important. Do you understand what I'm trying to say?*

The isolation, loneliness and purposelessness plaguing "the mentally ill" is ubiquitous in community mental health care and reinforced by the therapeutic focus on the self that contributes to the self-conscious, self-loathing, self-stigmatising *I*. Equally concerning, the vulnerable help seeker has little or no insight or education about the political complex of social, cultural, economic and legal forces which shape and reinforce her suffering. Her sense of responsibility to the other is consequently *denied* through her indoctrination in a reductive "therapeutic process" that keeps her blind to even its possibility. It is also denied when the treatment goal from an institutional standpoint is "remission" or "improved functionality".

Allies and companions for the journey

> Desire . . . is the experience of the self "transcended" above itself and toward the Other for the sake of the Other. Desire is insatiable, not because it is too great a lack to be satisfied, but because it is deepened by desire. The good of the Other is always more than what the self can know or can do for him or her. . . . While needs come from the self, desire is inspired by the Other.[141]

We close this chapter with a reflection on the emerging project for *Psychology and the Other*,[142] whose unique focus lies in exploring and connecting Levinas' ethical vision with psychology and praxis. Community mental health care differs significantly from the intensely relational therapeutic work of private therapists and psychotherapy itself—however it is construed. There is also—typically—a clear demarcation between the socio-economic status and privilege of those who pay for therapy and those who attend provincially funded institutions for "mental health" services and subsidised medication, within a medically driven jurisdiction. Nonetheless, the project of *Psychology and the Other* offers *any* mental health clinician a safe harbour from the storm. There, the clinician can gain insight into her moral injury, confess her dehumanisation of the help seeker and explore with others an-Other *possible* way forward.

The discussion begins, and must begin, with clinicians' stated disaffection with the status quo.

> It can plausibly be suggested that what we find in much of contemporary psychology is a kind of mirror image of the hoarded, depleted self. . . on both methodological and theoretical planes. In terms of the former, we need only consider the great welter of tools and techniques currently being employed in the discipline. These have their value, to be sure; they serve precisely to objectify experience, contain it, render it more manipulable, measurable, and useable. But in this very objectification and containment, they also serve to take us away from what is truly Other, beyond our own constricting schemes.[143]

Richard Williams condemns psychology's immaturity and ethical failure to promote moral development and behaviour. Relevance could be cultivated instead through a psychology dedicated to metaphysical questions related to intelligence, morality, agency, intimacy and a sense of the good.[144] Similarly, Frank Richardson and Andrew O'Shea claim the need for a "mature" psychology, sufficiently aware of its own shortcomings to "fully engage the debate between a purely secular outlook and affirmations of transcendence".[145] Goodman and Freeman argue that such maturity calls for new ways of seeing to "help us imagine what it might mean to live Otherwise, in closer proximity to the world's abundance and realness".[146] But, if "revisioning and reconstructing are the very foundations of psychological science", the inertia of the status quo is no less daunting on that account. Here, we cast back to Levinas' admonishment that the work lies in the "refusal to allow oneself to be tamed or domesticated by a theme".[147] What might that look like in praxis?

Goodman and Freeman describe the heartening emergence of the ever-broadening play of Other-centred therapeutic approaches that include "critiques of narcissism; attempts to think beyond hyper-individualistic therapeutic models and theories". These include the "ascendancy of intersubjective, dialogical, and relational thinking in therapy and beyond".[148] The problem of narcissism is of pointed interest, given the sheer volume of trauma seen in community mental health care, together with high prevalence rates of addiction that present co-morbidly with other "pathologies". But as Kunz suggests, the Other can play a purposeful role in helping the individual confront the "self-indulgence... that deceives itself", which is arguably as true for the clinician as for the help seeker. Even if we "resist the challenge... we cannot annihilate it", Kunz insists, because "our self-interest is put into question by the Other" and by "the experience of responsibility toward our neighbor who has rights over us".[149]

John Heaton also confirms the "crucial" importance of the Other to psychotherapy, which is continually occluded by our theories, writing and focus on treatments intended to cure pathology. No matter what, "psychotherapy... only finds itself: a form of violence to the Other", Heaton confirms. The clinician, perhaps especially the *mental health clinician*, is thwarted at every turn because she "works in the realm of pathology that originates from a classification system by which *she must at least appear to abide*".[150] Beyond any concerns of pathology is "the desire for the Other", for whom the help seeker is searching when she goes to an "analytic psychotherapist".[151] The same might well be said of the vulnerable help seeker attending community mental health care and, for that matter, the mental health clinician.

Most compelling is the humanity Levinas' vision extends the clinician through this non-reciprocal relationship. Within it, I am continually wrenched between my primacy, my "in the world", my "place in the sun", my "at home-ness" and the "usurpation of the places belonging to the other woman/man already oppressed and starved by me".[152] This double helix of relationality and responsibility is immutable and dynamic because it requires that I *act* on behalf of the other, *for* the Other. For this reason, the growing impact of Levinas on clinical interests is both fascinating and promising in its labour to move beyond psychology's focus on "being", towards the "ethical other". Nonetheless, Critchley cautions vigilance to those who are turning so hopefully to Levinas, lest we become disciples rather than critics. It is "all very nice" that Levinas' work has extended far beyond his own field of philosophy, but too much of this scholarship, Critchley insists, is confined to "exegesis, commentary, comparison with other thinkers, and. . . homage". His call for a "passage from ethics to politics"[153] is an urgent one, and it is to this theme we now turn in our concluding chapter.

Notes

1 R. House, 'Commentary: Taking Therapy Beyond Modernity? The Promise and Limitations of a Levinasian Understanding', *European Journal of Psychotherapy & Counselling*, 7 (2005), p. 104.
2 S. Critchley, 'Introduction', in *The Cambridge Companion to Levinas*, ed. by S. Critchley and R. Bernasconi (Cambridge: Cambridge University Press, 2002), p. 7.
3 "[T]he very phenomenon of suffering in its uselessness is, in principle the pain of the Other. . . . The justification of the neighbour's pain is certainly the source of all immorality". See: E. Levinas, 'Useless Suffering', *The Provocation of Levinas: Rethinking the Other*, ed. by R. Bernasconi and D. Wood, trans. by R.A. Cohen (London; New York: Routledge, 1988), p. 163.
4 E.R. Severson and others, 'Trauma Tragedy and Theatre: A Conversation with Simon Critchley', in *In the Wake of Trauma: Psychology and Philosophy for the Suffering Other*, ed. by E.R. Severson, B.W. Becker and D.M. Goodman (Pittsburgh, PA: Duquesne University Press, 2016), p. 28.
5 G. Jantzen, *Becoming Divine: Towards a Feminist Philosophy of Religion* (Manchester: Manchester University Press, 1998), p. 237.
6 E. Levinas, *The Levinas Reader*, ed. by S. Hand (Oxford: Basil Blackwell, 1989), p. 91.
7 Levinas asks: "Rational theology, fundamentally ontological, strives to take account of transcendence in the domain of being by expressing it with adverbs of height applied to the verb being; God is said to exist eminently or par excellence. But does the height, or the height above all height, that is thus expressed belong to ontology?" See: E. Levinas, *Collected Philosophical Papers*, Vol. 100, trans. A. Lingis (Dordrecht, The Netherlands: Martinus Nijhoff, 1987), p. 154.
8 R. Gibbs, 'Height and Nearness: Jewish Dimensions of Radical Ethics', in *Ethics as First Philosophy: The Significance of Emmanuel Levinas for Philosophy, Literature and Religion*, ed. by Adriaan T. Peperzak (New York; London: Routledge, 1995), p. 16.
9 Levinas, *The Levinas Reader*, p. 90.
10 See: Chapter 4, "Reciprocity and mutuality", pp. 94–5.
11 Levinas, *The Levinas Reader*, p. 72.
12 "For in consciousness everything is intentionally assumed", the answer to which "is a responsibility that is justified by no prior commitment". See: Levinas, *The Levinas Reader*, p. 92.
13 E. Levinas, *Ethics and Infinity: Conversations with Philippe Nemo*, trans. R.A. Cohen (Pittsburgh, PA: Duquesne University Press, 1985), p. 98.

158 *Clinical application and beyond*

14 Levinas, *The Levinas Reader*, p. 90.
15 Ibid. p. 91.
16 Ibid. See 'Notes', no. 2, pp. 119–20. The editor clarifies the argument that "[s]ubversion and revolution remain within order" and that the anarchy under consideration "has a meaning *prior* to the "political (or antipolitical) meaning currently attributed to it". In this context, anarchy is not understood as an anarchist would because "[i]t would be self-contradictory to set it up as a principle. . . . Anarchy cannot be sovereign, like an *arche*. It can only disturb the State".
17 Ibid.
18 Critchley, 'Introduction', p. 11.
19 Levinas, *The Levinas Reader*, p. 90.
20 E. Levinas and R. Kearney, 'Dialogue with Emmanuel Levinas', in *Face to Face with Levinas*, ed. by R. Cohen (Albany, NY: State University of New York Press, 1986) p. 17.
21 D.M. Goodman and M.P. Freeman, *Psychology and the Other* (Oxford: Oxford University Press, 2015), pp. 215–16.
22 Levinas, *The Levinas Reader*, p. 90.
23 My addition of feminine gender to Levinas' statement. E. Levinas, *God, Death, and Time* (Palo Alto, CA: Stanford University Press, 2000), p. 157.
24 R.P. Blum, 'Emmanuel Levinas' Theory of Commitment', *Philosophy and Phenomenological Research*, 44 (1983), p. 145.
25 P. Davies, 'On Resorting to an Ethical Language', in *Ethics as First Philosophy: The Significance of Emmanuel Levinas for Philosophy, Literature and Religion*, ed. by A.T. Peperzak (New York; London: Routledge, 1995), pp. 95–104.
26 Blum, 'Emmanuel Levinas' Theory of Commitment', p. 146.
27 The allusion of the box in which a lamb lies sleeping comes from Antoine de Saint Exupéry's *Le Petit Prince*. See: E. Levinas, *Alterity and Transcendence* (New York: Columbia University Press, 1999), p. 88.
28 Ibid. p. 89.
29 For a general overview of the issues raised by mystical experience in clinical practice, see: C. Racine, 'Loving in the Context of Community Mental Health Practice: A Clinical Case Study and Reflection on Mystical Experience', *Mental Health, Religion & Culture*, 17 (2014), pp. 110–16. The work being undertaken at the *Center for Spirituality, Theology and Health* at Duke University's Medical Center, <https://spiritualityandhealth.duke.edu/> and the *Centre for Spirituality, Theology and Health* at Durham University, UK. <www.dur.ac.uk/csth/> reflects the increasing legitimisation of this aspect of mental health research and care.
30 Jantzen, *Becoming Divine: Towards a Feminist Philosophy of Religion*, p. 107.
31 M. Jackson and K. Fulford, 'Spiritual Experience and Psychopathology', *Philosophy, Psychiatry, & Psychology*, 4 (1997).
32 Ibid.
33 C.C.H. Cook, 'Psychiatry and Mysticism', *Mental Health, Religion & Culture*, 7 (2004), p. 160.
34 The constraints imposed on such research are discussed by researchers who appear to bend over backwards to defend their use of *any* qualitative measures in their "scientific" work. See: N. Kohls, A. Hack, and H. Walach, 'Measuring the Unmeasurable by Ticking Boxes and Opening Pandora's Box? Mixed Methods Research as a Useful Tool for Investigating Exceptional and Spiritual Experiences', *Archive for the Psychology of Religion/Archiv für Religionspychologie*, 30 (2008).
35 Cupitt notes that these were among the first contemporary writers on mysticism whose works were produced mainly between 1890 and 1970, a period that coincided with the emergence of the psychology of Freud, Jung and James himself. See: D. Cupitt, *Mysticism After Modernity* (Malden, MA: Blackwell, 1998), p. 26.

Clinical application and beyond   159

36 See: R.W. Hood Jr, 'The Construction and Preliminary Validation of a Measure of Reported Mystical Experience', *Journal for the Scientific Study of Religion*, 14 (1975), pp. 31–32. For an example of research informed by this measure, see: K.R. Byrd, D. Lear, and S. Schwenka, 'Mysticism as a Predictor of Subjective Well-Being', *The International Journal for the Psychology of Religion*, 10 (2000).
37 W.T. Stace, *Mysticism and Philosophy* (London: Macmillan, 1961).
38 N. Kohls and H. Walach, 'Exceptional Experiences and Spiritual Practice: A New Measurement Approach', *Spirituality and Health International*, 7 (2006).
39 Ineffability, noesis, transiency and passivity. See: W. James, *The Varieties of Religious Experience*, Vol. 13 (Cambridge, MA: Harvard University Press, 1985).
40 Cook, 'Psychiatry and Mysticism'.
41 D. Lukoff, F. Lu, and R. Turner, 'From Spiritual Emergency to Spiritual Problem: The Transpersonal Roots of the New DSM-IV Category', *Journal of Humanistic Psychology*, 38 (1998), p. 26. See also: D. Lukoff, 'The Diagnosis of Mystical Experiences with Psychotic Features', *Journal of Transpersonal Psychology*, 17 (1985), pp. 160–66.
42 The *DSM* is the *Diagnostic and Statistical Manual* of *Mental Disorders*, published by the American Psychiatric Association (APA), and is the diagnostic "bible" of psychiatry.
43 Lukoff, Lu, and Turner, 'From Spiritual Emergency to Spiritual Problem: The Transpersonal Roots of the New DSM-IV Category', p. 26.
44 American psychiatrist Harold Koenig's phenomenal contribution to the classification and meta-analyses of hundreds of studies related to the field of spirituality, religion and health has put this field on the map. See: H.G. Koenig, D.E. King, and V.B. Carson, *Handbook of Religion and Health* (New York: Oxford University Press, 2012). Also: H.G. Koenig, M.E. McCullough, and D.B. Larson, *Handbook of Religion and Health* (New York: Oxford University Press, 2001).
45 M.A. McIntosh, *Mystical Theology: The Integrity of Spirituality and Theology* (Oxford: Blackwell, 1998), p. 49.
46 Ibid.
47 Ibid. p. 11.
48 B. McGinn, *The Foundations of Mysticism* (New York: Crossroad, 1991), pp. XV–XVI.
49 B. McGinn, 'Mystical Consciousness: A Modest Proposal', *Spiritus: A Journal of Christian Spirituality*, 8 (2008), p. 50.
50 J.K. Ruffing, ed., *Mysticism and Social Transformation* (New York: Syracuse University Press, 2001), p. 1.
51 The section of this chapter titled "Mystical experience and mysticism" draws on Racine, 'Loving in the Context of Community Mental Health', pp. 109–13. Reprinted by permission of the publisher. (Taylor & Francis Ltd, www.tandfonline.com).
52 E. Levinas, *Emmanuel Levinas: Basic Philosophical Writings* (Bloomington; Indianapolis: Indiana University Press, 1996), p. 139.
53 M.L. Morgan, *The Cambridge Introduction to Emmanuel Levinas* (Cambridge: Cambridge University Press, 2011), p. VII.
54 L. Hill, '"Distrust of Poetry": Levinas, Blanchot, Celan', *MLN*, 120 (2006), p. 988.
55 See: J. Caruana, 'Not Ethics, Not Ethics Alone, but the Holy', *Journal of Religious Ethics*, 34 (2006).
56 E. Levinas, *Difficult Freedom: Essays on Judaism* (Baltimore: Johns Hopkins University Press, 1990), p. 14.
57 This political aspect of mysticism has been examined by Grace Jantzen, whose feminist analysis draws on a number of postmodern thinkers, especially Luce

160 *Clinical application and beyond*

58. Irigaray, to formulate an argument for the divinisation of the immanent and embodied. See: Jantzen, *Becoming Divine: Towards a Feminist Philosophy of Religion.*
58. P. Benson and K.L. O'Neill, 'Facing Risk: Levinas, Ethnography, and Ethics', p. 32. See also: Critchley, 'Introduction', p. 6.
59. Hand, *Emmanuel Levinas*, p. 59.
60. J. Derrida, *Adieu to Emmanuel Levinas* (Palo Alto, CA: Stanford University Press, 1999), p. 30.
61. M.L. Morgan, *Discovering Levinas* (Cambridge: Cambridge University Press, 2007), p. 157.
62. See, for example: A.M. Hollywood, 'Preaching as Social Practice in Meister Eckhart', in *Mysticism and Social Transformation,* ed. by J.K. Ruffing (New York: Syracuse University Press, 2001), pp. 88–89.
63. Critchley, 'Introduction', p. 12.
64. Rubenstein's thoughtful work describes the complexity and controversy of this ever-evolving issue. See: M.J. Rubenstein, 'Dionysius, Derrida, and the Critique of "Ontotheology"', *Modern Theology*, 24 (2008), p. 726.
65. For a brief analysis of Eckhart's negative theology, see: Ibid. pp. 726–27.
66. Porete was believed to have belonged to the Beguines and claimed several astounding accomplishments for a woman of her time, not the least being her doctrine claiming that the direct apprehension of the divine was possible, essentially, without having to engage in the proscribed sacraments of the Church. Her work won favour among the most highly placed theological scholars of the day, although she was subsequently burned at the stake in Paris in 1310. Feminist scholars, among others, are working to understand how she and a few others like her gained access to the highest levels of ecclesiastical power, despite their gender. Their example is relevant to our interest in employing wonder—and Levinasian ethics—to infiltrate and subvert the grip of reductive orthodoxy. See: M. Porete, E. Colledge, J. Grant, and J.C. Marler, *The Mirror of Simple Souls* (Notre Dame, IN: University of Notre Dame Press, 1999). Also: A.M. Hollywood, 'Beauvoir, Irigaray, and the Mystical', *Hypatia*, 9 (1994), p. 169.
67. See, for example: E. Levinas, *Otherwise Than Being, or, Beyond Essence* (Pittsburgh, PA: Duquesne University Press, 1998), pp. 44, 181.
68. E. Levinas, *Totality and Infinity: An Essay on Exteriority* (The Hague; Boston; London: Martinus Nijhoff, 1979), p. 305.
69. E. Severson, *Levinas's Philosophy of Time: Gift, Responsibility, Diachrony, Hope* (Pittsburgh, PA: Duquesne University Press, 2013), p. 256.
70. Ibid. p. 295.
71. B. McGinn, 'The Language of Love in Christian and Jewish Mysticism', in *Mysticism and Language*, ed. by S.T. Katz (New York: Oxford University Press, 1992). See also: Cupitt, *Mysticism After Modernity*, p. 25. Cupitt suggests that medieval mystical writing appears to evoke union with God in terms of the female sexual response. See also: C.W. Bynum, *Jesus as Mother: Studies in the Spirituality of the High Middle Ages* (Berkeley; Los Angeles; London: University of California Press, 1982), p. 138.
72. McGinn, 'The Language of Love in Christian and Jewish Mysticism', pp. 225–27.
73. Ibid. p. 226.
74. See: L. Nelstrop, K. Magill, and B.B. Onishi, *Christian Mysticism: An Introduction to Contemporary Theoretical Approaches* (London: Routledge 2009), pp. 47–48, 57–58, 216. See also: S.T. Katz, 'Mystical Speech and Mystical Meaning', in *Mysticism and Language*, ed. S. Katz (New York: Oxford University Press, 1992), pp. 5–15.
75. McGinn, 'The Language of Love in Christian and Jewish Mysticism', p. 206.
76. Ibid. p. 205.

77 Ibid. p. 226.
78 J.K. Ruffing, 'Introduction', in *Mysticism and Social Transformation*, ed. by J.K. Ruffing (New York: Syracuse University Press, 2001), pp. 4–5.
79 Much has been said about the differences between apophatic and kataphatic mysticism and the perceived superiority of the former to the latter, which draws another essentialising dividing line between male rationality and female emotionality and has been strongly critiqued by feminist theologians. Hollywood offers an overview of the subject and argues that both are needed, and neither are mutually exclusive or gender exclusive. See: Hollywood, 'Beauvoir, Irigaray, and the Mystical', pp. 158–85.
80 Levinas, *Otherwise Than Being, or, Beyond Essence*, p. XII.
81 Vanier's PhD was titled "Happiness as Principle and End of Aristotelian Ethics". See: J. Vanier and C. Whitney-Brown, *Jean Vanier: Essential Writings* (London: Darton, 2008), p. 26.
82 George Vanier's career was in the military and diplomatic services. Together with his wife, Pauline, Vanier served as Canada's governor general from 1957 to 1967. See: J. Dunne, 'Sense of Community in L'arche and in the Writings of Jean Vanier', *Journal of Community Psychology*, 14 (1986), p. 41.
83 Vanier won the Templeton prize for 2015. See: <www.youtube.com/watch?v=qNxAVzICf-M>
84 Vanier and Whitney-Brown, *Jean Vanier: Essential Writings*, p. 43.
85 Ibid. p. 48.
86 J.L. Allen Jr, 'L'Arche Founder Reveals Face of Christ', *National Catholic Reporter Online*, (November 1, 2002) <http://ncronline.org/>.
87 For references to abortion and homosexuality, see: T. Kearney and J. Vanier, 'The Prophetic Cry: Interview with Jean Vanier', *The Crane Bag*, 5 (1981), pp. 81–82.
88 Vanier and Whitney-Brown, *Jean Vanier: Essential Writings*, p. 17.
89 In an inquiry undertaken by L'Arche, 14 witnesses and ten victims offered reliable testimony that Thomas Philippe had sexually abused adult women to whom he was ministering as spiritual director between 1970 and 1990, two years before his death. Philippe had a psychological and spiritual hold over these women that he used to enforce their silence. L'Arche opened the findings of this investigation to the public, but these have now been replaced with new findings about Vanier himself.
90 Vanier and Whitney-Brown, *Jean Vanier: Essential Writings*, p. 28. Vanier speaks of the "forces of darkness and hatred" in his own heart. "Elitism", he claims, "is the sickness of us all". Ibid. p. 75.
91 Vanier, *Becoming Human*, p. 40.
92 For a discussion on altruism and ambivalence, see: K. Reimer, 'Natural Character: Psychological Realism for the Downwardly Mobile', *Theology and Science*, 2 (2004).
93 Vanier and Whitney-Brown, *Jean Vanier: Essential Writings*, p. 103.
94 J. Dunne, 'Sense of Community in L'Arche and in the Writings of Jean Vanier', *Journal of Community Psychology*, 14 (1986), pp. 47–49.
95 J. Klostermann, 'L'Arche International Has a History of Exploiting Women', *The Toronto Star* (March 2, 2020). <www.thestar.com/opinion/contributors/2020/03/02/larche-international-has-a-history-of-exploiting-women.html> Klostermann, a former employee of L'Arche, paints a far less idealized picture of the expectations placed on paid workers living at L'Arche, and similar stories have begun to emerge on this issue following the revelation of Vanier's abuses.
96 T. Wright, P. Hughes, and A. Ainley, 'The paradox of morality: An interview with Emmanuel Levinas', in *The Provocation of Levinas: Rethinking the Other*, ed. by R. Bernasconi and D. Wood, trans. by A. Benjamin and T. Wright (London; New York: Routledge, 1988), pp. 172–73. (My gender changes in brackets.)

162 Clinical application and beyond

97 K.Q. Seelye, 'Jean Vanier, Savior of People on the Margins, Dies at 90', *The New York Times* (May 7, 2019). <www.nytimes.com/2019/05/07/obituaries/jean-vanier-dead.html>

98 E. Mbengue, 'Founder of French Charity Is Accused of Pattern of Abuse', *The New York Times* (February 23, 2020). <www.nytimes.com/2020/02/23/world/europe/jean-vanier-abuse-larche.html>

99 J. Vanier, *L'Arche International: Findings of Independent Inquiry Summary Report* (February 22, 2020). <www.larche.org/documents/10181/2539004/Inquiry-Summary_Report-Final-2020_02_22-EN.pdf/6f25e92c-35fe-44e8-a80b-dd79ede4746b>

100 J. Vanier, 'L'Arche founder Jean Vanier Sexually Abused Women-Internal Report', in *BBC News* (February 22, 2002). www.bbc.com/news/world-51596516

101 R.A. Cohen, 'Book Reviews of Emmanuel Levinas (2003) on Escape', *European Journal of Psychotherapy & Counselling*, 7 (2005), p. 111.

102 B. Nordtug, 'Levinas's Ethics as a Basis of Healthcare-Challenges and Dilemmas', *Nursing Philosophy*, 16 (2015), p. 51.

103 R. Kearney, 'The God Who May Be', in *Ideas*, ed. by David Cayley (Toronto, Canada: Canadian Broadcasting Corporation, 2006), pp. 1–22 (p. 20).

104 J. Bloechl, *Liturgy of the Neighbor: Emmanuel Levinas and the Religion of Responsibility* (Pittsburgh, PA: Duquesne University Press, 1999), p. 4.

105 D.V. Almeida, 'Humanization of Health Care: A Reflexive Theoretical Essay Based on the Philosophy of Emmanuel Lévinas', *Text Context Nursing, Florianópolis*, 23 (2014), p. 768.

106 Ibid. p. 771.

107 Ibid. p. 769.

108 Ibid. p. 774.

109 Ibid. pp. 772–73.

110 Almeida's paper is translated from Spanish to English, which might explain the absence of the article "the" that would otherwise precede "Other". Ibid. p. 774.

111 D. Vieira de Almeida and E. Corrêa Chaves, 'Teaching Humanization in Undergraduate Nursing Education Programs', *Journal Einstein*, 7 (2009), pp. 271–78.

112 J. Swinton, 'The Body of Christ Has Down's Syndrome: Theological Reflections on Vulnerability, Disability, and Graceful Communities', *Journal of Pastoral Theology*, 13 (2003), p. 75.

113 J. Swinton, 'From Inclusion to Belonging: A Practical Theology of Community, Disability and Humanness', *Journal of Religion, Disability & Health*, 16 (2012).

114 J. Swinton, *Does Evil Have to Exist to Be Real? The Discourse of Evil and the Practice of Mental Health Care* (London: Royal College of Psychiatrists Spirituality and Psychiatry Special Interest Group, 2002).

115 A comparable argument is made by Grace Jantzen. See: Chapter 5, "A brief critique", pp. 120–3.

116 C. Chalier, 'The Philosophy of Emmanuel Levinas and the Hebraic Tradition', in *Ethics as First Philosophy: The Significance of Emmanuel Levinas for Philosophy, Literature and Religion*, ed. by A.T. Peperzak (New York: Routledge, 1995), p. 10.

117 A.T. Peperzak, *Ethics as First Philosophy: The Significance of Emmanuel Levinas for Philosophy, Literature and Religion* (New York: Routledge, 1995).

118 Racine, 'Loving in the Context of Community Mental Health', pp. 113–14.

119 CBT stands for cognitive behavioural therapy.

120 A. Ben-Ari and R. Strier, 'Rethinking Cultural Competence: What Can We Learn from Levinas?', *British Journal of Social Work*, 40 (2010), p. 2156. For a brief analytic summary of cultural competence, see: A. Kleinman and P. Benson,

Clinical application and beyond 163

'Anthropology in the Clinic: The Problem of Cultural Competency and How to Fix It', *PLoS Medicine*, 3 (2006), p. 1675.
121 See: Ibid.
122 A. Ben-Ari and R. Strier, 'Rethinking Cultural Competence: What Can We Learn from Levinas?', p. 2158.
123 Bloechl, *Liturgy of the Neighbor: Emmanuel Levinas and the Religion of Responsibility*, p. 37.
124 Levinas, *The Levinas Reader*, p. 90.
125 Bloechl suggests that Levinas' ethical formulation cannot be reduced to the Jewish themes or inspiration found in his work, although such correlations have been made. Levinas himself claimed that his own work did not represent any specific dogma or religious tradition. See Bloechl, *Liturgy of the Neighbor: Emmanuel Levinas and the Religion of Responsibility*, pp. 7–9.
126 M. Kovan, 'Violence and (Non-) Resistance: Buddhist Ahiṃsā and Its Existential Aporias', *Journal of Buddhist Ethics*, 16 (2009).
127 For examples of such work and its ambitions, see: J. Kabat-Zinn, 'Mindfulness-Based Interventions in Context: Past, Present, and Future', *Clinical Psychology: Science and Practice*, 10 (2003).
128 See, for example, S.G. Hofmann, P. Grossman, and D.E. Hinton, 'Loving-Kindness and Compassion Meditation: Potential for Psychological Interventions', *Clinical Psychology Review*, 31 (2011).
129 See: P. Chödrön, *Comfortable with Uncertainty: 108 Teachings* (Boulder, CO: Shambhala Publications, 2008), pp. 180–81.
130 See one author's argument for loving her students that shows the overlap between Levinasian inter-subjectivity and the Buddhist practice of "Metta". This practice comprises loving-kindness, compassion, sympathetic joy and equanimity described as the "four abodes" of the Brahma Viharas. See: M.J. Hinsdale, 'Choosing to Love', *Paideusis*, 20 (2012). For a more comprehensive definition of these abodes, see: C. Eppert, 'Heartmind Literacy: Compassionate Imagining & the Four Brahmavihāras', *Paideusis,* 19 (2010), pp. 21–23.
131 See: Hofmann, Grossman, and Hinton, 'Loving-Kindness and Compassion Meditation: Potential for Psychological Interventions'.
132 Kovan, 'Violence and (Non-) Resistance: Buddhist Ahiṃsā and Its Existential Aporias', p. 46.
133 Levinas, *Difficult Freedom: Essays on Judaism*, p. 6.
134 Kovan, 'Violence and (Non-) Resistance: Buddhist Ahiṃsā and Its Existential Aporias', pp. 39–40.
135 For another example of such hybrid experiments, see: K.C. Krycka, 'Levinas and Gendlin', *Existential Analysis: Journal of the Society for Existential Analysis*, 20 (2009), pp. 94–108. The researcher brings together E.T. Gendlin's work on "focusing" with Levinasian ethics to negotiate a potentially volatile dialogue between Jews and Palestinians.
136 E. Levinas, *Entre Nous: On Thinking-of-the-Other* (New York: Cambridge University Press, 1998), p. 227.
137 Cohen alludes here to Levinas' dissatisfaction with Freud's view of the libidinal drive that Levinas apparently argued had failed to clarify its "ontological origins". R.A. Cohen, 'Book Reviews of Emmanuel Levinas (2003) on Escape', *European Journal of Psychotherapy & Counselling*, 7 (2005), p. 110.
138 Ibid.
139 S.J. Onken and others, 'An Analysis of the Definitions and Elements of Recovery: A Review of the Literature', *Psychiatric Rehabilitation Journal*, 31 (2007), pp. 17–18.

140 Cohen, 'Book Reviews of Emmanuel Levinas (2003) on Escape', p. 112.
141 G. Kunz, 'An Analysis of the Psyche Inspired by Emmanuel Levinas', *Psychoanalytic Review*, 94 (2007), p. 624.
142 See: www.psychologyandtheother.com/
143 D.M. Goodman and M. Freeman, 'Introduction: Why the Other?', in *Psychology and the Other*, ed. by D.M. Goodman and M. Freeman (Oxford: Oxford University Press, 2015), p. 4.
144 R.N. Williams, 'Self-Betraying Emotions and the Psychology of Heteronomy', *European Journal of Psychotherapy & Counselling*, 7 (2005), p. 10.
145 F. Richardson and A. O'Shea, 'Suffering and Psychology: Dilemmas and Possibilities', in *In the Wake of Trauma: Psychology and Philosophy for the Suffering Other*, ed. by E.R. Severson, B.W. Becker and D.M. Goodman (Pittsburgh, PA: Duquesne University Press, 2016), p. 175.
146 Goodman and Freeman, 'Introduction', p. 4.
147 Levinas, *The Levinas Reader*, p. 90.
148 Goodman and Freeman, 'Introduction', p. 7.
149 Kunz, 'An Analysis of the Psyche Inspired by Emmanuel Levinas', p. 621.
150 J. Heaton, 'The Other and Psychotherapy', in *The Provocation of Levinas: Rethinking the Other*, ed. by R. Bernasconi and D. Wood, trans. by R. Cohen (London; New York: Routledge, 1988), p. 6.
151 Ibid. pp. 5–6.
152 E. Levinas, 'Bad Conscience and the Inexorable', in *Face to Face with Levinas*, ed. by R.A. Cohen (Albany, NY: State University of New York Press, 1986), pp. 38–39.
153 S. Critchley, 'Five Problems in Levinas's View of Politics and the Sketch of a Solution to Them', *Political Theory*, 32 (2004), pp. 172–73.

References

Allen Jr, J.L., 'L'Arche Founder Reveals Face of Christ', *National Catholic Reporter Online*, November 1, 2002. www.natcath.org/NCR_Online/archives/110102/110102a.htm

Almeida, D.V., 'Humanization of Health Care: A Reflexive Theoretical Essay Based on the Philosophy of Emmanuel Lévinas', *Text Context Nursing, Florianópolis*, 23 (2014), 767–75. https://doi.org/10.1590/0104-07072014000340013

Ben-Ari, A., and Strier, R., 'Rethinking Cultural Competence: What Can We Learn from Levinas?', *British Journal of Social Work*, 40 (2010), 2155–67. https://doi.org/10.1093/bjsw/bcp153

Benson, P., and O'Neill, K.L., 'Facing Risk: Levinas, Ethnography, and Ethics', *Anthropology of Consciousness*, 18 (2007), 29–55. https://doi.org/10.1525/ac.2007.18.2.29

Bloechl, J., *Liturgy of the Neighbor: Emmanuel Levinas and the Religion of Responsibility* (Pittsburgh, PA: Duquesne University Press, 1999).

Blum, R.P., 'Emmanuel Levinas' Theory of Commitment', *Philosophy and Phenomenological Research*, 44 (1983), 145–68. https://doi.org/10.2307/2107213

Bynum, C.W., *Jesus as Mother: Studies in the Spirituality of the High Middle Ages* (Berkeley; Los Angeles; London: University of California Press, 1982).

Byrd, K.R., Lear, D., and Schwenka, S., 'Mysticism as a Predictor of Subjective Well-Being', *International Journal for the Psychology of Religion*, 10 (2000), 259–69. https://doi.org/10.1207/S15327582IJPR1004_04

Caruana, J., 'Not Ethics, Not Ethics Alone, but the Holy', *Journal of Religious Ethics*, 34 (2006), 561–83. https://doi.org/10.1111/j.1467-9795.2006.00285.x

Chalier, C., 'The Philosophy of Emmanuel Levinas and the Hebraic Tradition', in *Ethics as First Philosophy: The Significance of Emmanuel Levinas for Philosophy, Literature and Religion*, ed. by A.T. Peperzak (New York: Routledge, 1995), pp. 3–12.

Chödrön, P., *Comfortable with Uncertainty: 108 Teachings* (Boulder, CO: Shambhala Publications, 2008).

Cohen, R.A., 'Book Reviews of Emmanuel Levinas (2003) on Escape', *European Journal of Psychotherapy & Counselling*, 7 (2005), 109–15. https://doi.org/10.1080/13642530500087096

Cook, C.C.H., 'Psychiatry and Mysticism', *Mental Health, Religion & Culture*, 7 (2004), 149–63. https://doi.org/10.1080/13674670310001602436

Critchley, S., 'Introduction', in *The Cambridge Companion to Levinas*, ed. by S. Critchley and R. Bernasconi (Cambridge: Cambridge University Press, 2002), pp. 1–25.

——, 'Five Problems in Levinas's View of Politics and the Sketch of a Solution to Them', *Political Theory*, 32 (2004), 172–85. https://doi.org/10.1177/0090591703261771

Cupitt, D., *Mysticism After Modernity* (Malden, MA: Blackwell, 1998).

Davies, P., 'On Resorting to an Ethical Language', in *Ethics as First Philosophy: The Significance of Emmanuel Levinas for Philosophy, Literature and Religion*, ed. by A.T. Peperzak (New York; London: Routledge, 1995), pp. 95–104.

Derrida, J., *Adieu to Emmanuel Levinas* (Palo Alto, CA: Stanford University Press, 1999).

Dunne, J., 'Sense of Community in L'Arche and in the Writings of Jean Vanier', *Journal of Community Psychology*, 14 (1986), 41–54. https://doi.org/10.1002/1520-6629(198601)14:1<41::AID-JCOP2290140105>3.0.CO;2-T

Eppert, C., 'Heartmind Literacy: Compassionate Imagining & the Four Brahmavihāras', *Paideusis*, 19 (2010), 17–28.

Evans, H.M., 'Reflections on the Humanities in Medical Education', *Medical Education*, 36 (2002), 508–13. https://doi.org/10.1046/j.1365-2923.2002.01225.x

Gibbs, R., 'Height and Nearness: Jewish Dimensions of Radical Ethics', in *Ethics as First Philosophy: The Significance of Emmanuel Levinas for Philosophy, Literature and Religion*, ed. by Adriaan T. Peperzak (New York; London: Routledge, 1995), pp. 13–23.

Goodman, D.M., and Freeman, M., 'Introduction: Why the Other Psychology', in *Psychology and the Other*, ed. by D.M. Goodman and M. Freeman (Oxford: Oxford University Press, 2015), pp. 1–13.

Hand, S., *Emmanuel Levinas*, ed. R. Eaglestone, Routledge Critical Thinkers (London; New York: Routledge, 2009).

Heaton, J., 'The Other and Psychotherapy', in *The Provocation of Levinas: Rethinking the Other*, ed. by R. Bernasconi and D. Wood, trans. by R. Cohen (London; New York: Routledge, 1988), pp. 5–14.

Hill, L., '"Distrust of Poetry": Levinas, Blanchot, Celan', *MLN*, 120 (2006), 986–1008. https://doi.org/10.1353/mln.2006.0011

Hinsdale, M.J., 'Choosing to Love', *Paideusis*, 20 (2012), 36–45.

Hofmann, S.G., Grossman, P., and Hinton, D.E., 'Loving-Kindness and Compassion Meditation: Potential for Psychological Interventions', *Clinical Psychology Review*, 31 (2011), 1126–32. https://doi.org/10.1016/j.cpr.2011.07.003

Hollywood, A.M., 'Beauvoir, Irigaray, and the Mystical', *Hypatia*, 9 (1994), 158–85. https://doi.org/10.1111/j.1527-2001.1994.tb00654.x

———, 'Preaching as Social Practice in Meister Eckhart', in *Mysticism and Social Transformation*, ed. by J.K. Ruffing (New York: Syracuse University Press, 2001), pp. 76–90.

Hood Jr, R.W., 'The Construction and Preliminary Validation of a Measure of Reported Mystical Experience', *Journal for the Scientific Study of Religion*, 14 (1975), 29–41. https://doi.org/10.2307/1384454

House, R., 'Commentary: Taking Therapy Beyond Modernity? The Promise and Limitations of a Levinasian Understanding', *European Journal of Psychotherapy & Counselling*, 7 (2005), 97–108. https://doi.org/10.1080/13642530500130433

Jackson, M., and Fulford, K., 'Spiritual Experience and Psychopathology', *Philosophy, Psychiatry, & Psychology*, 4 (1997), 41–65. https://doi.org/10.1353/ppp.1997.0002

James, W., *The Varieties of Religious Experience*, Vol. 13 (Cambridge, MA: Harvard University Press, 1985).

Jantzen, G., *Becoming Divine: Towards a Feminist Philosophy of Religion* (Bloomington; Indianapolis: Indiana University Press, 1999).

Kabat-Zinn, J., 'Mindfulness-Based Interventions in Context: Past, Present, and Future', *Clinical Psychology: Science and Practice*, 10 (2003), 144–56. https://doi.org/10.1093/clipsy.bpg016

Katz, S.T., 'Mystical Speech and Mystical Meaning', in *Mysticism and Language*, ed. by S. Katz (New York: Oxford University Press 1992), pp. 3–41.

Kearney, R., 'The God Who May Be', in *Ideas*, ed. by David Cayley (Toronto, Canada: Canadian Broadcasting Corporation, 2006), pp. 1–22.

Kearney, T., and Vanier, J., 'The Prophetic Cry: Interview with Jean Vanier', *The Crane Bag* (1981), 79–85.

Kleinman, A., and Benson, P., 'Anthropology in the Clinic: The Problem of Cultural Competency and How to Fix It', *PLoS Medicine*, 3 (2006), 1673–76. https://doi.org/10.1371/journal.pmed.0030294

Klostermann, J., 'L'Arche International Has a History of Exploiting Women, The Toronto Star', March 2, 2020. www.thestar.com/opinion/contributors/2020/03/02/larche-international-has-a-history-of-exploiting-women.html

Koenig, H.G., King, D.E., and Carson, V.B., *Handbook of Religion and Health* (New York: Oxford University Press, 2012). https://doi.org/10.5402/2012/278730

Koenig, H.G., McCullough, M.E., and Larson, D.B., *Handbook of Religion and Health* (New York: Oxford University Press, 2001). https://doi.org/10.1093/acprof:oso/9780195118667.001.0001

Kohls, N., Hack, A., and Walach, H., 'Measuring the Unmeasurable by Ticking Boxes and Opening Pandora's Box? Mixed Methods Research as a Useful Tool for Investigating Exceptional and Spiritual Experiences', *Archive for the Psychology of Religion/Archiv für Religionspsychologie*, 30 (2008), 155–87. https://doi.org/10.1163/157361208X317123

Kohls, N., and Walach, H., 'Exceptional Experiences and Spiritual Practice: A New Measurement Approach', *Spirituality and Health International*, 7 (2006), 125–50. https://doi.org/10.1002/shi.296

Kovan, M., 'Violence and (Non-) Resistance: Buddhist Ahiṃsā and Its Existential Aporias', *Journal of Buddhist Ethics*, 16 (2009), 39–68.

Krycka, K.C., 'Levinas and Gendlin', *Existential Analysis: Journal of the Society for Existential Analysis*, 20 (2009), 94–108.

Kunz, G., 'An Analysis of the Psyche Inspired by Emmanuel Levinas', *Psychoanalytic Review*, 94 (2007), 617–638. https://doi.org/10.1521/prev.2007.94.4.617

Levinas, E., *Alterity and Transcendence* (New York: Columbia University Press, 1999).

——, 'Bad Conscience and the Inexorable', in *Face to Face with Levinas*, ed. by R.A. Cohen (Albany, NY: State University of New York Press, 1986), pp. 35–40.

——, *Collected Philosophical Papers*, Vol. 100, trans. A. Lingis (Dordrecht, The Netherlands: Martinus Nijhoff, 1987).

—— *Difficult Freedom: Essays on Judaism*, trans. S. Hand (Baltimore: Johns Hopkins University Press, 1990).

——, *Emmanuel Levinas: Basic Philosophical Writings* (Bloomington; Indianapolis: Indiana University Press, 1996).

——, *Entre Nous: On Thinking-of-the-Other*, trans. M.B. Smith and B. Harshav (New York: Cambridge University Press, 1998).

——, *Ethics and Infinity: Conversations with Philippe Nemo*, trans. R.A. Cohen (Pittsburgh, PA: Duquesne University Press, 1985).

——, *God, Death, and Time*, trans. B. Bergo (Palo Alto, CA: Stanford University Press, 2000).

——, *Otherwise Than Being, or, Beyond Essence*, trans. Alphonso Lingis (Pittsburgh, PA: Duquesne University Press, 1998).

——, *The Levinas Reader*, ed. S. Hand (Oxford: Basil Blackwell, 1989).

——, *Totality and Infinity: An Essay on Exteriority*, trans. A. Lingis (The Hague; Boston; London: Martinus Nijhoff, 1979).

——, 'Useless Suffering', in *The Provocation of Levinas: Rethinking the Other*, ed. by R. Bernasconi and D. Wood, trans. by R. Cohen (London; New York: Routledge, 1988), pp. 156–167.

Levinas, E., and Kearney, R., 'Dialogue with Emmanuel Levinas', in *Face to Face with Levinas*, ed. by R.A. Cohen (Albany, NY: State University of New York Press, 1986), pp. 13–33.

Lukoff, D., 'The Diagnosis of Mystical Experiences with Psychotic Features', *Journal of Transpersonal Psychology*, 17 (1985), 155–81.

Lukoff, D., Lu, F., and Turner, R., 'From Spiritual Emergency to Spiritual Problem: The Transpersonal Roots of the New DSM-IV Category', *Journal of Humanistic Psychology*, 38 (1998), 21–50. https://doi.org/10.1177/00221678980382003

Mbengue, E., 'Founder of French Charity Is Accused of Pattern of Abuse', *The New York Times*, February 23, 2020.

McGinn, B., 'Mystical Consciousness: A Modest Proposal', *Spiritus: A Journal of Christian Spirituality*, 8 (2008), 44–63. https://doi.org/10.1353/scs.0.0012

——, *The Foundations of Mysticism* (New York: Crossroad, 1991).

——, 'The Language of Love in Christian and Jewish Mysticism', in *Mysticism and Language*, ed. by S.T. Katz (New York: Oxford University Press, 1992), pp. 202–35.

McIntosh, M.A., *Mystical Theology: The Integrity of Spirituality and Theology* (Oxford: Blackwell, 1998).

Mohr, S., Gillieron, C., Borras, L., Brandt, P.Y., and Huguelet, P., 'The Assessment of Spirituality and Religiousness in Schizophrenia', *The Journal of Nervous and Mental Disease*, 195 (2007), 247–53. https://doi.org/10.1097/01.nmd.0000258230.94304.6b

Morgan, M.L., *Discovering Levinas* (Cambridge: Cambridge University Press, 2007).

——, *The Cambridge Introduction to Emmanuel Levinas* (Cambridge: Cambridge University Press, 2011).

Nelstrop, L., Magill, K., and Onishi, B.B., *Christian Mysticism: An Introduction to Contemporary Theoretical Approaches* (Surrey, England: Ashgate, 2009).

Nordtug, B., 'Levinas's Ethics as a Basis of Healthcare-Challenges and Dilemmas', *Nursing Philosophy*, 16 (2015), 51–63. https://doi.org/10.1111/nup.12072

Onken, S.J., Craig, C.M., Ridgway, P., Ralph, R.O., and Cook, J.A., 'An Analysis of the Definitions and Elements of Recovery: A Review of the Literature', *Psychiatric Rehabilitation Journal*, 31 (2007), 9–21. https://doi.org/10.2975/31.1.2007.9.22

Peperzak, A.T., *Ethics as First Philosophy: The Significance of Emmanuel Levinas for Philosophy, Literature and Religion* (New York: Routledge, 1995).

Porete, M., Colledge, E., Grant, J., and Marler, J.C., *The Mirror of Simple Souls* (Notre Dame, IN: University of Notre Dame Press, 1999).

Racine, C., 'Loving in the Context of Community Mental Health Practice: A Clinical Case Study and Reflection on Mystical Experience', *Mental Health, Religion & Culture*, 17 (2014), 109–21. https://doi.org/10.1080/13674676.2012.749849

Reimer, K., 'Natural Character: Psychological Realism for the Downwardly Mobile', *Theology and Science*, 2 (2004), 89–107. https://doi.org/10.1080/1474670042000196630

Richardson, F., and O'Shea, A., 'Suffering and Psychology: Dilemmas and Possibilities', in *In the Wake of Trauma: Psychology and Philosophy for the Suffering Other*, ed. by E.R. Severson, B.W. Becker and D.M. Goodman (Pittsburgh, PA: Duquesne University Press, 2016), pp. 175–97.

Rubenstein, M.J., 'Dionysius, Derrida, and the Critique of "Ontotheology"', *Modern Theology*, 24 (2008), 725–41. https://doi.org/10.1111/j.1468-0025.2008.00496.x

Ruffing, J.K., 'Introduction', in *Mysticism and Social Transformation*, ed. by J.K. Ruffing (New York: Syracuse University Press, 2001), pp. 1–28.

Seelye, K.Q., 'Jean Vanier, Savior of People on the Margins, Dies at 90', *The New York Times*, May 7, 2019. www.nytimes.com/2019/05/07/obituaries/jean-vanier-dead.html

Severson, E., *Levinas's Philosophy of Time: Gift, Responsibility, Diachrony, Hope* (Pittsburgh, PA: Duquesne University Press, 2013).

Severson, E., Critchley, S., Pellegrini, A., Kearney, R., and Skerrett, K., 'Trauma, Tragedy, and Theatre: A Conversation with Simon Critchley', in *In the Wake of Trauma: Psychology and Philosophy for the Suffering Other*, ed. by E.R. Severson, B.W. Becker and D.M. Goodman (Pittsburgh, PA: Duquesne University Press, 2016), 9–33.

Stace, W.T., *Mysticism and Philosophy* (London: Macmillan, 1961).

Swinton, J., *Does Evil Have to Exist to Be Real? The Discourse of Evil and the Practice of Mental Health Care* (London: The Royal College of Psychiatrists Spirituality and Psychiatry Special Interest Group, 2002).

——, 'From Inclusion to Belonging: A Practical Theology of Community, Disability and Humanness', *Journal of Religion, Disability & Health*, 16 (2012), 172–90. https://doi.org/10.1080/15228967.2012.676243

——, 'The Body of Christ Has Down's Syndrome: Theological Reflections on Vulnerability, Disability, and Graceful Communities', *Journal of Pastoral Theology*, 13 (2003), 66–78. https://doi.org/10.1179/jpt.2003.13.2.006

Vanier, J., 'Awarded 2015 Templeton Prize'. www.youtube.com/watch?v=qNxAVzICf-M

——, *Becoming Human* (Toronto, ON: House of Anansi, 1998).

——, 'L'Arche founder Jean Vanier Sexually Abused Women-Internal Report', *BBC News*, February 22, 2002. www.bbc.com/news/world-51596516

——, *L'Arche International: Findings of Independent Inquiry Summary Report* (February 22, 2020). www.larche.org/documents/10181/2539004/Inquiry-Summary_Report-Final-2020_02_22-EN.pdf/6f25e92c-35fe-44e8-a80b-dd79ede4746b

Vanier, J., and Whitney-Brown, C., *Jean Vanier: Essential Writings* (London: Darton, 2008).

Vieira de Almeida, D., and Corrêa Chaves, E., 'Teaching Humanization in Undergraduate Nursing Education Programs', *Journal Einstein*, 7 (2009), 271–78.

Williams, R.N., 'Self-Betraying Emotions and the Psychology of Heteronomy', *European Journal of Psychotherapy & Counselling*, 7 (2005), 7–16. https://doi.org/10.1080/13642530500087351

Wright, T., Hughes, P., and Ainley, A., 'The Paradox of Morality: An interview with Emmanuel Levinas', in *The Provocation of Levinas: Rethinking the Other*, ed. by R. Bernasconi and D. Wood, trans. by A. Benjamin and T. Wright (London; New York: Routledge, 1988), pp. 168–80.

7 The politics of need and desire

We have looked to wonder to problematise clinical reduction so we can *see* it from an insider's view and examine its underbelly. We have explored wonder's capacity to awaken the clinician from institutional entrancement to the stunning revelation of the vulnerable help seeker and her ineffable welcome. We have come some way in confronting the refractory nature of clinical reduction by examining the impact of medicalisation, asymmetry and dehumanisation on the clinician and clinical practice. We have also encountered the related problems of professional complacency and privilege and examined the toll of the emotional exhaustion and stress on those working in the under-resourced, high-pressure clinical environment of community mental health care. These stresses contribute undeniably to burnout, vicarious trauma and the "wonder-blindness" we are hoping to remediate. In turning to Levinas, I have also attempted to ground a final version of "wonder" capable of transcending the "institutional" reduction of the mentally ill—so-called. I have also employed autoethnography to clarify the theory, test the trustworthiness of my arguments and experience and illuminate the epiphany of the Face. In the wake of this excavation, we are left with a hauntingly poignant embodiment of the vulnerable help seeker whose potential devastation—*colonisation, indoctrination, stigmatisation and re-traumatisation*—are sobering within a marginalised clinical population that fuels the cultural and corporate interests of the institution and its many stakeholders.

In moving towards our conclusion, I have also been concerned that wonder appears to be a failed quantity that slides too predictably off the Teflon surfaces of community mental health care. That is, it still fails to enable the clinician to protect the vulnerable help seeker. Wonder may make a compelling moral impression, but not one substantial enough to destabilise the institution. Nor does it significantly affect the reasoning of all who maintain its boundaries. Indeed, both inside and outside institutional walls, our cultural entrancement with the "creep of mental illness" is ongoing. Its expanding territories are ever more "normalised" despite the undiminished stigma that anathemises the "mentally ill". The label of mental illness also comes with its own seductive rewards, particularly for those on the lower rungs of the socio-economic ladder involved with community mental health care. The most obvious of these may be guardedly described as "humane respite" and a constellation of social resources—including "free" medication—and someone who will listen, no matter how briefly, wearily or helplessly. Sociologist Philip Strong has argued for these rewards although they come at a high price.[1]

If the awe-full moral plea of wonder fails to overcome the truculence of the dominant discourse within community mental health care, wonder's capacity to help the clinician interrogate and apprehend the reductive system is unparalleled. Wonder does not *oppose* or argue so much as it *contrasts*, *contradicts*, *corrects* and *illuminates* by revealing the moral relationship and exposing the clinician to an almost irresistible ethical invitation beyond her ken but achingly familiar. Nonetheless, our earnest call for the remediation of clinical reduction and clinical distance is not without irony. For, this wonder-full "exposure" utterly shifts the power dynamic by *relocating* the clinician *below* the help seeker and confirming a stunning proximity. Here, the clinician may discover herself—in Levinasian terms—in a position of obeisance that very problematically *melts* her authority, status and privilege within a hierarchy that the clinician has no intention of forfeiting. Indeed, none of her professional or cultural markers would ever call these into question. Even so, this radical moral correction illuminates the fraudulence of the mental health clinician's work, her institution, her education and perspective, and her immediate relationship with the vulnerable help seeker. Because the reductive system is so well defended, the impact of wonder may leave the clinician moved and disturbed, but also confused, hamstrung and incapable of acting on the help seeker's behalf. Consequently, the clinician can be left distrusting herself, incapable of even discerning between the Other and the reduction. That is, of discerning between the moral and the immoral, the responsible and the irresponsible, as "James' Story" clearly illustrates.[2]

Herein lies the dissonance at the heart of this ethico-political matrix we have confronted that continually forecloses on *any* substantive argument attempting to go *beyond* the reduction. The consequences are all too evident in the predictable and maddening defilement of wonder itself, which is discovered in the conflation of *proximity* and *abuse*. Here the ethical proximity of the Other is *continually* conflated and confused with the threat of her potential *violation* and abuse. This conflation is inadequately interpreted, or ignored, even by those arguing for greater ethical protection of the vulnerable help seeker from the reductive system. Nonetheless, it prevails, leaving the soundest arguments for proximity diluted and defiled before they are absorbed back into the reductive bog. We must also remember that Levinas conceded that the vision for which he argued throughout his career was beyond the reach of a change that still lies in potential. "I have the idea of a possibility in which the impossible may be sleeping".[3] As noted earlier, this limitation has not stopped thinkers and researchers in growing numbers of fields of endeavour from trying. Others suggest that Levinas' work is too obscure to be adequately interpreted for any "purpose".

Our inquiry appears to sit midway between these two opposing perspectives of the "possible" and the "impossible", which is not to negate wonder's power or promise nor the value of our attempt to see beyond the obstacles in its way. Nevertheless, the obstacles are complex and fascinating in the context of community mental health care and the therapeutic relationship. These obstacles are the focus of our concluding chapter, together with the apparent *enslavement* of a notion we are attempting, in some ways, to wheel up to the institutional walls like a Trojan horse. As we will discover, wonder too is trapped in the same reduction as the help seeker. The problem resides in the totalising capacity of the reductive framework to colonise and defile *whatever* lies in its path, including those ethical strategies specifically aimed at its subversion. As Luce Irigaray compellingly suggests, our failure to adequately understand this problem is at the root of our inability to solve it with "secondary ethical tasks".

> It is not a matter of changing this or that within a horizon already defined as human culture. It is question of changing the horizon itself—of understanding that our interpretation of human identity is both theoretically and practically wrong.[4]

Like Levinas, Irigaray is not suggesting how this new horizon would be or should be, practically implemented, but her admonition offers a clear direction forwards. "If we fail to question what cries out to be radically questioned, we lapse or relapse into an infinite number of secondary ethical tasks", and such tasks, she accurately observes, will not "remove the exploitation".[5]

Connected to the obstacle of this conflation is the conscription of the help seeker as the *mule* of wonder. Here, the clinician construes her dazzled apprehension of the vulnerable help seeker as an "experience", a *consumable* that may overwhelm her with gratitude and awe but remains for her sole benefit. The clinician is also likely to find herself intimidated by the dominant discourse and tightly constrained in even attempting to bring a notion like wonder into the conversation. Indeed, the ultimate heresy is to *see* let alone *speak* or *act* beyond the reified—concretised—self-serving boundaries of the clinical enterprise. This is the enterprise that all but refutes the sanctity of the clinician's bond to the one to whom—as wonder so accurately insists—she *belongs*.

Thou shalt not love

> *I have been battling with the daughter of a chaotic and chronically suicidal mother who is under the care of my colleague, a nurse who has worked off and on with this woman for four years or more. This woman's child, barely 21, has made it through the first cut of intake and been assigned to me. She is now spitting bullets in my office because I am refusing to support her bid for mental health care in our Centre, which would entitle her to receive social*

assistance to which she believes herself entitled because, as she edgily informs me, she is unwell. "You are not ill," I tell her carefully, obliquely. "You need an education, employment and a better support system, not psychiatry, anti-depressants and a welfare cheque". It takes the best part of an hour to finesse this message to avoid appearing unsympathetic or negligent towards her or my line-manager, who this young woman will likely call to complain.

Surprisingly, my team supports my argument, but the young woman isn't having it and insists on another consultation, this time with her unemployed boyfriend in tow. She has no idea the suffering that lies well ahead of her, given her mother's profound instability and all that has gone before. I will not add to it by handing her over to a system that will make it almost impossible for her to motivate herself towards any real autonomy or recognise her potential. I also resent her for trying to take advantage of a service she does not require.

I wander down the hall to my colleague's office to discuss the matter, feeling caught in the moral vice of wanting this girl to fulfil her life and annoyed by her presumption, but also her willingness to leverage her mother's situation for such a wretched pay-off.

I lean against the doorframe of my colleague's office while she talks to me from her desk about this young woman's mother and the role she has played over several years with this tragically self-destructive woman and her family members. My colleague has been a constant, having attended this woman through many crises, visited her in her home and in hospital, and comforted and advised her family. It seems that the frequency of crises is beginning to lessen, the unstated hope being that my colleague's intervention has counted for something. Curiously, my colleague does not express the merest hint of impatience or ambivalence towards this woman. Her steady and unquestionable devotion and the significance of her place in this family constellation seem indisputable.

It's risky but I ask anyway, I want to know what she thinks. "Do you love her?" I say. She pauses before answering. The question is unnerving. It should not be asked it could mean anything, she does not like it, I have transgressed. "No, of course not," she answers shortly, while I come around from another direction to clarify the integrity of my meaning. "No," she protests again, looking at me, "No". Then, looking down at her desk she says, "I do not love her, I am her nurse," as though she might be trying out these words to test them for accuracy. And again, more forcefully, "I am her nurse," she says, looking up at the wall in front of her desk long enough to signal that it is time for me to go.

Wonder's enslavement:
Proximity and the conflation of violation

> *It is not by chance that the history of Western philosophy has been a destruction of transcendence.*[6]

The enigma of the clinician *belonging* to the help seeker, of her *desire* and *need* for the vulnerable other, is the most radical and problematic because it ruptures the status quo and opens the clinician's awareness to ultimacy and the astonishing *possibility* of a very different kind of ethical relationship. But not without the alarm being raised in the same instant by the spectre of violation that plagues such a notion within the reductive sphere. Resistance is predictable, swift and daunting. What about boundary violation? What about the clinician's abuse of power? What about the clinician having sexual feelings for the help seeker or of even "loving" her? What about the danger of role reversal? What about clinical distance? Is *some* distance not required for the clinician to be of any value to the help seeker? To which I can only agree.

More intriguing is *why* the clinician suddenly becomes such a high and *imminent* danger to the vulnerable help seeker whenever the issue of proximity is raised to address the issue of clinical reduction. This risk is presumably present in every single clinical encounter conducted behind closed doors. Moreover, we may confidently assume the unquestionable ability of every educated and licenced clinician to *fully* comprehend *why* she is never to misuse her power or position to violate the help seeker for her own gratification, sexual or otherwise. It is a rule so fundamental as to be elementary, redundant, even patronising. But *proximity*, not power, remains the focus of concern about the boundary violations that occur so predictably.[7]

Interestingly, gross clinical violations can be presented as though there is some good-enough psychological explanation why they occur and are *tolerated*. That is, without effectively shutting down the entire enterprise of mental health care as currently practised institutionally or privately. That they fail to do so might support the argument that the great concern about "proximity" has always been a red herring. But if proximity posed that great a threat to the help seeker why not eliminate the one-on-one consultative process? This strategy could be implemented or legislated simply enough if there was more focus on group therapy models. It could also be instituted through protocols requiring assessments and therapeutic sessions to be transacted in the presence of family members, close friends or even clinicians in training. Conversely, there could be far greater emphasis placed on the development and legitimisation of peer counselling models that have already proved their mettle.

I do not intend to problem-solve so much as to demonstrate the speciousness of the argument. Strategies like these could buffer many problems arising from the intractable power differential played out in the "private" consulting room while providing other substantial benefits. Among them would be a relaxation of the stranglehold on the notion of "mental illness" as something so exceptional and exclusive that its care is best conducted in private. Such strategies could also lighten the financial burden of a chronically underfunded system of care, help shorten wait lists and allow the institution to offer more service to higher numbers of people in less time. Arguments against the strategies I am suggesting are varied and predictable, including the purported inviolability of patient confidentiality. But this argument falls apart in the current reality of computerised patient files and a case management model of care. Indeed, the free flow of patient information within the system at large—among team members of the mental health centre and staff members providing additional resources from outside the system—certainly *seems* to destroy any possibility of legitimate confidentiality.

There is also the argument upholding the centrality of the "therapeutic" relationship that ostensibly requires the protection of privacy for it to be properly developed and maintained. In an environment like community mental health care, however, any semblance of the "psychotherapeutic" tradition characterised by a protracted "relationship" with one clinician has long since been replaced with "short-term", "solution-based" and "cognitive" modalities. Such is becoming the case even for those individuals suffering from SPMI (serious and persistent mental illness), generally viewed as requiring longer-term care. Additionally, the help seeker is likely to be shunted from one clinician to the next in the chaotic bustle of institutional care, which makes any substantial notion of a "therapeutic bond" an often tenuous one. That said, any number of simple strategies could help reduce the supposedly *dreadful* risk that looms in the shadow of proximity. Although, as we have seen, the physical proximity and *privacy* found in the one-on-one clinical relationship is woven, without question, into clinical praxis.

Violation "A"

The issue of *gross violation* identified here as violation "A" should be briefly clarified to understand what is being *primarily* conflated with ethical proximity. This violation amounts to the imposition and toleration of the gross exploitation of the help seeker through an abuse of power motivated entirely by the clinician's self-interest and gratification. It is no more complicated than this, despite whatever protestations might arise concerning the impoverished or overextended clinician and the many burdens he or she carries that might cause him or her to lose their way.

> [D]iscussions of boundary problems sometimes focus on the "bad apple" model: boundary problems and sexual misconduct occur only with a few bad apples, and the simple solution is to kick those persons out of the field. This simplistic view misses a central point of our discussion: boundary issues arise in all therapies and for all clinicians, apparently irrespective of the number of years of experience, and even for those practicing only psychopharmacology. The relevant question is whether the difficulties can be successfully surmounted.[8]

We have seen how the indisputable supremacy of the reductive system can straightjacket the clinician's ethical ability to subvert or resist the reductive institution on the help seeker's behalf. Nevertheless, we risk absolving the clinician of her unequivocal responsibility when we begin to enumerate the many causes of *gross* boundary violation. There is only *one* cause and to argue to the contrary is to deny the clinician's accountability, the inadequacy of the system to protect the help seeker and the primacy of the help seeker's human rights.

Of all the violating concerns, there is possibly none more hypnotising or scandalous than sexual violation, and I would suggest, it is around this violation that the clinician tiptoes the most carefully. Not surprisingly, there is only a modest amount of research on issues related to the sexual abuse of patients in the field of psychology as well as on love and loving in clinical practice. Pope et al. corroborate the great taboo of acknowledging having sexual feelings for a client and the resulting dearth of systematic research in this area.[9] It follows that there would be a corresponding dearth of literature on love (proximity) in the therapeutic relationship that is not interpreted as counter-transference, and indeed this is the case. The statistics speak for themselves.

An example of the statistics on the sexual abuse of vulnerable help seekers reported by one group of researchers estimates that 5%–10% of psychotherapists engaged in "sexual intimacies" in the course of their work as professionals.[10] Unsurprisingly, the occurrence of such abuse has a devastating impact on the help seeker.[11] An earlier prevalence study found that an average of 8.3% of men and 1.7 % of women working as psychologists and social workers had been similarly involved with help seekers.[12] Another study confirms the gravity of the situation by showing that false allegations were found in only 4% of the 958 cases where such abuses had been reported.[13] While the authors candidly admit that issues of validity make it necessary for such studies to be cautiously interpreted, their work shows remarkably high numbers. In this large study, there was a 50% return rate on a survey sent to 1,320 respondents in California. Of these, 647 professionals reported having seen at least one client who disclosed being previously engaged in "sexual intimacy" with a former therapist, with a total of 958 clients with such history being reported among them.[14]

The issue is fraught, particularly when researchers like Norris et al. and Pope et al. have called for more and better clinical education regarding sexual violation. However, the reader may be excused for wondering how this industry could imagine itself fit for purpose when its own practitioners have yet to learn how not to exploit the vulnerable help seeker in their "care". If the "relevant" question is "whether the difficulties can be successfully surmounted", as Norris et al. have claimed, I would suggest it comes very late in the day and, for that reason, has already been unequivocally answered.[15]

Whether more education would actually help is another issue beyond the remit of our inquiry. The main point is that even if these statistics were halved, *quartered*, research like this illustrates the appalling threat posed by the clinician. That this threat has yet to bring the practice of mental health care to its knees is remarkable and speaks to its own privilege. Norris et al. note that after suicide, the greatest number of malpractice suits are attributed to boundary violation and sexual misconduct among mental health providers.[16] In returning to our conflation, we can begin to appreciate just how averse the clinician may be to the apprehension of proximity under investigation and how easily

The politics of need and desire 177

conflated it can become with the threat of violation. It is the same threat, paradoxically, that our notion of proximity is meant to address and subvert.

Violations A, B and C

> *The distrust of introspection, of self-analysis, in our psychology, is perhaps only a consequence of the crisis of love and religion; it derives from the discovery of the true nature of the social.*[17]

Yecheskiel Cohen, who has written on love in the context of clinical practice, suggests that sexual feelings are actually less troubling for therapists to acknowledge and for this reason can be used as a *defence* against feelings of love.[18] It is a compelling argument, given a Levinasian perspective of wonder that points beyond institutional praxis and norms and consequently beyond the clinician's "role". Contributing to the ambivalence and confusion that the experience of love can create in clinical work is that "many psychological writers tend to identify love with sexuality".[19] Still, if love's appeal and its attending desire are reduced to sexual attraction, as Cohen suggests, then our problematic conflation is simply re-asserted. But Cohen also goes further in suggesting that:

> [T]he experience or feeling of love is not necessarily the result of drive energy but. . . another form of love, a nonerotic form. . . whose existence is difficult. . . to prove by. . . science. [E]rotic-driven love is directed toward an object or objects, whereby its aim arises from the wish that the object gratify. . . the subject. [N]onerotic. . . love is teleological. . . directed toward the object, the individual, for his or her sake, and not for that of the loving subject. The most characteristic form of love in this genre is that between parents and children.[20]

Cohen's strategic response to our problematic conflation *sidesteps* the misconstrual of desire as a sexual reduction by associating it with *parental love*. His approach may solve the problem but unfortunately infantilises the help seeker and maintains the dominance of—and presumably the need for—the (parental) therapist. Nonetheless, he formulates such love as being "beyond science", *purposeful* and, most significantly, aimed at the interests of the *other*. Cohen's argument shows how this conflation could be challenged by defining a type of relationship beyond the (scientific) reduction that is not inevitably or solely for the clinician's gratification.

Cohen's example is but one type of negotiation a clinician may attempt to address the conflation under analysis that points to the most feared—gross—category of violation identified here as type "A".[21] The very possibility of this violation provokes the clinician's hypervigilance and purportedly represents the industry's gravest concern for the welfare of the vulnerable help seeker

178 *The politics of need and desire*

who *must never be violated* but who *is*, routinely and predictably. It occurs not only through type "A" violations but also those violations *underwritten* in praxis and perpetrated in broad daylight under the guise of responsible and ethical clinical treatment. What can be called type "B" violations lie along a broad continuum of the ethically questionable, as seen in "Ladies' Shoes", where the main character is denied the right to end his dialysis treatment.[22] At one end of this continuum, we might find the fragile 18-year-old James being soundly humiliated in his first psychiatric consultation—ostensibly for his own good—for "pretending" to have read or understood a book of Kant's work that he carried around with him like an amulet.[23] At the other extreme end, would be my young friend Julia,[24] incarcerated and chemically subdued in a "state-of-the-art" Canadian psychiatric unit against her will for a week without a formal assessment. When I called the hospital to appeal for her rights, her sympathetic nurse wanted to assure me that in this lovely new institution, Julia was privileged enough to have a private room with its own toilet.

Stigma, the third type of violation—violation "C"—examined in Chapter 2,[25] is revisited here to underscore a violation so appalling that even clinicians dread its impact on their own professional lives. Stigma represents a remarkable ongoing hermeneutic injustice for the help seeker, about which she is likely to have exceptionally little understanding in entrusting herself to the care of the institution. Conversely, a clinician knows full well that an admission of mental illness is likely to result in significant stigmatisation by her own professional cohort.[26] The aversion to mental health diagnoses among health professionals and their concealment of mental illness, in themselves and their families, apparently contributes to the suicide rate among medical students and young doctors.[27]

Despite the ideal of the wounded healer, few mental health clinicians are willing to concede such vulnerability publicly.[28] Stephen Diamond's hyperbole about the "shocking and courageous public confession" of American psychologist, Marcia Linehan, is a case in point. Linehan, whose work with self-harming women brought her international recognition, spoke out about her own significant psychiatric history only near the end of her career because she did not want to "die a coward".[29] Her story made headlines in North America and testifies to the enormity of the fear of stigma that she avoided throughout her career.[30] Linehan's example also crystalises the imposition of a stigma so dreaded, that rather than claim membership with those she treats, a clinician will hide behind the socially distancing manoeuvre[31] of clinical reduction to avoid the very stigma she reifies in others.[32] As we have seen, it is type "A" violations—those criminal or abhorrent ethical breaches of trust perpetrated for the clinician's gratification—that tend to be the most readily conflated with the supposed threat of proximity. Nonetheless, types "B" and "C" are arguably more insidious because they are so tightly knit into "ethical" praxis and authorised by the privilege of the clinician that they are rendered invisible. These are violations that come in through the back door, so to speak, while our horrified focus remains on violation "A" and the convenient illusion that this is all the clinician has to fear and avoid in her "care" of the vulnerable help seeker.

Too much of a good thing: Another conflation

Another perspective on the issue of conflation emerges through the concern that our "wonder-full" ethical orientation might lead to unskilful practice and harm the help seeker with its *excess*. Here the fear is raised about the clinician who, with the best of intentions, might still violate the help seeker by "over-reaching" ethically or emotionally. Birgit Nordtug offers the example of a clinician who, in using a Levinasian framework to treat an eating disordered population, might harmfully impose "limitless love and care" on the help seeker.[33] As Nordtug reasonably argues, such an approach could stifle or smother someone from this exceptionally fragile clinical population. But such an approach would arguably be an unskilful response to *any* form of emotional or psychological suffering. More importantly, Nordtug appears to have misinterpreted Levinas' formulation of responsibility as something that could be somehow imposed or forced on *anyone*.

> The Other is radically other than I which is why she cannot be subsumed under totality or egoism. Nor do I dominate her in apprehending her. She always transcends my ability to bring her into my possession or my own identity. The desire for the other is not based on satiation. . . . My initial response is a generous impulse. It is ethical.[34]

Clifton-Soderstrom's summary statement above, neatly underscores the impossibility of Levinas' ethical vision being "imposed", which Nordtug's conflation appears to deny. It is also important to remember we are not dealing with a binary equivalent between distance and intrusion, which might seem to lie at opposing ends of a continuum. This ethical responsibility is *beyond* neglect *or* imposition in a Levinasian formulation of wonder that finds me consecrated by *and* indebted to the help seeker through her proximity. Proximity and violation are indeed—and very problematically—*conflated* within the reductive sphere. But they are *not* antithetical to one another as extremes located at opposing ends of a continuum because *they are on different planes altogether*.[35]

If my unskilful response reflects the gross nature and methods of the legalistic and reductive frame of my profession and workplace, Levinas' ethical vision can hardly be held accountable. Despite the justice, clarity and moral draw of his vision, I am still conditioned and constrained by the reductive sphere of my education, my institution and my world. All the more reason, it would seem, for the clinician to cling to this wonder-full proximity and the practice of what *ought to be*.

Beautiful girl

It was the second time in many months that the eating disorders therapist had asked me to meet with this young woman who was struggling with grief. My interest in grief and loss was known around the Centre and I was pleased to be asked. The knock came at my door. Did I have time? I did. We walked to my colleague's office and I greeted the downcast young woman whose face I hardly remembered from our first encounter. But the story came back as she reoriented me to its details while I sat and gazed at the girl, this lovely young tree felled by her own misery. She had no idea how perfect, how beautiful she was. She had struggled with an eating disorder and was still contorted by the sorrow of her sister's tragic and unexpected death. She felt abandoned by her mother who was half demented by the loss of her dead child while confronting the possible horror of losing her only other child to an eating disorder. The abyss, this young woman believed, could neither be crossed nor circumvented. There was nothing to turn to but time for its distant hope, and even that could not be guaranteed if she believed herself incapable of enduring.

The three of us sat together for little more than half an hour, but it was long enough for the thing to emerge, this wordless space, deeply quiet but definite as the latch of a door being opened. There was no emotional outburst, no lusting after outcomes. What could be said after all that she'd not heard a hundred times in the course of her therapy? Pauses ensued, during which she filled in a few more spaces of the story. My colleague and I, the witnessing women, sat grave faced, empty-handed and disturbed by the extreme suffering of this broken girl we could not even hold in our arms. But the opening continued to deepen through the play of our quiet voices, our attention, and the acknowledgment of the mystery of such annihilating sorrow, the possibility of enduring, the preciousness of life—her life.

At one point, the room became stagey with sunlight that strayed through the cloud cover of the overcast day and fell through the office window that was reinforced by thick black bars. The girl's long brown hair cascaded around her shoulders like a halo, its silken sheen momentarily captured by the sunlight, her tear-stained face iconic, her young hands quiet in her lap, the tissues she held like white flames.

I spoke a long while, it felt like a soliloquy memorised by heart, and told her what I knew and had to believe, which was little enough. But I was in the thing with her, we were swimming together in its vastness and the presence was all around. When I had finished saying what there was to be said, a moment came when the tender joy washed fully and finally over me, drawn up as it had been from this deep well. Then I said the only thing left to be said which was clinically inappropriate but wholly true. "Beautiful girl," I said, as though she was my own, as though I might never see her again and she met my eyes. Having nothing further to say and because it seemed that my part was done, I wished her well, said goodbye and left the room.

My colleague later commented on those two words she had noticed, above everything else, that had said more than they might seem to mean. Something about them and their saying had stayed with her that she wanted to explore.

It was months later in the noisy crush of our big city fair, on the midway amidst the screaming rides, the flashing coloured lights, the smell of frying food, that a lovely young woman rushed up to greet me, smiling, expectantly waiting for me to be equally happy to greet her. She was only vaguely familiar but her delight showed how clearly she remembered me, intimately enough to greet me like some long lost friend. I had to ask her to remind me who she was, but even this couldn't quell her joy in our unexpected reunion. Then she told me how it had all worked out, that it was better now, there was possibility and happiness and I had been part of that process and discovery for which she was so grateful.

I walked away from our encounter dazed, incredulous to have been found here, amid the deafening noise and glare of a midway at dusk by this beautiful girl. In whose life I had played so insignificant a role, whose name I had not even remembered, but who had come so far to recognise and bless me.

Tigers above, below and on all sides

When we begin to look, evidence of this conflation emerges wherever an attempt is made to *increase* the ethical integrity of practice by *decreasing* the distance between the clinician and the help seeker. How researchers stick-handle this problem is fascinating, given the intractable nature of the conflation and the variety of solutions forwarded for its subversion. These "solutions" are all the more fascinating, given the researcher's chronic fear—paranoia—that any attempt to address the issue of clinical distance will be *misunderstood* as potentially violating. Whatever solution is offered must *never* appear to pose a risk to the help seeker or, more importantly, to erase the line that *separates* the clinician from the help seeker. It is this line that must be monitored and defended, ostensibly for the protection of the help seeker but ultimately, it would appear, for the system and the privilege of its workers.

In the opening vignette of this chapter, evidence of this line is discovered in the stony resistance of my colleague to my query about her love for a self-harming patient.[36] Yecheskiel Cohen responds to this threat by *reconfirming* the clinician's dominant role in the guise of the benevolent parent. But this manoeuvre is achieved at the expense of the help seeker who now, in addition to being systemically reduced, is infantilised as well.[37] Birgit Nordtug's response is to deflect by raising concern over the possible violation of the help seeker by the well-intended but unskilful and over-reaching clinician and to dismiss the potential of proximity and a Levinasian approach to care, on these grounds.[38] John Swinton has confronted the threat of the conflation by forwarding the solution of *friendship* while acknowledging that his argument will likely raise the same defensive arguments we have already discussed here.[39]

Within Swinton's call for friendship, there is clearly *no* possibility for such friendship in the enterprise of community mental health care where the clinician's power *is* the law. Equally, friendship cannot be transferred or used to equalise power, even when hierarchical lines are *denied* by those in power, as the spectacular revelation of Vanier's sexual predations confirms. To imply otherwise is not only to spin our wheels in the kind of secondary ethical tasks Irigaray warns against, but to deny the breath-taking *legal* power wielded by any clinician in the institution. Even Clifton-Soderstrom, who speaks for a Levinasian approach to ethical medical care, cannot resist acknowledging this conflation by assuring the reader that what she intends with her Levinasian orientation is *not* for the gratification of the clinician. Nevertheless, within the reductive framework, *it will be* for her gratification and self-interest; it cannot fail to be.

It does not matter if the researcher assures the reader that she means proximity in an *ethical* way, a *good way*, intended only for the help seeker's benefit and the subversion of the reductive institution. The argument that *motivates* the researcher to urge her colleagues ethically forwards in the first place also, ironically and inevitably, requires her to warn them back again. *Get close! Not too close!* Because everybody knows what happens when we get too close. Or do we? The conflation triumphs nonetheless. For the dominant discourse relegates any notion greater than itself to the default position of its common denominator. This situation leaves even the most hallowed and radicalising notion of proximity as an abuse of power in the making because *there is no other* frame of reference. It effectively pre-empts the safe passage—*any* passage—of even a notion like wonder to its moral fruition. Consequently, the relational implications of this *wonder-fully* elevated vulnerable help seeker are lost on the abject and *ambivalent* clinician who confronts her.

So great is the aversion to this taboo—this *firewall*—against proximity that the clinician might appear to *prefer* the help seeker's reduction if only to avoid the risk of appearing to harm her. The greater concern for the clinician is that she will be perceived as a threat to the institution, which could cost her everything. The only alternative then, is for the clinician to continue to acquiesce, to *comply* with the reduction that will deflect, defile and dilute even her most genuine efforts on the help seeker's behalf while undermining her sense of integrity and trustworthiness. If the clinician is not to assume the wonderful clinical encounter for her own private and exclusive consumption, the proximity with which we are grappling will have to propel the clinician towards the work of change that will come at no small personal cost.

Palliation, transformation, mis-interpretation

Throughout our inquiry, a recurring question has been whether wonder should be understood as a refreshing *palliative* for the beleaguered clinician or an antidote—something transformational and morally galvanising. I have suggested that palliation is not sufficient to *transform* the clinician's perspective, fire her moral outrage or allow her to confront the horror of the help seeker's plight to which she contributes so substantially. But in the example of "Beautiful Girl", the question of transformation or palliation seems to be transcended. The story illuminates the ineffable in a moment of radiance and communion that makes this question irrelevant. The ineffable *melts* the constraints of the reductive imposition, the arbitrariness of the differing roles of the characters and the insufficiency of the therapeutic paradigm altogether. It does so to such an extent that all three characters are significantly "moved" or possibly refreshed *and* transformed. *Something happens* beyond the orchestration, imposition or control of any of the three players, and a profoundly satisfying—*socialising*—result occurs and not immediately, but also over time.

It would seem, then, that our Levinasian construal of wonder is no mere palliative nudge but a cataclysm of proximity capable of shattering the clinician's professional entrancement. Even if this cataclysm can only toss the clinician back up against the closed door through which even Levinas was unable to venture, it might at least keep her from running back through the institutional door of least resistance. This is the door behind which the mental health clinician hides and defends herself, and the status quo, from the *real* danger posed by this proximity and the help seeker's ethical call. This is the call that evokes the clinician's overwhelming yearning and compels a reverence that utterly contradicts the security of her privilege and the legitimacy of the enterprise in which she colludes and to which she clings.

In returning to Nordtug's example of the well-meaning but intrusively "responsible" clinician, we confront the real possibility of the clinician's failure to communicate or transact the ethical response she intends. Such failure might even be predictable, but Nortug's analysis still errs in conflating proximity with violation. We could equally credit our well-meaning clinician for her integrity and courage in *attempting* to counter-balance violations A and B, and C, no matter what the outcome. Even if our "misguided" clinician only wanted to assuage her sense of professional guilt, helplessness or fear in confronting the suffering of an eating disordered patient, *any* attempt at an ethical response should not be too readily dismissed. Otherwise, we risk vilifying, diminishing or overlooking the morality of her *desire*, and of conflating violation with proximity yet again. More importantly, we risk dismissing the ethical potential of Levinas' vision in our therapeutic project altogether.

Nordtug concludes that the risks involved in employing Levinasian ethics in a therapeutic context make his work ultimately unsuitable for our purposes because the possibility of misinterpretation is too great.[40] The risk, she claims, is that clinicians or theorists bringing his work into the therapeutic conversation are not immune to errors of interpretation or the temptation of making Levinas fit into *their* theories. However, the conversation with Levinas' ethical vision has hardly begun and *must not* be so quickly dismissed on those or similar grounds. None of these concerns, including the question of whether wonder is best understood as a palliative or antidote—moral refreshment or ethical and political transformation—indicates that the problem lies with Levinas or an ethical construal of wonder.

The difficulty clinicians may have, and surely *will have*, in learning to interpret, speak and practice an ethical language in and against the reductive clinical environment cannot mean they should not try. Great care and discernment will surely be needed to negotiate not only the risk but also the *fear* of harming the help seeker. Risk and fear are the deal breakers most likely to re-consign the clinician to the proven and familiar "ethics" of the institution and praxis where the help seeker's reduction is reified and her dehumanisation ensured. But the enigma that is my responsibility is never the problem, nor am I ever finished with it, as Levinas confirms. "[A]s responsible, I am never finished with emptying myself of myself".[41]

A ride on the mule of wonder

> As I turn and find my neighbour in proximity—in the turning—who I am most particularly becomes definitive in the proximity as well as in my word of response. In this turning and finding my neighbour to whom I belong . . . is where I will be with God or without God, where I will feel bereft or liberated in a fleeting absence of God. Here is where values feel their value, where the important things in life stand out, where rituals speak in silent, life giving meaning, where one knows nonreflectively how to live and die.[42]

Levinas' wonder-full proximity for which this inquiry is calling is, on closer investigation, scarcely if ever absent in even the most mundane and minute transactions between the mental health clinician and the help seeker. It features so prominently that the clinician might appear to be continually falling over the ethical issues it raises although these may not be immediately apparent. From the angle we are about to examine, the clinician's failure to ethically respond seems incomprehensible. For, the wonder that ignites the clinician's moral fire, that confirms her yearning and extends its tender reception to her, is under the aegis of the very person she is at most risk of harming.

In turning to wonder for moral authority, I find myself *under* the authority of the help seeker, the least endowed, to help me with the phenomenal task of remembering *who I am* so I can avoid harming her—and *she tells me*. The help seeker's misplaced trust in me and the institution cries out for my protection. Her willingness to nakedly, and unwisely, bare herself in *responsibly* seeking a reason and respite for her pain, exposes her defencelessness, which demands I dignify and protect her. *Nothing* is concealed. She is terrifyingly innocent of the machinations of an institution about which I am all too aware and which she desperately needs to understand at what is likely to be one of the lowest ebbs of her life. The "service" and "treatment" that await her, if she is successful in getting through the doors of the institution, will be endured at no small cost and without her full understanding of what she is undertaking. It is here, in this horrifying subtext, where the clinician discovers the help seeker's authorisation and prescription for a very different kind of dis-ease.

Herein, the enslavement of wonder is discovered again in a remarkable contortion of the awe-struck clinician believing that the *privilege* of accurately *seeing* the vulnerable help seeker is the endpoint of the moral vision. That is to say, that her profound experience and expression of awe are a sufficient response to the help seeker's question—her *plea*—that remains chronically *ignored*. How can we account for this astounding oversight? It appears related to the problem of the reduction beyond which the clinician cannot see, let alone imagine. If this is so, the clinician will only ever perceive the "Other" as a special privilege—hallowed perhaps—but meant entirely for *her* gratification. This remarkable convolution might seem to constitute the fatal flaw of any argument for wonder in clinical care, for here the help seeker becomes the *mule* who takes the clinician to and through the wonder-full encounter. This intractable problem, however, lies not with wonder but with the reductive system we wish to subvert that continually clones wonder to its purpose and perspective.

In failing to recognise wonder as the unequivocal ethical relationship Levinas describes, the clinician unknowingly submits the help seeker to an altogether invisible but *scandalous* level of mis-use. For, having survived everything she has endured as a result of her clinical reduction, the help seeker now becomes a radiant source of inspiration, fulfilment and *gratitude* for the dis-spirited and de-moralised clinician. We hear the echoes of this inspiration in the reverential murmurs of the clinicians and clergy described in "The church".[43] Indeed, clinicians can hardly resist sharing such enchanting, rewarding, experience, even while it jars with the implications of ownership and the shame of "privilege". Nonetheless, the clinician surely will find in the help seeker the respite to her own self-interest that she may even earnestly *wish* to relinquish but will likely fail to surrender. Instead, the help seeker is edified through a spiritual "experience" that humbles and overwhelms the clinician while leaving the help seeker empty-handed of everything except, perhaps, the clinician's expression of gratitude for the "privilege" of "serving" her.

Here, also, is the problem identified by feminist critics of Levinas' work, especially Luce Irigaray, who as previously noted, attempted to correct Levinas' formulation of the Other.[44] The interpretation of alterity that Levinas equated with the feminine enables the transcendence of the subject. As Irigaray has shown, this transcendence occurs at the expense of the feminine whose position remains subordinate and unchanged. We find an equivalent dynamic within the therapeutic relationship where this transcendence is accomplished *on behalf of* the clinician. Here, the subordinate help seeker—transfigured or luminous though she may appear to the reverent clinician—remains nonetheless outranked, disadvantaged and exploited.

There is no clinical equivalent or response for this peerless reception, which is ultimately "consumed" as a reward by the clinician for her privileged exposure to the vulnerable help seeker's most compelling injury—*the reduction itself*! This injury is also the one to which the clinician inevitably contributes and from which she *always* benefits. Of course, the clinician's response also *de*-moralises her, because it constricts and defiles her relationship to the help seeker even before it begins. Thus, wonder *and* the clinician remain as totalised as the vulnerable help seeker, bonsaied to the size of the very reduction the clinician wishes to remediate. It is this reduction into which wonder must *be made to fit* so it can pose no threat to anyone, least of all the clinician and the hierarchy.

As we can see, it is incredibly challenging to find a clear demarcation between the different "types" of violation we have examined here. They bleed together; the illegal and the legal, the gross and the implied, the unjustifiable and the legally defended. There is, in sum, little or no difference between the violated and the treated, the stigmatised and the rehabilitated, the exploited and the revered. Of course, these violations are devastating for the vulnerable help seeker. They are also devastating for the clinician standing in the shadow of the institution holding a broken moral compass while the promise of ethical proximity is erroneously and predictably cast as the prime suspect of violation.

Awareness, resistance and language

To see, speak and act beyond this conflation, clinicians must develop greater awareness, but the challenges are complex and significant. Patti Lather suggests that "piercing through the theory and the jargon and arriving at a greater understanding of social forces" is something we can only achieve with advanced education.[45] But this kind of political education does not lead the primary interests—or inform the methods—of a medically driven reductive enterprise like community mental health care. Instead, this enterprise separates the individual from her story and social context in order to accurately—*scientifically, measurably*—isolate and identify pathology and predict outcomes. *Any* clinician seeking the awareness that Lather recommends will have to work very hard to go against this grain if only to *see*. Similarly, Grace Jantzen suggests that members of oppressed groups—and those labelled as mentally ill surely qualify, including those who represent them—must exert real effort to become conscious of the situation in which they are mired. It will not occur, Jantzen observes "by simply contemplating but by being willing to work for liberation", which necessitates putting oneself in harm's way by working for justice with "its concomitant risks".[46]

These are risks associated with the clinician's moment-to-moment decision to look away, to endure, to keep her moral outrage and distress to herself, to decline the invitation to engage on behalf of the help seeker. It is also fair to say that the community mental health clinician is only reflecting how he or she has been groomed and girded by her education, authority, legal power and the sanctioned preserve of "clinical" distance. These are the privileges, which enable her to credibly and responsibly apply theories, labels and acronyms to people enduring lives of penury, violence, complexity and humiliation she is never likely to experience. Thus, the clinician can manipulate any affiliative emotion or gesture as a tool for *her* benefit[47] while remaining blind to an awareness of the help seeker as *herself* and deaf to the call that welcomes her into the wilderness of the Other.

As we can see, the clinician's moral response to the wonderful call of the Other remains problematic and unresolved. First, because it is conflated with the fear of violation, but also because there is no language within the reductive sphere capable of reflecting the integrity of this kind of consciousness.

Closing reflections

> *By virtue of its intentional structure gentleness comes to the separated being from the other. The Other precisely reveals himself in his alterity not in a shock negating the I, but as the primordial phenomenon of gentleness. . . . The welcoming of the Face is peaceable from the first, for it answers the unquenchable Desire for Infinity.*[48]

Despite the many nuanced complexities involved, the moral clarity of wonder is still unparalleled in interrogating the reductive scheme and illuminating the confinement against which Luce Irigaray rails in assessing the current state of affairs:

> Is not what is offered already within a horizon that annihilates my ability and my will? . . . I am, therefore, a political militant for the impossible, which is not to say a utopian. Rather, I want what is yet to be as the only possibility of a future.[49]

In working towards this unknown possibility, Levinas' wonder-full vision identifies the extreme relational implications of even the slightest "clinical" exchange such as we find in the example of "Daisy May".[50] In this autoethnography, May asks the group why she should bother getting up in the morning when her monumental efforts to do so have yielded no reward and left her as isolated and ignorant as ever. In response, I concede my private support to May through a shared, conspiratorial glance I hope will assure her of my alliance. But my gesture reduces her once again because I allow her to be humiliated.

In failing to publicly acknowledge May's courage and the accuracy of her observation, I protect myself, the therapeutic program in which she is enrolled and the institution, all at May's expense. This micro example illustrates the clinician's indelible connection to the help seeker in the most incidental of transactions. Through it, we observe the clinician's dishonest response to the defenceless help seeker whose proximity and entreaty the clinician is always ignoring, running from or unravelled by. There is no escape as Sharon's story confirms. "I am already in *up to my neck* with this woman before the question of how I am to help even emerges".[51]

It would be unfair and untrue to suggest that such private acts of heresy are lost on the help seeker or of no real credit to the clinician. But such gestures might be more accurately construed as apologies, confessions or acts of atonement because the clinician's privilege and power remain unscathed. This poignant truth was clarified near the end of my work with James, in my final heartfelt attempt to liberate him from his institutional oppression.

> *Ultimately it seemed to me that my most important task was to help James recognise and reclaim his place in the human community. I wanted him to grasp that we—the world around him—needed him to join us for his own benefit, certainly, but even more pressingly for ours. In one of our final*

> meetings, logic spun on its head the day I carefully explained to James that the very system he had come to for help was the same one that created and maintained his sense of exile—both inside and outside institutional walls. He listened carefully, quietly, the day I played that card, placed the final revelation of institutional complicity in his hand. "Do you understand me, James? Do you understand what I'm saying?" He was so young. Yet, even with this confession I could not sidestep my personal role in his alienation, despite what had been my best intentions and many attempts to subvert and resist the institution. Paradoxically, and painfully, my sense of guilt was further complicated by the very love that had emerged and driven my desire to keep him safe and help him understand and touch the transcendence he sought.[52]

Here again the vulnerable help seeker—James—is conscripted as the mule for this clinician's wonder. Despite accepting the ride ambivalently, even regretfully, I still ask him to absolve me of my guilt when I suggest that he can do more than I can do—for *either* of us. But I am obliquely encouraging him to challenge the system by resisting it, by not falling prey to a reduction that I help impose. This system also rewards me even while casting doubt on the value of the "metaphysical passion" James pursued and brought to our "therapeutic" conversations, to my great benefit and joy.

From whatever angle we examine wonder, it seems this consecrated "welcome home" of the clinician by the help seeker is deadlocked, its very prohibition enforced by a clinical relationship and a reductive enterprise that denies, distrusts—and *corrupts*—even its possibility. Such is the enormity of the threat posed *not* to the vulnerable help seeker but to the *clinician and the institution*. For what is hidden and must never show is what this relationship means *to the clinician*. The clinician can only warily state what this relationship means to her, for many reasons. Chief among them is the anathema of potential abuse and her daunting authority over the help seeker.

Such defensiveness might arguably confirm the clinician's unstated discomfort with the imbalance of power she reluctantly or ambivalently holds. Although, if we are to heed Levinas' denial of reciprocity and assert the elevation that is proximity, there can be no argument that the clinical relationship in community mental health care will ever be defensible. Indeed, the desecration of the holy Other is complete where the primary argument for clinical distance is upheld even less by the horror of harming the vulnerable help seeker than of actually loving her. This fatal flaw remains almost unaccountably elusive to the question raised by Jane Macnaughton who asks, "Why it is that the humanities (including philosophy) have not managed to lay the 'killer punch on medicine's atomistic viewpoint'?"[53] Her question suggests the need for the reductive viewpoint to be somehow "out-gunned" by all who, not incidentally, race to defend its primacy.

Paradoxically, the solution resides not in a punch but a sigh, a tender vulnerability, a whisper expressed in the welcoming regard of this defenceless help seeker. Her nobility is instructive and inviolable despite my pathetic attempt to shield myself from her beauty and protect her from my violence. Above all, the *welcome* of this help seeker's face demands a response from the clinician beyond gratitude and awe. By this I mean, something more than the grotesque assumption that having noticed, felt and articulated the "great privilege" of being called by the face of the other, the clinician has somehow morally responded to it.

Nor would I agree that wonder is a secondary ethical task, although our limited approach to its "deployment"—its "application"—enforces its current diminution.[54] Macnaughton's suggestion that the solution lies in the revisioning of medicine echoes Irigaray's warning. Such revisioning must also build on analyses related to the difficulty we have *seeing* this reduction and of *conceding* the personal costs of what we are not yet willing to sacrifice. As it stands, the transcendent notion of wonder delivers much less than we might reasonably expect while constantly referring us back to the issue of its enslavement and exploitation by the clinician and the authorising institution.

Consequently, we must be careful in promoting any definition of wonder towards re-humanising the vulnerable help seeker. To assume wonder's potential as an antidote to clinical reduction, or refreshment from its impact, is to misunderstand the predictable defilement of *anything* introduced into the clinical dialogue intended to interrupt, or subvert the status quo, no matter how pristine or novel. We may agree that the final evidence for an ethics of wonder capable of surpassing the help seeker's reduction lies tantalisingly close to the paradox of the clinician being *found* by the Face of the other. But, this is still not close enough to ensure the success of our wonder-full humanising project, which is to *protect the help seeker from the clinician and the institution*.

Wonder *annihilates* the cherished illusion that the most, and *only*, needful member in the clinical relationship is the vulnerable help seeker. This point is laid bare by the transfigured face of the help seeker who is *not* served first and best by the clinician within a hierarchy that subordinates and reduces them both. Paradoxically, the clinician's recognition of her need and desire for the help seeker is the most subversive in challenging clinical reduction and the hierarchy that ratifies it. This recognition is powerful and persuasive for any ongoing consideration of wonder towards which Levinas' vision continually points. It is also an admittedly slippery notion to grasp and sell within a hierarchy that requires the reductive framework to survive and that shows little interest in relinquishing its power.

Notes

1 See: Chapter 2, "Medical imperialism and medicalisation", pp. 26–28.
2 See: Chapter 1, "James' Story".
3 E. Levinas, *Alterity and Transcendence* (New York: Columbia University Press, 1999), p. 89.
4 L. Irigaray, *I Love to You: Sketch for a Felicity Within History* (New York: Routledge, 1996), p. 20.

190 *The politics of need and desire*

5 Ibid.
6 E. Levinas, 'God and Philosophy', in *Emmanuel Levinas Basic: Philosophical Writings*, ed. by A.T. Peperzak, S. Critchley, and R. Bernasconi (Bloomington; Indianapolis: Indiana University Press, 1987), p. 130.
7 For an example of such literature, see: D.M. Norris, T.G. Gutheil, and L.H. Strasburger, 'This Couldn't Happen to Me: Boundary Problems and Sexual Misconduct in the Psychotherapy Relationship', *Psychiatric Services*, 54 (2003).
8 Ibid. p. 518.
9 K.S. Pope, P. Keith-Spiegel, and B.G. Tabachnick, 'Sexual Attraction to Clients: The Human Therapist and the (Sometimes) Inhuman Training System', *American Psychologist*, 41 (1986), pp. 150–51.
10 Ironically and unfortunately the term "sexual intimacies" used in this research implies a symmetrical relationship of mutuality, trust and consent, which this is not.
11 K.S. Pope, 'How Clients Are Harmed by Sexual Contact with Mental Health Professionals: The Syndrome and Its Prevalence', *Journal of Counseling & Development*, 67 (1988), pp. 224–25.
12 Ibid. p. 222.
13 K.S. Pope and V.A. Vetter, 'Prior Therapist-Patient Sexual Involvement among Patients Seen by Psychologists', *Psychotherapy: Theory, Research, Practice, Training*, 28 (1991), p. 429.
14 Ibid. p. 431.
15 Norris, Gutheil, and Strasburger, 'This Couldn't Happen to Me', p. 518.
16 Ibid.
17 E. Levinas, *Entre Nous: Essais Sur Le Penser-À-L'autre* (Paris: Bernard Grasset, 1991), p. 23.
18 Y. Cohen, 'Loving the Patient as the Basis for Treatment', *American Journal of Psychoanalysis*, 66 (2006), pp. 144–46.
19 Ibid. pp. 140–41.
20 Ibid. pp. 141–42.
21 Reprinted by permission of the publisher. (Taylor & Francis Ltd, www.tandfonline.com) The opening paragraphs in the section titled "Violations A, B and C" are devoted to Cohen's argument. See: C. Racine, 'Loving in the Context of Community Mental Health Practice: A Clinical Case Study and Reflection on Mystical Experience', *Mental Health, Religion & Culture*, 17 (2014), pp. 113–14.
22 See: Chapter 3, "Ladies' Shoes", pp. 59–61.
23 See: Chapter 1, "James' Story".
24 See: Chapter 4, "My flower", pp. 89–93.
25 See: Chapter 2, "Infra-humanisation, stigma and the heartsink patient", pp. 37–41.
26 See: A.J. Gray, 'Stigma in Psychiatry', *Journal of the Royal Society of Medicine*, 95 (2002), p. 72.
27 Ibid. p. 74.
28 In my years of education and work in this field, I heard of only two mental health professionals within my "extended" workplace in British Columbia who publicly acknowledged having "mental illness". Frederick Frese, an American psychologist, is one of very few clinicians to speak openly about his own mental illness in an attempt to invite other professionals to acknowledge their diagnoses and psychiatric histories. See: F.J. Frese and others, 'Integrating Evidence-Based Practices and the Recovery Model', *Psychiatric Services*, 52 (2001), p. 1468.

According to Frese, a very small minority of clinicians are willing to take this professional risk. Frese himself has acknowledged knowing only ten people among 137,000 members of the American Psychological Association to speak openly about their psychiatric histories. See: H.P. Lefley, ' "Prosumers" and Recovery', *Psychiatric Services*, 64 (2013).

The politics of need and desire 191

29 See: S. Diamond, 'Linehan and Jung as Wounded Healers', *Psychology Today* (December 30, 2011); B. Carey, 'Expert on Mental Illness Reveals Her Own Fight', *New York Times*, (June 23, 2011).
30 Linehan's book was used at my Centre in running DBT (Dialectic Behavioural Therapy) groups for (mostly) women who were required to understand and agree with their diagnosis of Borderline Personality Disorder to be accepted into a therapy group. This diagnosis is one of the most derogating and damaging to the mostly female cohort to which it is attributed. See: M. Linehan, *Cognitive-Behavioral Treatment of Borderline Personality Disorder* (London; New York: The Guilford Press, 1993).
31 The need for professionals to address this issue is briefly discussed in: N. Sartorius, 'Iatrogenic Stigma of Mental Illness: Begins with Behaviour and Attitudes of Medical Professionals, Especially Psychiatrists', *British Medical Journal*, 324 (2002).
See also: O. Wahl and E. Aroesty-Cohen, 'Attitudes of Mental Health Professionals About Mental Illness: A Review of the Recent Literature', *Journal of Community Psychology*, 38 (2010), p. 58. In one review discussed in this paper, 14 of 19 studies showed that while mental health professionals held more positive views about mental illness than the general public, some negative attitudes prevailed throughout. "Negative attitudes were particularly apparent for social distance measures (and) tended to be similar to the public in being reluctant to accept those with psychiatric disorders within their social and occupational circles".
32 Linehan's late "confession" is all the more troubling because of the derogating implication of the "Borderline Personality" diagnosis represented by the cohort with whom Linehan worked.
33 B. Nordtug, 'Levinas's Ethics as a Basis of Healthcare-Challenges and Dilemmas', *Nursing Philosophy*, 16 (2015), p. 61.
34 M. Clifton-Soderstrom, 'Levinas and the Patient as Other: The Ethical Foundation of Medicine', *The Journal of Medicine and Philosophy*, 28 (2003), p. 452.
35 See: Levinas, *Ethics and Infinity: Conversations with Philippe Nemo, 1982*, pp. 8–10.
36 See: This chapter, "Thou shalt not love", pp. 172–3.
37 See: This chapter, "Violations A, B and C", pp. 177–9.
38 See: This chapter, "Too much of a good thing: Another conflation".
39 J. Swinton, *Does Evil Have to Exist to Be Real? The Discourse of Evil and the Practice of Mental Health Care* (London: Royal College of Psychiatrists Spirituality and Psychiatry Special Interest Group, 2002).
40 Nordtug, 'Levinas's Ethics as a Basis of Healthcare-Challenges and Dilemmas', p. 62.
41 Levinas, 'God and Philosophy', p. 144.
42 C.E. Scott, 'A People's Witness Beyond Politics', in *Ethics as First Philosophy: The Significance of Emmanuel Levinas for Philosophy, Literature and Religion*, ed. by A.T. Peperzak (New York: Routledge, 1995), p. 31.
43 See: Chapter 5, "The church", pp. 116–17.
44 See: Chapter 5, "A brief critique", pp. 120–3.
45 P. Lather, 'Issues of Validity in Openly Ideological Research: Between a Rock and a Soft Place', *Interchange*, 17 (1986), p. 76.
46 G. Jantzen, *Becoming Divine: Towards a Feminist Philosophy of Religion* (Manchester: Manchester University Press, 1998), p. 121.
47 For an exceptional synthesis of this issue, see: M.T. Taussig, 'Reification and the Consciousness of the Patient', *Social Science & Medicine, Part B: Medical Anthropology*, 14 (1980).

48 E. Levinas, *Totality and Infinity: An Essay on Exteriority* (The Hague; Boston; London: Martinus Nijhoff, 1979), p. 150.
49 Irigaray, *I Love to You: Sketch for a Felicity Within History*, p. 9.
50 See: Chapter 6, "Daisy May", pp. 150–1.
51 See: Chapter 5, "The paradox of authority and weakness", pp. 113–15.
52 See: Chapter 1, "James' Story".
53 J. Macnaughton, 'Medical Humanities' Challenge to Medicine', *Journal of Evaluation in Clinical Practice*, 17 (2011), p. 927.
54 Amy Hollywood notes that Simone de Beauvoir and Luce Irigaray both claim that individual change is impossible without societal transformation. See: A.M. Hollywood, 'Beauvoir, Irigaray, and the Mystical', *Hypatia*, 9 (1994), p. 174.

References

Carey, B., 'Expert on Mental Illness Reveals Her Own Fight', *New York Times*, June 30, 2011.
Clifton-Soderstrom, M., 'Levinas and the Patient as Other: The Ethical Foundation of Medicine', *The Journal of Medicine and Philosophy*, 28 (2003), 447–60. https://doi.org/10.1076/jmep.28.4.447.15969
Cohen, Y., 'Loving the Patient as the Basis for Treatment', *American Journal of Psychoanalysis*, 66 (2006), 139–55. https://doi.org/10.1007/s11231-006-9012-8
Diamond, S., 'Linehan and Jung as Wounded Healers', *Psychology Today*, 2011.
Frese, F.J., Stanley, J., Kress, K., and Vogel-Scibilia, S., 'Integrating Evidence-Based Practices and the Recovery Model', *Psychiatric Services*, 52 (2001), 1462–68. https://doi.org/10.1176/appi.ps.52.11.1462
Gray, A.J., 'Stigma in Psychiatry', *Journal of the Royal Society of Medicine*, 95 (2002), 72–76. https://doi.org/10.1177/014107680209500205
Hollywood, A.M., 'Beauvoir, Irigaray, and the Mystical', *Hypatia*, 9 (1994), 158–85. https://doi.org/10.1111/j.1527-2001.1994.tb00654.x
Irigaray, L., *I Love to You: Sketch for a Felicity Within History* (New York: Routledge, 1996).
Jantzen, G., *Becoming Divine: Towards a Feminist Philosophy of Religion* (Bloomington; Indianapolis: Indiana University Press, 1999).
Lather, P., 'Issues of Validity in Openly Ideological Research: Between a Rock and a Soft Place', *Interchange*, 17 (1986), 63–84. https://doi.org/10.1007/BF01807017
Lefley, H.P., '"Prosumers" and Recovery', *Psychiatric Services*, 64 (2013), 1278. https://doi.org/10.1176/appi.ps.201300382
Levinas, E., *Alterity and Transcendence* (New York: Columbia University Press, 1999).
——, *Entre Nous: Essais Sur Le Penser-À-L'autre* (Paris: Bernard Grasset, 1991).
——, *Ethics and Infinity: Conversations with Philippe Nemo, 1982*, trans. Richard A. Cohen (Pittsburgh, PA: Duquesne University Press, 1985).
——, 'God and Philosophy', in *Emmanuel Levinas: Basic Philosophical Writings*, ed. by A.T. Peperzak, S. Critchley and R. Bernasconi (Bloomington; Indianapolis: Indiana University Press, 1987), pp. 129–48.
——, *Totality and Infinity: An Essay on Exteriority*, trans. Alphonso Lingis (The Hague; Boston; London: Martinus Nijhoff, 1979).
Linehan, M., *Cognitive-Behavioral Treatment of Borderline Personality Disorder* (London; New York: The Guilford Press, 1993).

Macnaughton, J., 'Medical Humanities' Challenge to Medicine', *Journal of Evaluation in Clinical Practice*, 17 (2011), 927–32. https://doi.org/10.1111/j.1365-2753.2011.01728.x

Nordtug, B., 'Levinas's Ethics as a Basis of Healthcare-Challenges and Dilemmas', *Nursing Philosophy*, 16 (2015), 51–63. https://doi.org/10.1111/nup.12072

Norris, D.M., Gutheil, T.G., and Strasburger, L.H., 'This Couldn't Happen to Me: Boundary Problems and Sexual Misconduct in the Psychotherapy Relationship', *Psychiatric Services*, 54 (2003), 517–22. https://doi.org/10.1176/appi.ps.54.4.517

Pope, K.S., 'How Clients Are Harmed by Sexual Contact with Mental Health Professionals: The Syndrome and Its Prevalence', *Journal of Counseling & Development*, 67 (1988), 222–26. https://doi.org/10.1002/j.1556-6676.1988.tb02587.x

Pope, K.S., Keith-Spiegel, P., and Tabachnick, B.G., 'Sexual Attraction to Clients: The Human Therapist and the (Sometimes) Inhuman Training System', *American Psychologist*, 41 (1986), 147–58. https://doi.org/10.1037/0003-066X.41.2.147

Pope, K.S., and Vetter, V.A., 'Prior Therapist-Patient Sexual Involvement Among Patients Seen by Psychologists', *Psychotherapy: Theory, Research, Practice, Training*, 28 (1991), 429–38. https://doi.org/10.1037/0033-3204.28.3.429

Sartorius, N., 'Iatrogenic Stigma of Mental Illness: Begins with Behaviour and Attitudes of Medical Professionals, Especially Psychiatrists', *British Medical Journal*, 324 (2002), 1470–71. https://doi.org/10.1136/bmj.324.7352.1470

Scott, C.E., 'A People's Witness Beyond Politics', in *Ethics as First Philosophy: The Significance of Emmanuel Levinas for Philosophy, Literature and Religion*, ed. by A.T. Peperzak (New York: Routledge, 1995), pp. 25–35.

Swinton, J., *Does Evil Have to Exist to Be Real? The Discourse of Evil and the Practice of Mental Health Care* (London: Royal College of Psychiatrists Spirituality and Psychiatry Special Interest Group, 2002).

Taussig, M.T., 'Reification and the Consciousness of the Patient', *Social Science & Medicine, Part B: Medical Anthropology*, 14 (1980), 3–13. https://doi.org/10.1016/0160-7987(80)90035-6

Wahl, O., and Aroesty-Cohen, E., 'Attitudes of Mental Health Professionals About Mental Illness: A Review of the Recent Literature', *Journal of Community Psychology*, 38 (2010), 49–62. https://doi.org/10.1002/jcop.20351

Index

abuse 42, 53, 117, 150, 171, 188; and dehumanisation 115; of power 24, 44n9, 117, 174–6, 182; sexual 112, 176
addiction(s) 23, 43n7, 44n10, 92, 156
aesthetic account of wonder *see* Fisher, P.
allied-health 21, 23, 28; and para-professional 23, 27
Almeida, D.V. 147–9
Allport G. 21, 36
alterity 107–8, 110, 122–3, 148, 151, 185, 187
apophatic *see* mysticism
ambivalence 5, 9, 82, 84, 95, 115, 139, 149, 173, 177; and ambivalent 79, 81 84, 115, 182
anarchy 117, 137, 158n16; *see also* the Face/face
anti-psychiatry 24, 139
approach: of the ethical 54; of the face 136; Levinasian 181–2; minimalist 56; to moral research 54; reductive 42; of the transcendent 107
l'Arche *see* Vanier, J.
ASTAT (Adult Short Term Treatment and Assessment) 3, 15n7
asylum(s) 22–4
asymmetrical relationship 28, 32; *see also* dehumanisation
asymmetry 21, 29–31, 33, 43, 94, 109, 170; and height in Levinasian terms 136; *see also* dehumanisation
autoethnographic vignettes: Beautiful girl 180–2; The church 116–17; Daisy May 150–1; The dark blue file 40–1; The insulin coma 42; Ladies' Shoes 59–61; My flower 89–93; The Nitobe Garden 76–7; Safe as in church 154; Sharon 112–13; Staff toilets only! 34; Thou shalt not love 172–73; Tread lightly 30–31; What do you do? 153
autoethnography: analytic 54, 65, 72n94; an approach to research 54–7, 61; and criteria 55, 58, 61–2, 66; and criticism 59, 65–68; and ethnography 54–5, 57, 65, 68; evocative 53–5, 57–9, 62, 65, 67; incommensurability 62, 65; and language 55, 59, 64; and membership; 53, 55–6, 65–6; and the moral 53–4, 56–9, 61, 64–66, 68; and narrative 53–5, 57–9, 61, 65; and reflexivity 53, 55, 57–8, 65; and thick description 53, 55–6; trustworthiness 53, 57–8, 70n41; validity 56, 58, 62, 64, 69; and the vignette 55, 70n55, 88
awe 76, 78, 81, 84, 88–9, 95, 116, 122, 147, 171–2, 184, 189

Beautiful girl *see* autoethnographic vignettes
Behar, R. 55, 57–8, 67
being *see* ontology
being-for-the-other 117, 129n98
Beloved 113, 115, 140
Bloechl, J. 108, 151
Bochner, A.: 53–4, 56–58, 61, 64, 66
borderline personality disorder (BPD): 3, 5, 14–15n5, 39, 40, 47n100, 191n30
boundary/boundaries and violation(s) 10, 17n26, 34, 64, 83, 136; and gross abuse 149, 174–5, 77
Buber, M.: *See* Rogers, C.
Buddhism 7, 10, 152
Buddhist 6–8, 10, 12–13, 17n27, 98n59, 151–2, 163n125

Carel, H.: and testimonial injustice 32–3
case management 22, 43n2, 174
case study 63, 111–12; and Sharon 112–15
Chanter, T. 103, 123–4
The church *see* autoethnographic vignettes
Clifton-Soderstrom, M. 94, 179, 182
clinical: application 135, 138, 144, 151; care 33, 147–9, 151, 185; counsellor 2, 22; dehumanisation 35, 67, 120; distance 171, 174, 181, 186, 188; education 112, 176; encounter 33, 78, 83, 94, 174, 182; environment 42, 89, 170, 183; populations 39, 141, 170, 179; practice/ praxis 2, 35, 78, 135, 137, 139, 170, 176–7; professionals 2, 83, 120; role 61, 115, 118, 136; reduction 138, 141, 148–9, 170–1, 174, 178, 185, 189; relationship 57, 94–5, 110, 175, 188–9
clinical wonder 78, 83, 88, 94–5
cognitive(ly) 32, 36–7, 41, 43, 85, 175; *see also* Piaget, J.
Cohen, R.A. 115, 129n98, 143, 153–4
Cohen, Y. 177, 181
collusion: 8, 118, 146
community mental health care 13, 21–3, 28, 33, 37, 39–43, 56–7, 68, 76, 78, 92–3, 95, 109, 112, 123, 147, 151, 154–6, 170–2, 175, 181, 186, 188; *see also* mental health care
conflation (of proximity and abuse) 45, 171–3, 176–7, 179, 181–82, 186
Conrad, P. 25; *see also* medicalisation
counselling: and allied health 21; and peer counselling 174; and mutuality 94; and talk-therapy 82; and theory 82; *see also* Egan, G.
Critchley, S. 103, 120–1, 135, 142, 157; *see also* Levinas
criteria: and autoethnography 53–5, 58, 61–62, 66; and extrovertive mystical experience 7; and medical imperialism 26; and qualitative approaches to research 70n41
cultural competence 151
curiosity 79, 85–9, 98n76; an account of 86–87

Daisy May *see* autoethnographic vignettes
Dawkins, R.: a scientific account of wonder 87
dehumanisation 21, 33–5, 38, 41–3, 47n100, 54, 67, 93–4, 107, 109, 115, 120, 135, 144–5, 149, 155, 170, 184; and clinical dehumanisation 35, 47n76, 67, 120
de-moralisation 21, 27, 107, 118, 124
disgust 34, 115
Denzin, N. 53–4, 57, 62–3, 65, 68; *see also* autoethnography
Derrida, J. 34, 103–4, 118–19, 142
Descartes 86, 103, 109, 142
desire 6, 12–13, 63, 89, 95, 114–15, 119, 124, 141, 143, 148–50, 153–6, 170, 173, 177, 179, 183, 187–9
dialectic behavioural therapy 41, 191n30
discrimination 22, 32, 36, 121, 151
disinterest 104, 116; *see also* Levinas
dissimilarity 34–5; *see also* dehumanisation
dissymmetry 113, 118; *see also* responsibility
divine 70n34, 76, 79, 81, 110, 113–14, 140, 142–3, 147, 160; and divinised 119, 124; and divinity 85, 120; *see also* Levinas
dominant discourse 18, 64, 139, 171–2, 182; and status quo 37, 59, 95, 124, 137, 155–6, 173, 183, 189; *see also* reduction
The dark blue file *see* autoethnographic vignettes
DSM 25–6, 45n33, 140, 159n42

Egan, G. 16n19; and SOLER 83, 98n58
Ellis, C. 54, 56–7, 67; *see also* autoethnography
empiricism 106; empirical 41, 58, 79
enigma 59, 81, 111, 115, 138, 173, 184; enigmatic 8, 81, 86, 104, 138; enigmatically 88, 136; *see also* Levinas
entrancement 124; cultural 25, 170; institutional 170; of medicalisation 26; professional 95, 183; wonder blindness 136
epiphany 55, 59, 76, 82, 111, 138, 170; and epiphanic 55, 86, 88, 123, 135; *see also* transfiguring; the Face/face; *see* Levinas; wonder

epistemic injustice: *see* injustice
erotic: language of love 143, 160n71
ethics 9, 68, 104, 122–3, 135, 148, 157, 183; and autoethnography 68; and Buddhist 151–152; and dual relationship 10, 17n26; as first philosophy 123, 127n67, 135; and Levinas 103–4, 120, 122–3, 125, 135, 136–8, 142, 144, 147–8, 151, 183; and ontology 104, 115; and wonder 88, 189
ethical 88, 93, 95; language 138–9; and Levinas 141–2, 149; yearning 151; and responsibility 93, 118, 179
ethical relationship 103, 107–9, 136, 141, 173, 185
ethical vision: and Levinas 78, 94, 96, 103, 109–10, 121, 135–6, 141, 149, 155
ethnography: autobiographical 54; confessional and memoir 57; as field of practice 55; and performance 68; *see also* autoethnography
etymology of wonder 80–82; *see also* genealogy
Evans, H. M. 40, 78, 81, 83, 88–9, 93, 100n106; mutuality and reciprocity 94–5; *see also* clinical wonder
experience: lived 55, 59, 106, 141; *see also* mystical
exploitation 17n26, 27, 172, 175, 189

the Face/face 112–14, 115, 123–4, 136; and the anarchical 137; and approach 110, 136; of Christ 109; features of 113, 124; and desire 149–50; epiphany of 170; face to face 109, 111, 114, 142; orders and ordains 114; plea of 124; of the stranger, the widow, the orphan 110; transfigured 77, 114, 185, 189; welcome of 106, 121, 115, 187, 189; and wonder 84; *see also*: responsibility
formulation: of being 107; Levinas' ethical 112–14, 116, 118, 148, 163n125, 179, 185; of reflexivity 57; of wonder 88–9
feminism 125n4; and feminine 103, 122–3, 185; and feminist(s) 72n97, 146, 159–60n57, 160n66, 161n79; feminist therapy 44n9
Fisher, P. 79, 86; an aesthetic account of wonder 86, 88

Fricker, M. 31–3; and sexual harassment 31; *see also* injustice
friend(s) 105, 113
friendship: and fraternity 120; and kinship 97n43; in Levinas 100, 110, 120–1, 137, 143, 145, 157; in praxis and research 56–57, 66, 83, 120–1, 149, 174, 181

Geertz, C.: ethnography and thick description 55–56
genealogy of wonder 78–80; *see also* etymology
generalisation *see also* clinical reduction
genocide: and Allport, G. 36; and dehumanisation 33; and infra-humanisation 38
God 137, 140–143; *see also* mysticism; and trace
grief 79, 84, 118, 180; and complicated grief (CG) 25–6; *see also* medicalisation
guilt 12, 57, 111, 113, 188; and survivor's 118; professional 183

harpies 79, and Aello and Oypetes 79; *see also* wonder
heartsink patient 22, 37, 39–40, 114; *see also* stigma
Heidegger: and Nazism 107, 126n41; and onto-theo-logy 107–9
help seeker *see* vulnerable help seeker
height 136; and moral height 111, 124; and proximity 136
heresy 62, 66, 172, 187
hermeneutic injustice *see* injustice
hierarchy 28, 104, 171, 185, 189; of care 29; clinical 114; institutional 5, 21, 30; legalised 120; mental health 94; and team 23; sinning against 31
hinge: (the mysterious hinge) 84–5, 87; or node 114
Hollywood, A. 142, 161n79, 192n54
Holy/holy, 104, 108, 117, 124, 136, 137; and desecration of 188; desire for 148; and ethics 142; function of 135, 141; and the wholly/holy 103, 104, 123; and language 137; and praxis 148, 151–2; *see also* anarchy
homeless/ness 34, 39, 48n103; *see also* heartsink patient
horror 61, 78, 84, 105, 115, 149, 182, 188
hospitality 119–20, 143

hostage: 119–20, 123, 135, 142, 148–9; held hostage and ordained 119, 135
humanising 120, 141, 149, 189; and re-humanising 43, 94, 123, 145, 148, 189; *see also* dehumanisation
Husserl, E.: and epoché 126n26, 126n31; Husserl and Heidegger 103–4, 108–9; and phenomenology 105–107

ineffable 88, 114, 122, 139, 143, 145, 170, 182,
infra-humanisation 22, 37–8; *see also* dehumanisation; genocide
injustice 31–33, 42, 117, 144; epistemic 32–3, 68; hermeneutic 31–3; and stigma 178; and testimonial 31–33
intimacy: in praxis 16n19, 82–4, 156, in research 57; and sexual 176; and the welcome of the face 115
Irigaray, L. 103, 129n106, 159–60n57, 172, 181, 185, 187, 192n54
irreducible: and Levinas 104, 108, 115, 145
The insulin coma *see* autoethnographic vignettes

Jantzen, G. 103–4, 118, 129n106
justice 24, 122; and the face 112; and social 54, 67; and Levinas 105, 113, 124, 179; and the work of 106, 186

kataphatic *see* mysticism
Kearney, R. 127n66, 147
Keen, S. 78–9, 84–5
Kidd, I.: and testimonial injustice 32–33
to kill (murder) 113, 118, 136; and the 6th commandment 129n114

Ladies' Shoes *see* autoethnographic vignettes
Laing, R. D. 23–4, 139
language: and dehumanising 37, 40, 48n103; and Levinas 103, 107, 109, 122, 136–9, 141–3; and resistance 186–7; untrustworthy 122; *see also* autoethnography; erotic; ethical; holy; ineffable; love; power; wonder
Lather, P. 58, 66, 68, 69n29, 72n89, 186
Levinas, E.: early life 105; critique 120–3; feminist interpreters 103–4; feminist critics 122–3, 185; *see also* alterity; ambivalence; anarchy; beloved; desire; disinterest; divine; epiphany; ethics; ethics as first philosophy; ethical relationship; ethical vision; epiphany; the Face/ face; friend/ship; God; guilt; height; the holy; hospitality; hostage; language; love; moral; neighbour; ontology; onto-theo-logy; the Other/ other; passivity; phenomenology; proximity; responsibility and substitution; the saying and the said; the trace; transcendence
Linehan, M.: and borderline personality disorder 178, 191n30-n32
loneliness: the lonely self 152; of the "mentally ill" 154; of the strong 149
love 86, 145, and approval 82–3, being in 83, 97n49, 143; in clinical practice 82–4, 97n45, 149, 176–7; and the erotic 143; desire 149–150; and God 143; and justice 84, 124; and language of 143, 96; and mindfulness 98n76; and my neighbour 114, 124; and nonerotic 177; and parent(al) 177, 181; and psychotherapy 97n49; of truth 86; of wisdom 79; without concupiscence 114, 152; and wonder 83
loving 77, 163n130, 174, 177, 188; professional prohibitions of 141

Maynard, D. 29, 31; and perspective display sequence 29; *see also* asymmetry
medical 23, 25–6, 28, 30, 40, 59, 88 and asymmetry 29–33; biomedical 29, 40; and care 40, 89, 182; and education 82; humanities 78; and model 21, 28; and imperialism 26–8; paramedical 22; practice 40, 78, 88, 103; profession(al) 29, 33, 93–4; psychiatry and 24; and sociology 26, 28; and staff 23
medical imperialism 21, 25–8
medicalisation 21, 24–8, 39, 43, 44n10, 45n27, 30, 109, 170
membership *see* autoethnography
mental health care 8, 33, 43, 76, 82, 89, 141, 172, 174, 176; *see also* community mental health care
mental health clinician 43, 82, 104, 116, 155–6, 183–4, 186; and professional(s) 16n13, 43, 77, 190n28, 191n31
mental health institution 24, 30, 39, 66, 77, 84, 114, 118, 124, 154, 170–1, 174–5, 178–9, 182–4, 186–9

Index

mental illness 3, 7, 21, 23, 42–3, 154, 174; and complicated grief (or CG) 25–6; the creep of 170; failure of clinicians to acknowledge in themselves 190; and homelessness 39; and iatrogenic stigma of 190n1; and medicalisation 25; and misdiagnosis of spiritual/religious/mystical experience 139; as moral flaw 39; and ranking of 16n12; and somatic illness 32; serious and persistent 175; stereotyping and employment 38; *see also* stigmatisation; suicide
metaphysics 108; and Heidegger 107; and Levinas 116; and paradigm 62; and Western culture 88
mindfulness 17n27, 87, 98n76; and psychosis 17n25; and meditation 95; *see also* curiosity
Moncrieff, J.: and the Critical Psychiatry Network 24
moral: blindness 124; and discourse 65; and disengagement 35, disease as flaw 39; exclusion 38, process of clinician 53, 59, 66, 84, 104, 115, 118, 150, 152, 155, 171, 179; refreshment 89; research 54, 56, 58, 61, 65, 68; and social activism 57, 68; and wonder 78, 171
Morgan, M. 109, 111, 119, 142; *see also* the Face/face; passivity
mutuality and reciprocity *see* Rogers, C.
My flower *see* autoethnographic vignettes
mystic 86–7
mystical experience, 8, 16n16, 139–41, 158n29; of a counsellor; and pathology 16n20; and psychosis 139
mysticism: affective 141; apophatic 16n16, 142–3, 161n79; Dionysius 140; early 135, 140, 142; and God 140–1; kataphatic 16n16, 143, 161n79; medieval 81, 97n30, 160n71

narrative 35, 58, 65, 82; and presence 59; and research 53–5, 57, 82; and integrity of 58, 61; and the problem of power 68; *see* vignette
neighbour: and Levinas 104, 114, 123–4, 128n74, 136–8, 142
Nemo, P. 117–18
The Nitobe Garden *see* autoethnographic vignettes
Nordtug, B. 179, 183

object: subject-object distinction 117, 142, 148
objectification 35, 122, 155
ontology 104, 107–9, 115–16, 122, 135–7, 148; deterrents of 143
onto-theo-logy *see* Heidegger
Orange, D. 103, 137
the Other/other 103–4, 109, 122, 127n66, 136, 189; *see also* the Face/face

paradox 59, 81, 96, 189; of authority and weakness 113–115
paradigm: of the same 150; and positivism 63–4, 66; and post modernism 63–4; and reductive 97n45; and the third 64; and wars 53, 62–3, 65
passivity 117–19, 141, 143; *see also* responsibility
personality disorders: borderline 30, 39–40, 47n100, 191n30; antisocial 16n13
perspective display sequence *see* Maynard, D.
phenomenology: of sociality 110; *see also* Husserl
Piaget, J.: a cognitive account of wonder 85
Plato 79, 85, 103, 108
post-traumatic *see* trauma
power 66–7, 94, 171, 174; abuse of 117, 174, 175, 182; clinical 28, 139; and domination 66; imbalance 21, 29, 35, 188; institutional 95; legal 94, 114, 154, 181, 186; of language 144; medicine's 27; and objectification 35; over beings 108; and privilege 187; and reciprocity 94; and relationship 67, 84, 94; and responsibility 66–8; and structure 148; voice and authority 67; *see also* boundary/boundaries and violation(s)
praxis, 28, 58, 70n34, 72n97, 77–8, 82–3, 98n56, 135–6, 144, 155–6, 175, 177–8, 183
prejudice 21–2, 31, 35–7, 43; *see also* Allport, G.
proximity: and ethical 171, 175, 186; and conflation of abuse 172; conflation of violation 173–5; *see also* height
psychiatry: and antipsychiatry 23–24, 139; and mysticism 140; spirituality and theology 138–9; *see also* medicalisation

psychology: Psychology and the Other 70n34, 155; *see also* Allport, G.; Rogers, C.; Strong, P.
psychosis 15n9, 16n12–13, 17n25, 48n101, 139
psychotropic medication 24, 154; and antipsychotics 3, 6, 16

qualitative: and equivalent 58; and measures 158n34; and research 53, 62, 67
quantitative: and criteria 58, 70n41; and research 53, 62–4, 141
Quinn, D. 78–81, 83, 85–6

rainbow 79, 86–87; *see also* Fisher, P.
reduction/reductive: approach to care 42, 112, 125, 151, 155; and mental health system 94, 171–2, 174–5, 179, 182–3, 185–9; and hierarchy 104; and positivism 63; and violation 136; and worldview 54, 56, 66, 99, 109, 138, 97n45, 99n91, 104, 109, 112, 125, 136, 138, 151, 155, 160n66, 171–2, 174–5, 179, 182, 186; *see also* clinical
reflexivity *see* autoethnography
reciprocity and mutuality *see* Rogers, C.
relationship *see* ethical; therapeutic
responsibility 117–120; of the clinician 112, 114–15, 137, 147, 157; and disinterest 116; and desire 149; to the face 150; and justice 124; and Levinas, E. 108, 111, 113, 121, 135–6, 138, 143, 153, 194; and the vulnerable help seeker 155–6; and Rogers, C. 95; *see also* hostage
reverence 21, 81, 83, 88–9, 94, 115–16, 183
rigor: as measure of quantitative merit 58; and trustworthiness 58, 70n41
Rogers, C.: and Buber, M. 94–5; and mutuality and reciprocity 17n22, 82, 94; and "other realities" 82; and his theory of change 82–3
Rubenstein, M-J. 78–83, 86

Safe as in church *see* autoethnographic vignettes
saintliness 142, 145
saying and the said 128n74, 138, 142–3, 180
scientific account of wonder *see* Dawkins, R.

Index 199

sexual: and abuse 112, 176; attraction 177; feelings of clinician 174, 176–7; harassment 31; misconduct/violation 175–6; orientation 151; sublimation 143; and comparison to mystical union 160n71
Safe as in church *see* autoethnographic vignettes
Sharon *see* autoethnographic vignettes
Socrates 79–80, 83
reflexivity *see* autoethnography
Severson, E. 106–8, 126n31, 129n102, 136, 143; *see also* Husserl
sociology 27–8, 120, 123; and autoethnography and 54; medical 26, 28
social activism *see* autoethnography
SPMI- serious and persistent mental illness 16n12, 175
spiritual 7–10, 58, 87; and experience 185; and friendship 137; and practice 82, 84, 140; or mystical experience 139; and psychospiritual needs 141
spirituality religion and mental health 8, 16n17–18, 140, 159n44
spirituality, theology and health 139, 141, 158n29; in psychiatry 138
spirituality, religion and psychosis 139
Staff toilets only! *see* autoethnographic vignettes
stigma 22, 25, 37–39, 95, 154, 170, 178, 186; self-stigmatisation 39
stereotyping: *see* stigma
Strong, P. *see* medical imperialism
substitution 118–19; and the unsubstitutible 119, 152; *see also* responsibility
suicide 15n10, 17n23–24, 48n101, 153, 178
Swinton, J. 149, 181
Szasz, T.: 23–4; *see also* mental illness

taboo: and boundary violation 10; and sexual feelings 176; and proximity 182; *see also* injustice
therapeutic relationship 11, 22, 40, 57, 82–3, 94, 150, 172, 175–76, 185
thick description *see* autoethnography
Thou shalt not love *see* autoethnographic vignettes
trace (of the eternal) 109, 124, 137
transcendence 12, 108, 111, 119, 136, 141–2, 156, 157n7, 173, 185, 188

transcendent 7, 11, 13, 16, 86, 106, 107, 109–11, 114, 122, 136–8, 143–5, 147, 149, 151, 153, 189
transfigure: and transfiguring 83, 88–9; *see also* Face/face
transformation(al) 54, 61, 82, 182–3; and narrative and social 54; and utopian 68
Tread lightly *see* autoethnographic vignettes
trauma 14n4, 16n12, 41–43, 44n9, 110, 156; and burnout 41, 170; and compassion fatigue 41; and post-traumatic stress disorder 41; and secondary traumatic stress 41; and vicarious trauma 41, 170
treatment 22–3, 25–6, 29–30, 47n100, 89, 139, 148, 184; and clinical 178; and coercive 1, 14n2; and concurrent disorders 43n7; and plan 8, 32, 154
trustworthiness *see* autoethnography

Vanier, J: history of L'Arche 144–145; Vanier's fall from grace 146–147
validity in qualitative research, *see* autoethnography
vignette *see* autoethnography
violence 53, 105, 114, 118, 124, 138, 149–50, 186, 189; and autoethnography (performance) 53; and dehumanisation 33; and disinterest 116; institutional 95, 109, 136–7; and Jantzen, G. 104, 123, 129n106, 139; and Levinas 136, 138, 142, 152; and predictors of 16n13; and psychotherapy 156; Severson, E. 143; systemic 104, 154; and trauma 41–3; and Vanier, J. 144–7
vulnerable help seeker 21, 26, 28–9, 31, 35, 38, 41–3, 56, 66, 82, 84, 89, 94–5, 110, 118–20, 142, 149–50, 152, 154–6, 170–2, 174, 176–7, 179, 182, 184–6, 188–9

What do you do? *see* autoethnographic vignettes
wonder: and the clinician 88–89; enslavement of 173–175; the hinge of 84–85; the mule of wonder 172, 184–85, 188; origins of 79–8; as a palliative in the clinic 182–83; and praxis (light, love, openness, ambivalence) 82–84; as the seat of wisdom 85–86; sources of entry 95–96; *see also* ambivalence; awe; clinical wonder; curiosity; Dawkins, R.; etymology; Evans, M.; Fisher, P.; genealogy; the hinge to wonder; horror; the Nitobe Garden; Piaget, J.; reciprocity and mutuality; Rubenstein, M-J.; transfiguring